FIRST IN THE FIELD
America's Pioneering Naturalists

Books by Robert Elman

THE GREAT AMERICAN SHOOTING PRINTS

THE HIKER'S BIBLE

THE ATLANTIC FLYWAY

THE LIVING WORLD OF AUDUBON MAMMALS

FIRST IN THE FIELD
America's Pioneering Naturalists

by Robert Elman

Foreword by Dr. Dean Amadon,
Curator Emeritus, Department of Ornithology,
The American Museum of Natural History

MASON/CHARTER · NEW YORK · 1977

500, 922
Elma

Library of Congress Cataloging in Publication Data

Elman, Robert.
   First in the field.

   Bibliography: p.
   Includes index.
   1. Naturalists—United States—Biography.
I. Title.
QH26.E44   500.9'2'2   [B]   77-3437
ISBN 0-88405-499-3

JUL 3 '77

8/77

To Ellen

Contents

Foreword

As our country enters its third century it is a time to take stock of our heritage—to evaluate past successes and failures as a factor in formulating a program for the future. One insight is to be found in the lives and accomplishments of the pioneering naturalists and explorers who made known the physical features, the fauna, and the flora of our continent. Mr. Elman's approach has been to select nine outstanding naturalists and analyze their careers in depth. As he notes, it was these naturalists of the eighteenth and nineteenth centuries who paved the way for today's specialists—ornithologists, geologists, foresters, and many others. No longer is it possible for a single individual to make outstanding contributions in a number of related disciplines. Science, technology, and theory have advanced so far that specialization, involving intensive study and preparation, has become mandatory.

This, of course, is not true of the out-and-out amateur or hobbyist, but his avocation has become increasingly a form of recreation rather than a scientific pursuit, though nonetheless rewarding for that. An exception must be made, too, for the conservationist and environmentalist. Here a broad general approach is not only permissible but desirable. To be sure, a conservationist who is also a specialist in some branch of natural history or ecology will profit much from his specialization. Made thus aware of the complexity of science (and, on the other hand, of the shortcomings of human society), he will be less apt to espouse cranky or infeasible points of view.

The case histories set forth in this book will give an added breadth of perception both to the general reader and the professional. Mr. Elman begins by telling us of some of the dabblers in natural history—for many of them were no more than that—of the colonial period. The chapters that follow, each devoted to an outstanding naturalist (or in one case father and son and in another case two collaborators), are packed with information and reflect painstaking research. There is a biographical thread in each account, but beyond that an overall survey of the development of natural science and a conservation ethic on our continent.

These men form a highly varied group. Some, like Louis Agassiz of Harvard and John Wesley Powell, the intrepid explorer of the Canyon of the Colorado, were energetic leaders, organizers, and innovators who left a permanent impact upon entire disciplines and institutions. Others, like John James Audubon, were equally ebullient but dedicated to a more restricted goal—in Audubon's case the publication of artistic and technical masterpieces on the birds and mammals of North America.

Contrasting with such meteoric careers, one has the moody, obscure, and ill-starred Alexander Wilson whose *American Ornithology*, brought to fruition under incredible difficulties, antedated and in many respects rivaled the productions of Audubon. Presenting other kinds of contrasts are the accounts of the quiet, scholarly Bartrams, John and his son William, horticulturists and naturalists. The elder Bartram was the most accomplished botanist in North America. His son, if anything, surpassed him, and his literary skills have made his *Travels* a classic. One of the discoveries of the Bartrams in their Appalachian rambles was a small flowering tree which they named Franklinia in honor of their friend Benjamin Franklin. This tree must have been on the verge of extinction from natural causes, for it has never been found in the wild again. But seedlings were taken back to John Bartram's gardens in Philadelphia; thus saved from extinction, the descendants of those trees are still to be found in estates and parks.

The book concludes with a somewhat different and more recent figure, John Burroughs, who died in 1921. The author calls Burroughs a "publicist," and so he was in the sense that his numerous volumes enjoyed an enormous public vogue at the turn of the century, and are now making something of a comeback in this ecology-conscious age. Yet Burroughs did not enjoy publicity, he loathed it, and after fame pursued him he sought escape in his rustic hideouts, Slabsides and Woodchuck Lodge.

Though he was not a scientist, a sound realization of the value of science underlies John Burroughs' writings. His profound respect for scientific evidence made him an extraordinarily objective and perceptive observer of natural phenomena. He did not repeat Louis Agassiz' egregious error of rejecting evolution, and his geological insights were sometimes superior to those of his more formally trained friend, John Muir. And more than the others portrayed in this volume he sensed that the rampant destruction of forests, the overexploitation of fuels and minerals would, in time, make the world as barren as a "sucked orange."

Is it too late to heed his warning? More of us, certainly, are becoming concerned, but the forces of destruction, aggravated by a worldwide population explosion, are also accelerating. A recent cosmopolitan opinion poll reveals some sobering but not unexpected attitudes. It is precisely in the undeveloped countries, the "Third World," that "progress" is measured in terms of increased population, urbanization, and industrialization. In the most critical areas, then, the destructive forces may be welcomed for the sake of apparent short-term benefits. What will happen as the multitudes proliferate, together with the environmental problems that sometimes appear to be gaining an irreversible momentum?

"Being in a boat," Dr. Johnson said, "is like being in jail with the chance of drowning added." One might, in this nuclear age, paraphrase him and say that being on the spaceship Earth is increasingly like being in jail with the chance of being blown to smithereens added. If there is to be a turning away from disaster, it will be when enough of us acquire a kinship with nature; an appreciation comparable to that of the naturalists depicted in this thought-provoking volume.

Dean Amadon, Curator Emeritus
Department of Ornithology
The American Museum of Natural History

Introduction

One has only to sit down in the woods or fields,
or by the shore of the river or lake,
and nearly everything of interest will come round to him,
the birds, the animals, the insects. . . .
                                    John Burroughs
                                    West Park, New York
                                    January 5, 1882

John Burroughs was, as usual, percipient in asserting that a great many of nature's most intriguing creatures will reveal themselves to the patient observer who merely sits and waits. Of course, merely sitting and waiting—with sufficient patience, unflagging alertness, scientific objectivity, and a grasp of the possible meanings of what may be seen and heard—is a kind of sitting and waiting that can be a difficult technique to master. Its demands are confirmed by every field investigator who has sweated or frozen in a blind for hours, days, or weeks, in order to learn some new detail of animal behavior or to interpret some previously observed fact.

Burroughs was as precise in his use of language as in his habits of observation. *"Nearly* everything of interest" might present itself to the observer sitting in the woods or by the waters, but not everything. He referred specifically to animate creatures, and even within that context there were small, hidden, secretive, remote, ephemeral, or protean marvels that must be sought out rather than awaited. Not many aquatic creatures would come to the sitter by the shore, nor would the subterranean life tunneling invisibly and silently below. Nor would the inanimate "productions of Nature," as earlier naturalists had called them: the secret-laden rocks on the far shore, the distant vegetation beyond the rocks, the elements themselves, and the glaciers of the north, flowing slowly enough to make one think about geologic processes, geologic time.

An able naturalist is driven by an insatiable yearning for knowledge of his still-mysterious planet. He is therefore as indefatigable in his active pursuit of revelations as in his observation and analysis of them. The layman cannot, as a rule, experience so intense a yearning for scientific answers (or for the propounding of new questions); his interest in nature is diluted by other interests and by the demands of his own life. What a naturalist feels is akin to the composer's obsession with music, the painter's with art, and cannot be fully shared by the rest of us, who are satisfied to understand the nuances of a sonata, appreciate the textures of a painting, or realize that a bird's song is all the more beautiful because it has been evolved for a purpose more profound than melody. But if our perception of the natural scientist is less than complete, our appreciation of his achievements increases with our interest in his discoveries, and currently that interest is greater than ever before.

The interest to which I refer is undoubtedly a kind of enlightened self-interest, growing out of a well-reasoned fear that unless we gain a fuller understanding of our planet, we may destroy it. Writers at the turn of the century detected a "renaissance" of concern for nature, and this concern has been a recurrent phenomenon, as will be seen in these pages. Usually it has accompanied a new level of exploitation of natural resources, or a new awareness of such exploitation, as it did in the colonial period and again in the late nineteenth century. But never has this concern been as strong as it is now, for never have the threats to the environment been greater, and never have those threats been so widely publicized or so well grasped by the public.

This latest renaissance of interest in nature has been a direct outgrowth of the modern conservation movement—"environmentalism," as it is called now—a grasp of the significance of ecology, or "Oekologie," as it was termed by some scientists over a century ago, much earlier than most environmental novitiates realize. The conservation movement, in turn, owes much of its impetus to the widely publicized discoveries of American naturalists, and it is therefore fitting in this time of unprecedented concern to review the lives and accomplishments of the pioneers in American field studies.

A major problem in planning this work was to define the word *naturalist*. A consensus of lexicographers shows that the word's connotation is at least as important as its denotation. Dictionaries agree in principle that a naturalist is any person versed in natural science—that is, a student of natural history. And "natural history," they agree, is an almost obsolete term for "the study, description, and classification of animals, plants, minerals, and other natural objects, thus"—as Webster phrases it—"including the modern sciences of zoology, botany, mineralogy, etc., insofar as they existed at that time—now commonly restricted to the study of these subjects in a more or less unsystematic way."

But the "unsystematic way" was necessarily the only way among the pioneering naturalists who are the protagonists of this volume and whose work led to specialization and very systematic ways. Furthermore, modern investigators in the natural sciences still commonly use the terms naturalist and natural history despite Webster's implication of obsolescence, and they tend to add their own less pejorative implications. To them, as a general rule, a naturalist is an investigator, usually but not always trained in at least one scientific discipline, who may or may not specialize in a single discipline or a single aspect of nature, but who usually delves to some degree into many aspects. Finally, he is an individual who puts great emphasis on field investigations as opposed to pure laboratory work.

Nature and *field* are the key words here, and the two general areas of effort are field biology and field geology. Of course, each of the two involves many more specific areas. Biology, for example, encompasses botany, biochemistry, animal psychology, genetics, ichthyology, ornithology, mammalogy, paleontology (a discipline of which the geologists often become equally enamored), and a multitude of other studies.

Thus, a naturalist inevitably becomes an ecologist and an environmentalist. Alexander Adams, an astute popular writer on this subject, has remarked that in our present age of technological miracles, the greatest miracle remains one "that has been with us unchanged for many millennia—the miracle of the interrelationship of all life-forms and of their dependency on their environments." This is the essence of the study of natural history and, as Adams points out, it has awakened an ever stronger public interest "because man is slowly becoming more conscious of these delicate ties that bind him to the natural world."

Naturalists have been seeking answers ("more or less unsystematically" until recent times) for as long as man has been curious about the ways of nature. In primitive societies the priests, witch doctors, or sorcerers were interpreters of natural history. More sophisticated early societies very soon produced philosophers of a scientific inclination surprisingly close to that of modern investigators. And some of the ancient discoveries, though not readily accepted in their own time, have been confirmed in later centuries. Aristotle, for example, in his *Historia Animalium*, dismissed the misconception that the dolphin was a fish and declared it to be a mammal. "The dolphin, the whale, and all the rest of the Cetacea"—Aristotle also observed—"all, that is to say, that are provided with a blow-hole instead of gills, are viviparous." The quest for knowledge of the natural world is an ancient one.

The efforts of Aristotelian thinkers did not, however, sweep away many of the myths, superstitions, and misconceptions that shrouded the natural world until the eighteenth century—the Age of Reason, the period of the philosophical movement known as the Enlightenment, which was characterized by an almost religious belief in the power of human reason. The Enlightenment produced revolutionary scientists, many of the first "modern" investigators, and it led to the emergence of America's pioneering naturalists in the eighteenth and nineteenth centuries. The work of these men had a significance that far exceeded national progress; it added immeasurably to the fundamentals of progress in the natural sciences throughout the world.

Such men are the heroes of this book—some, undeniably, more publicists or artists or explorers than scientists in the modern sense, and all of them flawed despite the bowdlerizing of some biographers. It seems to me that their flaws make them all the more interesting, and certainly more accessible, to the rest of us flawed humans. I have tried to tell their stories without deleting the blemishes, but with an emphatic focus on the great achievements that form the thread, indeed the entire fabric, of this book: the progress, overcoming great odds, of the study of natural history in America.

A few readers—particularly those who profess to be "nature lovers" without being conversant with nature—may be mildly dismayed to read about the methods and attitudes prevalent among these heroic naturalists. Catesby, the Bartrams, Wilson, Audubon, Bachman, Burroughs, all of them but Powell and Agassiz, were hunters who killed animals not exclusively for use as scientific specimens or even for food but for the pleasure of the hunt. Agassiz, for that matter, was an angler who delighted in the catching—that is, killing—of fish; and Powell, who shot game for food, was not opposed to doing so for sport. Those who have come no closer to nature than a manicured urban park, a tilled field, or fictionalized presentations in print and on film have difficulty comprehending how a man can so love nature that he devotes his life to its study and yet feels no pangs at the killing of nature's creatures. The uninitiated have been morally and esthetically influenced by the fantasists of nature reportage—"nature fakers," Theodore Roosevelt called them; "sham naturalists" in the words of John Burroughs.

If I am not addressing an audience of zealous vegetarians (who may or may not feel remorse over the killing of plants), I think no defense is needed in behalf of a naturalist or anyone else who kills in order to feed himself. With regard to the collecting of specimens, I will quote the eminent ornithological painter George Miksch Sutton: "It's simply a fact of my life, a necessity. . . . I've argued tirelessly for the protection of wildlife and habitat, and delighted in the wilderness. But I have to have models; I must see for myself how a bird is put together, what its muscles are like, what it eats. . . . The more we learn from specimens we take from the wild—whether it's to show other people the beauty of the creature in a painting, or to teach students—the more we'll contribute to the well-being of a species on the whole. Understanding must come first." The argument is valid—and still more valid for a Wilson or an Audubon or any pioneering scientific investigator than for later artists such as Seton, Fuertes, or Sutton.

The question of killing for sport—the pleasure of the chase —is a more difficult philosophical and moral problem. A number of modern writers of natural history have declared (in defiance of current journalistic fashion) that hunters are hardly the villains portrayed by the popular press. Victor B. Scheffer has written that "it was the naturalists, from career scientists to organic gardeners, bird watchers, and a great many hunters, who early saw the important changes [in natural habitat] and who are now so terribly upset at the degradation of wildlife environments." Though Scheffer is by no means a zealous advocate of hunting, there is an implication here that a hunter (or at least a competent and concerned hunter) can be one kind of bona fide naturalist, whether amateur or professional. In reply to a letter from a dismayed lady in Vermont who felt that Theodore Roosevelt could not have much regard for the wildlife he killed, John Burroughs said that Roosevelt's regard for the larger mammals was probably deeper than his own, since Roosevelt's was based on a hunter's knowledge. (Burroughs himself hunted only birds and various small game.) To be successful, a hunter must, after all, learn the ways of his game, and with learning comes regard. Aldo Leopold held that both hunters and fishermen usually begin as mere enthusiastic tyros, grow into efficient harvesters, and finally become philosophers more interested in future than in present harvests. The early American naturalists, and many who are working today, would agree with Ortega y Gasset's philosophical approval of the chase in *Meditations on Hunting*. They would agree, too, with Paul Shepard (though they might scoff at his Dartmouth College title of Visiting Professor of Environmental Perception and would certainly oppose many of his mystical views) that man is the "tender carnivore," whose ancient hunting heritage is responsible for more good than evil human traits and for whom the pursuit of prey is the closest remaining link with the natural world—an act almost sacred as a method of participation in that world and a way of penetrating its secrets.

These naturalists, being of scientific temperament, were less inclined than today's romantic and innocent urbanites to assign moral values to nature. They did not simplistically condemn all predators as evil and laud all prey as meek and good, even when they surrendered to the temptation to anthropomorphize. What they perceived—albeit dimly—was an overall good, an order or plan of nature not yet fully revealed. They accepted it (and reveled in it) as it was, and accepted themselves as predatory but compassionate and reasoning participants in it. Had they not done so, they could not have come to know nature intimately enough to amass their great achievements.

One other question remains with regard to value judgments in this volume—a question of selection. Of necessity, a book like this must be a very personal work, and I have relied solely on my own researches and conclusions in choosing the naturalists to be included. Why did I not include the visionary William Beebe or the great botanist Asa Gray (a contemporary of Agassiz at Harvard)? Why not Spencer F. Baird? Why not Elliott Coues? Why not Ellen Swallow, one of this country's first ecologists and the first woman to enter Massachusetts Institute of Technology? Why not Aldo Leopold? Why not Rachel Carson? The list could be lengthened enormously—too much so for the confines of a single book—and that is the essential answer. An addition that tempted me perhaps more than any other was Elliott Coues, who combined great scholarship with a penchant for exploring, and whose contributions to ornithology and mammalogy have been called monumental. One reference drew my attention to the fact that some of his work in the West was without question pioneering, and certainly Coues merits a full modern biography which is yet to be written. But in his own writings, Coues made it clear that his work extended the investigatory roads cut by earlier explorers of nature who had no previously blazed trails to follow— men such as Catesby, the Bartrams, Wilson, and Audubon. These men were the true pioneers, less knowledgeable than their successors, less scientific for the very reason that they were the pioneers. The most knowledgeable, the most scientific and scholarly of the lot was Agassiz, and he, too, was a pioneer—a revolutionary, in fact, first in paleoichthyology and then in geology. I have chosen my heroes not for their scholarship but for their courageous and significant explorations of then unknown realms of nature.

Within that scientific context I permitted myself one exception—John Burroughs. Scientifically he was no pioneer, nor did he contribute anything monumental to the scientific study of natural history. But he worked during the twilight of the pioneering era and he was preeminent among a new breed of naturalists—the literary publicists who dramatized and popularized the natural world without resorting to the sham of the romanticists. He was called the philosopher of the naturalists and the chief architect of the latest renaissance of public interest in the natural world—a renaissance that seemed for a while to be dimming but is burning in the public consciousness and conscience with greater intensity than ever. To some of us who are concerned with the uses of science and the future of this planet as a wild and beautiful creation, a chapter devoted to the Seer of Slabsides is not an inappropriate ending for a volume such as this.

Greentown, Pennsylvania   *Robert Elman*

Chapter 1
THE FORERUNNERS

To the Europeans who first explored and settled a narrow coastal strip of this continent—probing no more than fifty miles inland, establishing hardly more than a precarious beachhead— the New World was a new wilderness. If they encountered this unknown realm with all the courage they could muster, they did so, too, with all the trepidation they could not overcome. For some, optimism may have been more a form of needed bravado than of hope, as when explorers reaching Roanoke, unaware of what hardships lay ahead, reported to Sir Walter Raleigh that they had "found such plenty . . . on the sand and on the green soil of the hills . . . in the plains . . . on every little shrub . . . in all the world the like abundance is not to be found." For others, such optimism seemed insane. Oliver Cromwell, responding to the settlers' accounts of New England, called the land "that desert and barren wilderness." In the minds of those settlers, it was a wilderness to be conquered, literally smashed and tamed, rather than a strange but friendly world to be penetrated by the curiosity of the pure scientist.

The first explorations of this continent's flora and fauna, therefore, were timorous probings, tentative and fantasy-ridden, sometimes disdainful of forms unlike those of the Old World or of no direct use to man. Observations of natural life were incidental to the quest for riches or for the means of survival.

But all the same, those observations, preserved in the accounts of explorers, administrators, and settlers, disseminated new knowledge and whetted a thirst for more, thus laying a founda-

1

tion for the investigation of nature in a strange and seemingly fabulous world. Eventually such investigation would grow into one of the world's most important sciences—or rather, groups of specialized, related, sophisticated sciences such as entomology, ichthyology, mammalogy, ornithology, botany, ethology, ecology, geology: in fact, all the divisions and subdivisions and sub-subdivisions of natural history that help to reveal the world in a grain of sand or in a hummingbird feather, the universe in an atom or an estuary.

It is tempting to award the glorious title Father of American Natural History to some early and farsighted investigator—a Mark Catesby or a John Bartram—as some writers have done. Actually, however, each of the pioneering naturalists built his little wilderness outpost of knowledge on still earlier, simpler, often random observations, somewhat in the way common law built itself on custom, precedent, and the testing of previous concepts. First came the observers, then the collectors, then the explainers, the more diligent examiners, the systematists, the insatiable experimenters and researchers.

The Spaniards were the first to broadcast detailed descriptions of new life forms discovered on this continent. It was not a scholar but a conquistador, Francisco Vásquez de Coronado, who first observed *el tigre,* the jaguar, in what is now New Mexico. That was forty-eight years after Columbus sighted the island of San Salvador, the first landfall of the New World. By the time of Coronado's exploration of New Mexico, the Spanish colonists had become acquainted with a great many of the more easterly and tropical animals and plants indigenous to America. Coronado's 1540 expedition also brought back the first full reports of the vast herds of ponderous bison and the far-stretching colonies of plump little prairie dogs. How strange the contrasts of these closely associated animals must have seemed to the Spaniards: bison bulls weighing a ton or more, making the earth tremble as they wallowed in the dust near burrows dug by two-pound prairie dogs.

About a year later, Hernando de Soto's expedition reached the Mississippi and there discovered a fish to vie with the legends of sea serpents: a toothless, scaleless, shark-tailed gray-blue monster sometimes five feet long and weighing well over a hundred pounds, equipped with a long, paddle-shaped snout with which it stirs up mud in order to feed on plankton, insect larvae, algae, and such. Its skeleton is chiefly cartilage, like that of a shark. The species is a living fossil called the paddlefish (*Polyodon spathula*), a primitive and distant relative of the sturgeons on which the colonists at Jamestown feasted. It has only one near relative among living species, the Chinese paddlefish of the Yangtze River.

Assiduous explorers though the Spaniards were, they proved to be neither innovative agriculturists nor ardent gleaners of nature's provender. Other European groups, settling to the north, contributed more plentiful and detailed, though not at first more accurate, studies of unfamiliar flora and fauna. "These Penguins are as bigge as Geese, and flie not," reported Richard Whitbourn in 1618 of the auks that helped to feed the English and other colonists. The "penguins," together with deer, various kinds of waterfowl, fishes, and a "great store of Pease," were described as being wonderfully plentiful on Cape Cod. Almost a decade before, the English navigator Henry Hudson had reported to his Dutch employers with comparable enthusiasm that the Island of Manhattan was a fine woodland full of "sweet water and deer." Native plants and animals, giving promise of food in lean times, were hungrily investigated and recorded.

Still earlier, beginning in 1585, John White had used watercolors to record the images of such creatures as the frigate bird, pelican, loggerhead turtle, alligator, and various fishes encountered in the West Indies and in the area of North Carolina's Roanoke Island. Most of his works were unpublished, but they were deposited in the British Museum and it is known from surviving examples that he painted at least sixteen species of fish, a skink (probably *Eumeces fasciatus*), and one reptile that appears to be a milk snake. White was governor of the doomed Roanoke colony. He soon went back to England for supplies, and when he returned to the island in 1590 the only remaining trace of the colony was a word, "Croatoan," carved into a tree; it was the name of a friendly Indian tribe with whom the starving colonists may have departed. They were never found.

In 1608, Captain John Smith became governor of the Jamestown colony and he, too, attempted to study and record American wildlife. In his *Map of Virginia* he described a score of birds. Between 1678 and 1692, a later Virginia settler, John Bannister, drew detailed pictures of plants and mollusks in the area of the James River. A number of art historians as well as chroniclers of natural history have felt that Bannister, John White, and Mark Catesby were the only artists of substantial merit to precede William Bartram in delineating specimens of American nature.

It has been said that Plymouth, like Jamestown, survived initial hardships where previous settlements had failed because the inhabitants quickly learned to live off the land. In doing so, of course, they took note of the land's "production," as plants and animals were once aptly called. Plymouth's first year, 1620, began with the menace of starvation, but by September of the following year Governor Edward Winslow was sending exultant letters to England: "For fish and fowl we have great abundance. Fresh cod in the summer is but coarse meat with us. Our bay is full of lobsters all the summer, and affords a great variety of other fish."

Near Plymouth, an Anglican trader named Thomas Morton established a little settlement called Ma-re Mount. Simultaneously, he established a reputation for shrewd bargaining with the Indians and for an unseemly propensity to engage in such merriment as reveling about a Maypole. Inevitably, Ma-re Mount came to be called Merry Mount, and many years later Nathaniel Hawthorne would base a story, "The Maypole of Merry Mount," on Morton's adventures and misadventures. Somehow Morton reserved time from bartering and merrymaking to observe wildlife. When the scandalized Plymouth Pilgrims sent Miles Standish to arrest and deport him back to England, he had amassed copious notes and, apparently, very little bitterness toward the scene of his eviction. In a book entitled *New English Canaan,* published in England in 1637, he confirmed Winslow's assessment of America's living riches. It was among the first books to devote close scrutiny to American animals. In it, he celebrated the sight of "millions of Turtledoves" and recounted his discovery of "pide Ducks, gray Ducks, and black Ducks in great abundance."

The "pide Ducks" he described could have been buffleheads, old-squaws, eiders, or some other pied species, but it is just as likely that he referred to the now extinct Labrador duck (*Camptorhynchus labradorius*) whose numbers were devastated by the feather-gathering voyages of New England merchantmen to the nesting grounds on the southern coast of Labrador in the 1750s. These handsome black and white sea ducks, which had once wintered as far south as Chesapeake Bay, were becoming rare by the first quarter of the nineteenth century. John James Audubon reported that the species sometimes "enters the Delaware River, in Pennsylvania, and ascends . . . at least as far as Philadelphia." But when he sought specimens to describe and draw he had to settle for a pair shot by Daniel Webster off Martha's Vineyard and later enshrined at the Smithsonian Institution.

Men like Thomas Morton, inquisitive observers and admirers of wildlife, were among the first heralds or fashion-setters of the Age of Enlightenment, and they laid a foundation for more systematic study of nature. Understandably, few of these amateur naturalists had the foresight to perceive that they might be observing doomed species amid the land's bounty—species like the Labrador duck, destined to be extinguished by the rapacity of civilization. Among the minor exceptions to the rule of heedlessness was another of Plymouth's governors, William Bradford, who astutely foresaw a waterfowl decline. Bradford was an advocate of the need to live off the land, and he therefore understood and asserted the concomitant need to keep the habitat productive. But he also understood the more dominant attitudes of the colonists. "What could they see," he asked in 1620, "but a hideous and desolate wilderness, full of wild beasts and wild men? And what multitudes there might be of them they knew not."

Other observers, though diligently studying and recording the New World's treasures, could not visualize a reduction in the seemingly endless production of nature. Thus George and Leonard Calvert, enumerating Maryland's wildlife, wrote in 1633 of "infinite" numbers of birds, "diversely colored . . . eagles, bitterns, swans, geese, partridge, ducks. . . . By all which it appears, the country abounds not only with profit but with pleasure."

The reports of men like the Calverts in Maryland and Thomas Morton in Massachusetts sharpened the curiosity of readers in England. And books like Morton's were received well enough to encourage other writers—for example, John Josselyn, whose notes on his travels in Massachusetts formed the content of his *New England Rarities Discovered*, published in 1672. Such works, despite the inclusion of natural curiosa, might later be dismissed as more travelogues than natural histories, but they did nourish an interest in the elucidation of nature's secrets.

Still another amateur (or in this case merely self-styled) naturalist was the grim sermonizer Cotton Mather, to whom hindsight has assigned the role of villain in terms of wildlife as well as witchery. One of his pronouncements was to the effect that "what is not useful is vicious," an opinion that pertained to any plant or creature that could not be eaten, worn, sold, or otherwise utilized. Like other observers, Mather took note of the annual disappearance and reappearance of certain species of birds. But unlike the others who commented on the migrations, he felt no need to speculate or investigate, for he had been granted divine knowledge. Among the revelations he deigned to share with the public was one presented in the Royal Society's usually more reliable *Philosophical Transactions* to the effect that wild pigeons did, indeed, accomplish their seasonal disappearance by migrating; they betook themselves to an unknown satellite, an undiscovered moon "accompanying the Earth at a near Distance."

Later naturalists (notably Catesby and Audubon) were possessed of sufficiently less assurance and more curiosity to doubt such edicts and to discover the truth through experimental investigation. Audubon's bird-banding experiments were as brilliant as they were simple. Perhaps, then, even Mather's brand of natural history served a purpose, if only the negative purpose of spurring refutation.

In a more positive way, at least one more amateur naturalist prefigured the great explorations of Mark Catesby and his scientific heirs. This man was John Lawson, Surveyor-General of North Carolina, whose *History of Carolina* included long passages of *natural* history and preceded by two decades Catesby's study of the same general region. Between 1701 and 1708, Lawson spent considerable time describing and drawing a menagerie of the New World. His drawings were sometimes more imaginative than realistic, as when he drew an unusually large bobcat astride a stylized stag reminiscent of English heraldry rather than American zoology, and a fox-faced raccoon using its tail as bait to catch a crab, and a rattlesnake with its head hungrily probing beneath a turtle's carapace while its berattled tail lashes the victim from above.

Such fantasy notwithstanding, Lawson's achievement was significant. He contributed accurate observations regarding the presence and regional prevalence of such creatures as the wolf, cougar, beaver, sturgeon, turkey, trumpeter swan (which was never very abundant), passenger pigeon, and Carolina parakeet. The parakeet, doomed by its need of unspoiled habitat as well as by its propensity for raiding fields and orchards, was to be extirpated even sooner than the Labrador duck and the passenger pigeon.

Among the mammals Lawson drew was a somewhat stunted, bovine, and excessively curly coated bison. At that time, woods bison grazed in the East. Darker than the Plains bison and almost humpless, they were sometimes seen in herds numbering more than a hundred, though they were never incalculably plentiful, as were their western counterparts. East of the Appalachians, the last one was killed in Pennsylvania in 1801, at a place ironically called Buffalo Cross Roads, near Lewisburg. East of the Mississippi, the last two—a cow and her calf—were killed in what is now West Virginia in 1825. Audubon recalled seeing bison in Kentucky when he was a young man, but Lawson was correct in his earlier surmise that eastern bison were never exceptionally plentiful. The species, he wrote, "seldom appears among the English inhabitants, his chief Haunt being in the land of Massiassippi."

He was pardonably less astute in his notes regarding cougars, for he was biased by the agriculturist's fear of depredations on livestock. Thus he characterized the species as "the greatest Enemy to the Planter of any Varmine in Carolina." He must have been influenced by the almost universal fear of the cougar, the bear, and the wolf, yet his attempts at objectivity were more successful—indeed admirable—in the case of the wolf than in that of the cougar. Scoffing at the legendary blood lust of wolves, he insisted that they "are not Man-slayers, neither is any Creature in Carolina unless wounded."

Such a statement must have made him, in turn, the victim of other scoffers, but of course he was quite correct. The wolf's harmlessness to man is a behavioral fact of which modern naturalists are still trying valiantly to convince those who are less familiar with nature than with myth.

There was, perhaps, one exception to Lawson's rule that Carolina's "Creatures" were not "Man-slayers." If, as Peter Matthiessen points out in his book *Wildlife in America*, Lawson shared the common view of Indians as "Creatures"—a species of wild beast though related to the human (European) species—then surely he acknowledged one dangerous variety of wildlife in eastern America. For Lawson was sufficiently familiar with the friction between the natives and the settlers to be distrustful of Indians, and he met his death at the hands of men: Indians. One can only speculate whether he was so much more objective than his peers that he understood what provocations would wound and arouse any "Creature," the human species included.

Perhaps he was not that far ahead of his time. Perhaps he was more understanding of the wolf than of that more dangerous example of nature's "productions," man. He was, nevertheless, a missionary of the scientific attitude—the attitude that rejects old myth in favor of new discovery—and a precursor of men like Catesby who would establish this continent as the world's richest vein for the prospector of nature's mysterious creations.

Chapter 2
MARK CATESBY

In the last quarter of the seventeenth century and the first years of the eighteenth, there were many who, like Cotton Mather, arrived at their opinions of natural phenomena through cogitation that intermittently seemed to kindle divine revelation; and there were still more who contented themselves with received dogma or wild surmise. But the light of the Age of Reason was already glimmering in the minds of many. In Europe, particularly, intellectualism was acquiring a new and, indeed, fashionable respectability. For more than a century, many kinds of skepticism, ranging from that of Columbus to that of Galileo, had been influencing the search for knowledge.

Building on the works of Galileo and Kepler, the English philosopher and mathematician Sir Isaac Newton—who, significantly, considered himself a natural scientist—in 1665 discovered the binomial theorem of algebra; shortly afterward developed the elements of differential calculus; and began to ponder the problems of gravity that would be fully expounded in the 1680s, when he wrote his great *Principia*. In the solution of natural mysteries, the power of logic was becoming manifest and was being extended to all branches of inquiry.

Partly because of the needs of agriculture and partly because the medical practice of the time depended heavily on "botanicals," plant research was gaining new adherents and was among the beneficiaries of the new scientific spirit. Systematic principles of botany were being formulated by men like the

9

French scientist Joseph Pitton de Tournefort, and still more important work was being done in England by John Ray.

At about the time Newton was writing his *Principia*, Ray was preparing his *Methodus plantarium*, in which he presented a system of plant classification that greatly influenced the development of systematic botany, and, in fact, helped to form a fundamental basis for modern classification. Ray, like most naturalists, delved into more than one field of inquiry. A century later Georges Cuvier, the French anatomist, called another facet of Ray's work "the basis of all modern zoology." Ray and his patron, Francis Willughby, were also credited with helping to found scientific ornithology. Their classifications of birds, and of fishes as well, were followed in large part by the Swedish botanist and systematist Carl Linnaeus in his *Systema naturae* and in his subsequent works which established the system of binomial nomenclature for all living creatures.

Today a trinomial nomenclature prevails in order to designate subspecies after stating the genus and species, and the criteria for differentiation have become far more accurate and sophisticated. (Linnaeus, for example, classified many plants merely according to the number of their stamens and pistils, a basis he recognized as artificial and oversimplified but one that was expedient in a period when so many new plants were being discovered that a scientist could not afford the time for more careful examination and classification.) But in spite of modification to conform to new knowledge, the fundamental Linnaean method remains valid and essential to modern taxonomy. Ray and, in later years, Mark Catesby furnished precious data for Linnaeus.

It is significant that scientific explorers like Newton and Ray were members of the Royal Society, the oldest scientific organization in Great Britain and one of the oldest in the world. Through the presentation and publication of discoveries and through the subsidies of wealthy patrons, the Society made possible a great many scientific advances. Mark Catesby was another fellow of the Society and he, too, provided many of the ornithological classifications used by Linnaeus.

Catesby was also an adept artist whose wildlife paintings have been compared to those of William Bartram, Alexander Wilson, and John James Audubon; in fact, Audubon's portrayals reveal Catesby's strong influence. Like a growing number of his illustrious colleagues, Catesby was a skeptic of untried scientific dogma. As both artist and field investigator, he was too close an observer to accept contemporary notions about the seasonal disappearance of migratory birds, for example. He rejected the common belief that swallows hibernated in hollow trees or caves or in the muddy bottoms of ponds. He dismissed the notion that some other birds hid their migrations from human eyes by flying high above the atmosphere. And he had little use for Matherian dicta to the effect that passenger pigeons wintered on an undiscovered moon.

In his great work, *The Natural History of Carolina, Florida, and the Bahama Islands*, Catesby included a far more down-to-earth commentary in connection with his plate depicting "The Pigeon of Passage," as he called the species:

> In their passage the People of New-York and Philadelphia shoot many of them as they fly, from their balconies and tops of houses; and in New-England there are such numbers, that with long poles they knock them down from their roofs in the night in great numbers.
>
> The only information I have had from whence they come, and their places of breeding, was from a Canada Indian, who told me he had seen them make their nests in rocks by the sides of rivers and lakes far north of the river St. Lawrence, where he said he had shot them. It is remarkable that none are ever seen to return, at least this way; and what other rout they may take is unknown.

Probably Catesby's greatest single contribution to the scientific archives of the Royal Society was a paper he read in 1747, a few years after publication of his *Natural History*. Entitled "Of Birds of Passage," it put to rest the legends about avian hibernation and supernaturally high migratory flights. (In this latter regard, he was ahead of even the revered Linnaeus.) Typically, Catesby conceded his paper's own chief flaw, "the want of occular testimony," but the treatise was a major advance in that it presented a rational view, though it contained errors regarding details of the causes, manner, and extent of migrations.

Catesby declared that birds flew south when they were urged on by cold and diminished food. This is, of course, an oversimplification and may strike modern readers as an astonishingly obvious speculation, but it is a fundamentally true over-simplification and evidently not very obvious since it had eluded other investigators. Because Catesby knew little about climatology and because he shared the passion of his time for uniformity among creatures—a "grand design" of Providence that seemed to necessitate symmetry in nature—he blundered regarding where and how far the various birds migrated. But these understandable errors detracted little from the value of Catesby's contributions, either in this paper or in his revolutionary two-volume *Natural History*, a pioneering work in scientific illustration, the most complete and authoritative work of its time, and for a century the best account of North American flora and fauna.

An outstanding characteristic of early naturalists in America—Catesby, John and William Bartram, Wilson, Audubon—was their patient and unquenchable enthusiasm for personal observation of nature, even under trying circumstances. In 1714, on a voyage to the West Indies, shipboard accommodations were so scant that Catesby was forced to share close quarters with a flock of sheep. He cheerfully bore his odorous and unsanitary plight, so intrigued was he with the physiological adaptations of the sheep, "which," he noted, "as they approached the South, gradually dropt their Fleeces, which by the Time they arrived at the Island [Jamaica], was all fallen off and was succeeded by Hair like that of Goats."

On another occasion, in September of 1725, he lay for three nights on the deck of a sloop at Andros Island, listening to passing "rice birds"—bobolinks. He came to the conclusion that the long migrations of these handsome little black, white, and yellowish songbirds could be explained in terms of the ripening time for rice from Cuba to Carolina. His notes at this time were themselves like grain slowly ripening; they would mature into his later theories on bird migration.

There was little in Mark Catesby's English background to foretell his role as a bold, pioneering chronicler of American natural history. His baptismal record, surviving in the parish register of St. Nicholas Church, Castle Hedingham, Essex, shows that he was born on March 24, 1682, according to the Julian calendar then favored in England—a date corresponding to April 3, 1682, on the Gregorian calendar subsequently adopted and still in use. Historians have sometimes reported his place and year of birth as Sudbury, 1679, or 1680, an error perhaps arising from the later adoption of the new calendar and the fact that the Catesby family moved from Sudbury to Hedingham shortly before he was born. He was the youngest son of John and Elizabeth Catesby, the fourth of five children still alive (several others having died in infancy) when their father drew up his will in 1700. John Catesby, like many of his relatives and ancestors, was a prosperous solicitor, farmer, landlord, and minor politician. He was mayor of Sudbury for four years. His surname, derived from the Parish of Catesby, dated to the twelfth century. His wife's family, the Jekylls, also included a number of lawyers and politicians, as well as antiquarian scholars, and their pedigree could be traced to Lincolnshire in the region of Henry VI. Notwithstanding an indulgence in political controversy by some of the Catesbys, the family typified rural England: complacent and genteel.

Mark Catesby probably attended the Sudbury Grammar School and he may have been tutored by a nonconformist preacher named Samuel Petto, whom John Catesby protected during the period of political hostility toward religious dissenters. The Reverend Petto was a minor scientific figure whose studies of the phenomena known as parhelia—luminous halos associated with the sun—appeared in the *Philosophical Transactions* in 1699. It is likely that the boy enjoyed an early exposure to the challenges of natural science.

Perhaps even more important were frequent visits to the home of his uncle, Nicholas Jekyll, a studious local historian and a friend of England's foremost naturalist, John Ray, who probably ranked second to no English scientist of the time except Newton. Though Jekyll was not an accomplished scientist, he shared Ray's interest in botany. (Some years later the celebrated English naturalist and ornithological illustrator George Edwards, who edited the great second edition of Catesby's *Natural History* which appeared in 1754, and who also collaborated with William Bartram, wrote that John Ray had inspired young Catesby to take up natural history.) Another friend of Ray and the Catesbys was Samuel Dale, a physician, amateur botanist, and patron of science. Dale was to help finance Mark Catesby's American explorations.

Mark Catesby thus passed a good deal of time during his

youth in the company of England's new intelligentsia—part of the circle of late seventeenth and early eighteenth century intellectuals who helped to inaugurate the Age of Reason.

In 1705 his father died, leaving him a modest income. It was probably then that he began making trips to London to study botany with gifted nurserymen such as Thomas Fairchild, to whom he later shipped plants and seeds from Virginia. In the preface to his *Natural History*, Catesby recalled his yearning first to study in London and then in more distant places. In a sense, the chance to satisfy the latter desire was provided by his sister Elizabeth, characterized by John Catesby as "my disobedient daughter," because she had married Dr. William Cocke and settled with him in Virginia. As noted in the first of the two volumes of Catesby's *Natural History*, her residence there made possible his first American sojourn. It was probably during a visit at Nicholas Jekyll's home in 1711 that arrangements were discussed for him to sail to Virginia and send back botanical specimens for Samuel Dale.

Catesby arrived in Williamsburg on April 23, 1712, and stayed at the home of Dr. Cocke, a successful physician and politician who was soon appointed Secretary to the Colony and in 1713 became one of Her Majesty's councilors. Here he met several influential colonists, and he subsequently visited for nearly a month at the Westover plantation of William Byrd, a member of the Virginia Council. Byrd evidently was an inquisitive though not very adept naturalist; he and his guest strolled about the plantation observing hummingbird nests and such, and he noted in his diary that "Mr. Catesby directed how I should mend my garden."

After a second visit that autumn, Catesby accompanied Byrd to an Indian town on the Pamunkey River where Byrd had an appointment with Governor Alexander Spotswood to attempt settlement of a dispute they were having over quitrents. Dr. Cocke sided with Spotswood in this dispute, which was not quickly ended, and Catesby must have exercised considerable diplomacy in order to maintain a cordial neutrality, antagonizing neither his brother-in-law nor the Governor.

The Pamunkey River trip afforded Catesby his first view of Indians (discounting a few at Williamsburg). He developed his observations then and later into an impressive discourse on American aborigines in the second volume of his *Natural History*. To him, as to several other early naturalists in this country, Indians were "Productions of Nature," as deserving of investigation as any other living creatures. Anthropology—cultural and physical anthropology intertwined—was a legitimate branch of natural history, and in this regard it can be said that Mark Catesby, William Bartram, the artist George Catlin, and John James Audubon were among the pioneering American anthropologists. This view of all inhabitants of a natural environment as interrelated was surprisingly common, almost taken for granted, until the rise of extremely specialized, self-isolating scientific disciplines caused the overall approach to be neglected. Modern ecologists have by no means founded a new science or even a new approach but have revived and refined an old one.

Catesby's theories about the aborigines were in some respects simplistic—a reflection of contemporary views. He believed, for example, that all Indian groups were parts of a single group and essentially alike, regardless of differences in customs, linguistics, physiognomy, geography, and so on. This uniformist view hardly encouraged lengthy investigation, and, in fact Catesby was content to borrow a good deal of material (with due acknowledgment) from John Lawson's *History of Carolina*. Yet he was astonishingly far ahead of his time in certain of his perceptions about Indians. Having noted similarities to Asian peoples, he concluded that American aborigines were of Asian origin. And even though he did not have a particularly firm grasp of geography or geology, he wrote that "there is a probability that the Continent of the northeast Part of Asia, may be very near, if not contiguous to that of America." Reading these words, written when pre-Columbian views regarding the size of the globe and the nearness of Asia had been discredited, and when nothing was yet known of the now-vanished land bridge that crossed the Bering Strait to link Asia with Alaska, one is reminded that great scientists are reputed to temper their skepticism with an insight akin to intuition.

For more than a year, Catesby collected Virginian botanical specimens. In the spring of 1713, Governor Spotswood sent a packet of Catesby's seeds to Henry Compton, Bishop of London, whose garden was notable for its exotic plants. Catesby also sent botanicals for apothecary use to Samuel Dale; and seeds to

Thomas Fairchild, the horticultural essayist and nurseryman; and specimens to Nicholas Jekyll, who succeeded in bringing some of them to maturity as flowering acacia trees at Hedingham.

At about this time, Catesby seems to have been inspired by the work of Sir Hans Sloane, Court Physician, colleague of John Ray, editor of the Royal Society's *Philosophical Transactions*, writer of natural history, and the man whose collections of books, manuscripts, plants, and curiosities formed the original basis of the British Museum. Sloane was one of the influential Englishmen who encouraged the work of naturalists in America. In 1687–1688 he had visited Jamaica as physician to the Duke of Albermarle, and while there had collected some eight hundred new species of plants. By 1707 he had completed the first volume of an important work on the flora and fauna of the West Indies, and was working on the second volume, which was published in 1725. The full title of this seminal work, commonly called *The Natural History of Jamaica*, was *A Voyage to the Islands Madera, Barbados, Nieves, S. Christophers and Jamaica with the Natural History of the Herbs and Trees, Four-footed Beasts, Fishes, Birds, Insects, Reptiles, &c.* Sloane's work was an immediate and strong influence. In 1714 Catesby voyaged to the West Indies, primarily to explore Jamaica, and it is believed that his impetus was the first volume of Sloane's account. At this early date, Catesby could not have known that Sloane was to be a patron as well as an example when he began his own work on a similar treatise covering Carolina, Florida, and the Bahamas.

It was on this voyage that Catesby shared his berth with sheep and managed to concentrate his attention on the phenomenon of their molting pelage rather than their mounting odor. He was now beginning to record his observations of such things as the "Plat Palmetto" in Bermuda and "Cacao-Walks" planted by the Spaniards in Jamaica. On the latter island and perhaps in Bermuda, he also collected specimens to confirm and supplement Sloane's findings. He then returned to Virginia, and though he remained until 1719, little more is known of his years there. Bits and pieces have survived: a passage in the Cocke family genealogy showing that Catesby spent much time at Windsor, Major William Woodward's plantation in Carolina County; brief observations by the naturalist regarding shells found seventy feet down in a well shaft at Windsor—more of that sort of thing, nothing significant. In Volume I of his *Natural History* he was to speak ruefully of that first American exploration:

I thought then so little of prosecuting a Design of the Nature of this Work, that in the Seven Years I resided in that Country, (I am ashamed to own it) I chiefly gratified my Inclination in observing and admiring the various Productions of those Countries . . . only sending from thence some dried Specimens of Plants and some . . . in Tubs of Earth, at the Request of some curious Friends, amongst whom was Mr. Dale of Braintree. . . .

Apart from the shipment of those specimens and some seeds, he said, he had also sent Dale a "few observations on the Country," but he evidently felt he had accomplished little, though he had gained valuable experience and had begun to make the drawings that would play a pivotal role in his great opus.

Soon after Catesby returned to England in the autumn of 1719, Dale discussed his abilities and prospects with William Sherard, founder of the Chair of Botany at Oxford and, in Catesby's words, "one of the most celebrated Botanists of this Age." Sherard brought Catesby's collecting talents to the attention of the Royal Society. It was an instance of the right man appearing at the right time to undertake a major scientific venture.

For a decade or more, English scholars and scientists had been contemplating an extensive specimen-collecting project in the American colonies. The idea had been considerably stimulated by Surveyor-General John Lawson of North Carolina in 1709, when he had published *A New Voyage to Carolina*. The 1714 edition and those that came after were significantly retitled *The History of Carolina: Containing the Exact Descriptions and Natural History of that Country: Together with the Present State Thereof.* This account, if somewhat credulous in its acceptance of popular beliefs, was the most comprehensive description so far attempted of the region's flora and fauna. Less than a year after publication of the first edition, Lawson was persuaded by another of the prominent English naturalists, the apothecary James Petiver, to compile a complete natural history of Carolina. But the work had barely begun when, in 1711, Lawson was killed by Tuscarora Indians. Upon Petiver's death in 1718, Sherard became the leading promoter of American scientific explorations, and he judged

Catesby to be a promising replacement for Lawson. Through Dale, he offered to find support for further explorations by Catesby.

One of the first patrons recruited was Colonel Francis Nicholson, Governor of South Carolina, who declared he would grant the naturalist a pension of twenty pounds per annum to pursue the work. Other potential subscribers were approached, and the Council Minutes of the Royal Society for October 20, 1720, duly noted that Mr. Catesby was to "observe the Rarities" of South Carolina. The prestige of the Royal Society's approval attracted additional subscribers. Among the major patrons were Sloane and Sherard, Charles Dubois (treasurer of the East India Company), and James Bridges, Duke of Chandos. For a brief period they were inclined to send Catesby off to Africa rather than America, but they reverted to the original plan and Catesby sailed for Charles Town in February, 1722.

The crossing required three months, for the vessel detoured far southward to avoid North Atlantic storms, and Catesby must have been elated when he finally stepped ashore in May. By June he had set to work, journeying "40 miles up the country"—country that was a largely unknown frontier. During this period he began writing to his patrons, and his letters revealed a descriptive aptitude—as when he told how a storm "disrobed the trees"—that would aid him in the writing of his *Natural History*. In December, he sent Sherard a description of the storm and its aftermath: "About the middle of September here fell the greatest flood attended with a Hurricane that has been known since the country was settled. Great numbers of Cattle, Horses, Hogs, and some people were drowned. The Deer were found frequently lodged on high trees."

For a while, the damage to vegetation hampered his collecting activities, and he was also perplexed by the choice between quantity and variety in finding specimens to be sent to Sloane and Dubois, "especially," he remarked, "when I am several hundred miles off." That spring, in sore need of manual assistance to handle his supplies and collection, he purchased a slave, then resumed his explorations. The ardors and dangers of these explorations occasionally emerge in notes and letters. At Newington he saw a rattlesnake eight feet long (but evidently did not collect it) and, the following winter, a Negro woman who was making up his bed found a smaller but aggressive rattler between the sheets. "Probably it crept in for warmth in the night," he wrote to Sherard, "but how long I had the company of [the] charming Bedfellow I am not able to say."

Most physicians of the time believed in one kind of snakeroot or another as an antidote for rattler venom. Catesby himself was not quite sure such remedies might not be efficacious under certain circumstances and he dutifully sent snakeroot specimens to England, but he cautioned that "where a vein or Artery is pricked by the bite of a Rattle Snake no Antidote will avail anything, but Death certainly and suddenly ensues, sometimes in 2 or 3 minutes, which I have more than once seen." Though it is hard to imagine so fast a death from a rattler bite, Catesby's doubts about snakeroot show him to be better informed than most chemists, physicians, and other scientists of the age.

In March of 1723, he traveled a hundred and forty miles through the backwoods to Fort Moore, an outpost on the Carolina side of the Savannah River. In this area he encountered a band of sixty Indians. Fortunately, they were at peace with England at the moment, and Catesby got on well with Indians. He soon hired one to guide him, help carry equipment and specimens, and help shoot the game on which Catesby and any companions sometimes subsisted. After this he did not mention the slave—his "Negro Boy"—again. Perhaps he freed or sold him. Again in the area of Fort Moore in late August, Catesby told of fishing for enormous sturgeon and witnessing a run of them up the Savannah. He wrote to his patrons of his experiences, and later described them in the preface to his *Natural History*:

> I then went to the Upper uninhabited Parts of the Country, and continued at and about *Fort Moore*, a small Foretress on the Banks of the River *Savanna*. . . . I was much delighted to see Nature differ in these Upper Parts, and to find here abundance of things not to be seen in the lower parts of Country. This encouraged me to take several Journeys with the *Indians* higher up the Rivers, towards the Mountains, which afforded not only a succession of new vegetable Appearances, but the most delightful Prospects imaginable, besides the Diversion of Hunting Buffaloes, Bears, Panthers, and other wild Beasts.

During this period, Catesby spent most of his time in the field, exploring the lowlands and the Piedmont bordering the Appalachians. He dried a great many plant specimens and sent them to England pressed in books and between sheets of paper, and he sent live ones in tubs of earth. He also shipped seeds in small wooden boxes and in gourds. Some of his bird specimens were sent in alcohol, but more often he dried them slowly in an oven, then stuffed and covered them with tobacco dust. Snakes, insects, and other small animals were sent in wide-mouthed bottles of rum or other spirits. A great many alcoholically preserved specimens survived the voyage to England in good condition, although sailors sometimes drank off the rum.

Early in the spring of 1724 he made a brief trip into the Cherokee country but evidently returned without having reached the principal Cherokee settlement of Keowee. Next he made plans to explore Mexico with a friend, Dr. Thomas Cooper, but failed to raise sufficient funds and instead sailed for the Bahamas in the spring or summer of 1725. It was during this expedition that he lay on a sloop deck for three nights listening to passing flights of bobolinks and pondering the mysteries of migration.

The following year he returned to England to begin the task of communicating what he had seen in words and paintings. Having spent about a fourth of his forty-three years exploring America's wilderness, he was eager to begin a new kind of labor. He had many field sketches and paintings, and had resisted most of his patrons' demands for them, but he was unsure of his drafting and coloring skill. He therefore took instruction from Joseph Goupy, a French-born etcher and watercolor painter. The informality and brevity of his artistic training was perhaps beneficial, for his work shows not only a quasi-primitive vigor but a dynamic freedom unusual in previous illustrations of natural history. Few of his birds, for example, were drawn in the customary stiff profile. A famous and exemplary plate was one showing a bald eagle—called "White-headed Eagle" by Catesby—diving to catch a falling mullet dropped by an osprey. The osprey soars in the distance, haplessly watching the aerial robbery of its prey.

Catesby also had the wisdom to show plants and different orders of creatures in relation to one another—a swallowtail butterfly hovering about a hop tree, a catbird about to snatch an insect, animals depicted with plants forming an appropriate background rather than a stylized setting. He included plants (more often than not in their proper ecological context) in all of his plates except those depicting fishes and a few birds.

His art is inferior to Alexander Wilson's and hardly comparable to Audubon's, yet better than that of his contemporaries and realistic enough to influence Audubon. Thus his pioneering work has been judged vastly significant in the development of ornithological illustration. In the preface to his first volume, Catesby himself explained his intention:

> I humbly conceive that Plants, and other Things done in a Flat, tho' exact Manner, may serve the Purpose of Natural History, better in some Measure, than in a more bold and Painter-like Way. . . . The Animals, particularly the Birds, I painted while alive (except a very few) and gave them their Gestures peculiar to every kind of Birds, and where it could be admitted, I have adapted the Birds to those Plants on which they fed, or have any relation to.

Catesby planned an immense two-volume encyclopedia of the natural history he had observed in the southeastern part of continental North America—"Carolina and Florida," as he styled it—and the Bahamas. Since this would require years, he determined to publish it in sections, each containing twenty plates together with their descriptive texts. The projected total price of the work, with two hundred plates, would be twenty guineas, and he was able to support himself in part by selling the installments to subscribers at two guineas each. During the early stages of production, he engraved the copper and colored the finished pages himself. At the same time he augmented his income by working at Thomas Fairchild's Hoxton nursery, and he obtained a substantial loan from Peter Collinson, a Quaker merchant and patron of American natural history, who was to be instrumental in furthering the careers of the Bartrams.

Three sections of the book were completed by 1730 and a fourth by 1731. The fifth and final section of Volume I, bringing the number of plates to one hundred, was presented to the Royal Society on November 23, 1732, although the volume's title page bore the date 1731 and this is usually given as the year of publication. Thus, one occasionally sees references to new species, such as the ivory-billed woodpecker, "first described by Mark Catesby in 1731." This rare, beautiful black and white bird with its fiery-red crest, brought to the verge of extinction since Catesby's time, appeared in association with the willow oak in

Plate 16. Catesby straightforwardly named it "The largest white bill Wood-pecker." He had, of course, discovered and described it long before, as he had many other American birds and plants, but the year of publication is customarily used to date such discoveries.

The first volume firmly established Catesby's scientific reputation, and a year after its presentation to the Royal Society he was elected a fellow of that august body. He was an active member. In 1734, the year he completed the sixth part of his *Natural History*—the first section of Volume II—he presented the Society with the skin of an animal known to many Carolineans as the "Black Fox." He explained that it was a "Polecat" (an eastern spotted skunk, *Spilogale putorius*). This animal was probably the model for a spotted skunk portrayed in the second volume. In the following year, 1735, the Society invited him to review the first edition of Linnaeus's *Systema naturae.* He declined, not because his Latin was weak (which it was) but because he felt he lacked other qualifications—he was not a systematist or even a consistent follower of the classification system being developed by Linnaeus.

Sherard, before his death in 1728, had provided much of the Latin classification for Catesby's text. Some of Catesby's vernacular names for newly described birds ("Blew Bird, Blew Jay, Hairy Wood-pecker, Red-headed Wood-pecker) have endured. A number of them were already in common American usage; others he named "after European Birds of the same Genus, with an additional Epithet to distinguish them." His pre-Linnaean Latin designations were fashioned, with Sherard's help, by taking the initial Latin nouns from the great three-volume *Ornithology* by John Ray and Francis Willughby and adding Latin versions of his "Epithets."

By 1758, Linnaeus had so refined and expanded his system that his binomials rendered Catesby's Latin designations obsolete. Yet Linnaeus retained some elements of Catesby's designations, and based an impressive number of his classifications on Catesby's descriptions and illustrations (as well as a few specimens that evidently reached him). At least a dozen Linnaean plant classifications were based on Catesby, as were designations (whole or in part) of seventy-five mainland American birds and several Bahaman birds.

It is possible that Catesby's timidity about reviewing Linnaeus for the Royal Society was reinforced by the initial hostility of English botanists toward the young Swedish systematist. His expedient but botanically simplistic classification of plants by their reproductive organs was not universally accepted, and on one occasion Sir Hans Sloane had received a letter from Johann Amman suggesting that if plants were to be grouped in that manner one might as well classify animals by their penises. During a visit to England in 1736, Linnaeus overcame much of the hostility. He had read Catesby's first volume and at this time the two probably met. Thereafter each was influenced by a respect for the other's achievements.

Having published the sixth section of his masterpiece in 1734, Catesby completed three more parts in the next four years and the last of the projected installments, plus an introduction, in 1743. Even then, however, he was not quite satisfied with the scope of the work, and a twenty-plate appendix was added in 1747. Thus, he had worked more than twenty years to complete a work that remained definitive through almost the first half of the nineteenth century. Without doubt, it influenced and encouraged other investigators even before the appearance of the second volume. There was, for example, the two-volume *Flora virginica*, by Johann Friedrich Gronovius and John Clayton, published in Leyden in 1739–1743. A second, much improved edition appeared in 1762, and except for Catesby's work, it was the century's finest study of plants in Britain's American colonies.

During all the years of his labor, Mark Catesby had evidently been too busy, too preoccupied with his investigations, to think of marriage. To those who knew him only casually, he was a solemn, withdrawn man—tall, thin, nearsighted, somewhat stubborn and morose in manner, though cordial with friends. In 1747, at last, he took a spouse. He was then sixty-four years old, and he had only two years to live. He married Mrs. Elizabeth Rowland, a widow with a grown daughter. There is some evidence (and hope on the part of at least the present biographer) that they had lived together for a time before the nuptials. Before his death in 1749, she bore him two children, Mark and Ann.

He died without any suspicion that his fame as a botanist would be nearly eclipsed by his ornithological contributions. He was, after all, the century's most important plant collector; he introduced a number of new botanical species to England and went so far as to grow American poison ivy in his English garden for examination by the Royal Society. He pictured plants carefully, named them descriptively, and in his text noted where he had found them growing and sometimes in what kinds of soil.

His mammal portrayals were not uniformly successful and some of his fishes were bereft of a fin or two, or otherwise inaccurate. His insects, reptiles, and amphibians were generally well depicted and described, but neither these efforts nor his botanical contributions compared with his ornithology. No one—not even John Lawson (whose bird list had been admirable for its time) or John White (who had meticulously painted some of Virginia's birds)—had combined fine illustration with reasonably accurate descriptive text or had matched Catesby's scope. He portrayed one hundred and thirteen birds representing one hundred and nine species.

"I believe," he wrote, "very few Birds have escaped my Knowledge, except some Water Fowl and some of those which frequent the Sea." He was not quite right but he underestimated the diversity of American bird species only because he was overenthusiastic in applying his (essentially correct) theory that, except for aquatic species, "Animals in general, and particularly Birds, diminish in numbers of species so much nearer they approach the Pole."

He contributed extraordinarily advanced speculations regarding migration; he provided relatively detailed data regarding coloration and size; and he furnished comparisons with similar European birds. Oddly, the descriptions accompanying some of the most detailed paintings are sketchy, but for those birds he had been able to observe carefully, he included comments on migratory, feeding, and sometimes breeding habits. His exquisite delineation of "The Summer Duck" (a wood-duck drake) is enhanced by a description of the male, a note that "The Female is all over brown," and a commentary that is vivid and reasonably accurate until, in the last lines, it relies on hearsay. "They breed in Virginia and Carolina," he wrote, having no way of knowing where else they might breed, "and make their nests in the holes of tall trees (made by Wood-peckers) growing in water, particularly Cypress Trees." This interesting and valid observation was marred only by the acceptance of the legend that the young are flown from the nest on the backs of the adults and escape danger in the same manner.

Regardless of such occasional errors, the text—in parallel English and French columns, the French translation by an unknown writer—outstrips all eighteenth-century efforts. Without Catesby, more than one authority has declared, the work of Linnaeus and other pioneering taxonomists would have been far less complete. In a monograph on American ornithology before Audubon, Elsa G. Allen has called Catesby the "founder of American Ornithology." And in a monograph on the nomenclature of American birds, the ornithologist Witmer Stone averred that Catesby's work "forms the basis of the ornithology not only of the Southern States, but the whole of North America."

Chapter 3
THE BARTRAMS

In 1813, a thirty-nine-year-old botanist named Frederick Traugott Pursh completed a comprehensive listing of American plant species. His work was published the following year in London in two octavo volumes with the title *Flora Americae Septentrionalis, or a Systematic Arrangement and Description of the Plants of North America*. Linnaeus had published his *Species Plantarium* in 1762, just over a half-century earlier. During that half-century, the number of known plant species in Britain's former American colonies, in the territories to the west, and in Canada had multiplied to 3,076—a threefold increase. Botanical historians have attributed this tripling of knowledge to four major factors: reinterpretations of earlier findings; discoveries in the Pacific Northwest; the penetration of the prairies in the Missouri River Basin; and the southeastern travels of John and William Bartram.

Linnaeus called John Bartram "the greatest natural botanist in the world." Bartram's son William was an exceptionally gifted illustrator of plants and, in the judgment of later scholars, an even better botanist than his father. And both father and son made significant contributions to field studies other than botany. John Bartram collected and described shells, birds, insects, fishes and turtles for the edification of English and Continental scientists. In his journals and many letters he also recorded sound new ideas in geology. For example, in a letter written in 1755 to Alexander Garden, a Scottish-American physician, naturalist, and plant collector, Bartram proposed the borings and mappings of underground strata, which became a major undertaking of the Geological Survey many years later. "Contrary to the beliefs of his time," as the *Dictionary of American Biography* points out in a brief synopsis, "he conceived limestones and marbles to have been formed as geologists now believe they were." And on the banks of the Schuylkill River near Philadelphia, John Bartram established this country's first educational and experimental botanical garden.

His son William, who significantly expanded the famous garden, was the first native-born American artist-naturalist. Some two dozen of his meticulous botanical drawings represented the first full descriptive reports of species new to science. A number of them served in lieu of actual type specimens, furnishing proof of priority in scientific reportage and acceptance of a taxonomic name. In his book *Travels,* published in 1791, he included a *Catalogue* of two hundred and fifteen birds of the eastern United States, the fullest and most accurate ornithological listing prior to Alexander Wilson's; in the same book, he proposed one hundred and twenty-three new binomial designations for American flora and fauna; and he presented the first detailed physical and behavioral descriptions of such little-understood animals as bullfrogs and alligators. Finally, his work, personality, and encouragement served as inspiration for Alexander Wilson and other young naturalists who were to make important contributions.

The patrilineal grandfather after whom John Bartram was named left England in 1682 and settled with his family on a farm near Darby, in Delaware County, Pennsylvania. Of old John's three sons and a daughter, only the youngest son, William, married, and he in turn begat a daughter and three sons, one of whom was John Bartram the future botanist, born at the farm near Darby on March 23, 1699, according to the "old calendar"—April 2, 1699, by Gregorian reckoning. Like his father and grandfather, he was a Quaker farmer, possessed of more piety than schooling, but he had an inquiring and very independent intellect that would bring him into conflict with the Society of Friends, while leading him to the frontiers of scientific observation.

In a letter to one of his patrons, Peter Collinson, he recalled having had a passionate interest in botany from the age of about ten, and his early botanical curiosity was also mentioned in a biographical sketch by his son William. A concurrent interest in medicine, probably awakened during his adolescence, prompted him to study the properties of plants reputed to have healing powers. "He had a very early inclination," William wrote, "to the Study of Physics and Surgery. . . . He gave great relief to his poor neighbors who were unable to apply for medicine and assistance to the Physicians of the city [Philadelphia]. . . . Most of his medicines were derived from the vegetable Kingdom. . . ."

As a young man, John Bartram made frequent journeys to Philadelphia to find books on medicine and botany. In Philadelphia he met James Logan, a civic leader, bibliophile, amateur gardener, and founder of the Loganian Library, who procured for Bartram a copy of John Parkinson's *Herbal* and other influential botanical treatises. Though never bookish or even very scholarly, Bartram was sufficiently inspired to engage a tutor in Latin so that, a few years later, he could read the newly published *Systema naturae* of Linnaeus.

In Philadelphia, too, Bartram met young Benjamin Franklin, who had organized a debating club known as the Junto, or Leather Apron Club, in 1727 and four years later helped to organize the Library Company of Philadelphia in order to obtain books for club members. Franklin gave Bartram a share of the Company, which became the first American subscription library, and Bartram later shipped seeds, specimens, and even clothing under the care of this organization. Franklin became his lifelong friend and a valuable promoter of his reputation.

But even before that, Bartram had decided that he must live closer to the cultural and scientific activity of Philadelphia. He was no longer satisfied with farming his land near Darby, the legacy of an uncle. In 1723, he had wed Mary Maris, who had given him two sons before she died in 1727. As a moderately prosperous farmer and stonemason, the young widower was able to buy a small piece of farmland in 1728. It was situated on the west bank of the Schuylkill at Kingsessing. The buildings and garden survive, a quiet oasis surrounded by low-cost housing, deteriorating tenements, and Philadelphia's sprawling industrial maze. It was then a rural village three miles from the city's outskirts. Bartram, who enjoyed manual labor and was almost as proud of his masonry as of his gardening, erected four stone buildings. One was the main house at Kingsessing, his home and that of his celebrated son. He carved a pious inscription in faulty Greek over the door, and in front of it he began to lay out his garden. In 1729, soon after buying the little farm, he was ready to marry again. His second wife, Ann Mendenhall, was to give him five sons and four daughters. William Bartram was the third of Ann's sons. He and his twin sister Elizabeth were born in the stone house on the Schuylkill on April 20, 1739.

Ann Mendenhall Bartram was content as the wife of a comfortable farmer and mason. When James Logan began encouraging John Bartram to become a professional botanist, she expressed fears that he could not earn a livelihood in such work. Perhaps, too, she foresaw that botanical investigation would take him on extended journeys while she would be left to tend family and farm. But Logan persisted in his conviction that Bartram "had a genius perfectly well turned for Botany." At first, Bartram seemed indecisive. Apparently he had no intention of amassing an important herbarium or describing new species; he simply liked to gather, distribute, grow, study, and experiment with living plants. With introductions supplied by Logan, he began to correspond with English gardeners, naturalists, and potential patrons. One of these was Peter Collinson, a fellow Quaker, botanical collector, and friend of American naturalists. Bartram and Collinson were never to meet but their correspondence, begun in 1733, continued until Collinson's death in 1768, and Collinson became one of Bartram's chief patrons. They traded both plants and information, and by letter they discussed the success or failure of every bulb or cutting. In 1735, Collinson offered Bartram his patronage by arranging to buy seeds for himself and other English gardeners and naturalists. Bartram was to supply boxes of seeds, one hundred species to a box, at five guineas for each such shipment. He sent about twenty boxes a year until 1760.

As soon as botany began to sustain him, Bartram intensified his studies. By 1739, he was able to write to Colonel William Byrd of Virginia about his "microscopical observations on the malle and femall parts in vegetables" and his "several Successful experiments of joyning several species of the same genus whereby I have obtained curious mixed Colours in flowers never known before." He had produced a flesh-colored lychnis and perhaps other curiosities. There in his garden on the Schuylkill he was performing the first American experiments in cross-fertilization and hybridization.

The following year he sent Johann Friedrich Gronovius a specimen which Gronovius determined to be a new genus of moss. It was appropriately named *Bartramia*. (Curiously and somewhat ironically, subsequent reclassifications have resulted in the use of the name for an entirely different moss, which Bartram did not discover.) Gronovius also credited Bartram with several fossil discoveries, and Hans Sloane, too, made use of "petrified representations of seashells" supplied by Bartram. Soon the Shuylkill farmer was corresponding with Catesby, Linnaeus, Queen Ulrica of Sweden (Linnaeus's patroness), the German-born botanist Johann Jakob Dillenius (who directed the botanical garden at Oxford), Philip Miller (director of the famous Physic Gardens at Chelsea and author of the *Gardener's Dictionary*), and other naturalists, thus enhancing his knowledge and theirs. Often the exchange must have been more to his benefit than theirs, as when Collinson—for the sake of Bartram's "improvement in the knowledge of plants"—sent him seeds, roots, tree cuttings, vegetables, and flowering plants cultivated in England, as well as goods and clothing for his family, directions for collecting and drying specimens, and packages of paper for their preservation. Lord Petre, an enthusiastic horticulturist and owner of extensive private gardens, sent a stipend of twenty pounds a year until his death in 1742, and Bartram also received funds from Philip Miller and the Duke of Richmond. The total income was not large but it sufficed.

In the mid-1730s Bartram began making collecting trips, at first exploring the Schuylkill and sending his patrons a journal and maps. To Collinson, he shipped such "Rarities" as insects, birds, eggs, nests, turtles, snakes, shells, a hornet's nest, wasps, and fossils that were regarded as "evidence of the Deluge." His first long journey was made in 1738, first to Williamsburg, Virginia, then up the James River and across the Blue Ridge— eleven hundred miles covered in five weeks with only one day of rest.

This expedition and many subsequent trips took place in autumn, the best season for gathering viable seeds, roots, and bulbs. Bartram usually rode alone, and he often belled his horse so that he could locate it, then dismounted and let the animal graze freely while he explored the woods. His genius for recognizing and gathering unfamiliar plants is evident in the fact that in three decades he sent over three hundred species to England.

By 1743, he was a celebrity. In that year, Bartram helped the eminent English naturalist George Edwards prepare a treatise on the mineral licks and "licking ponds" frequented by deer. And that was also the year when the American Philosophical Society was founded, with Benjamin Franklin's name at the head of its roll of nine original members, each representing a different branch of study. Immediately following Franklin's name was that of John Bartram, representing the science of botany.

The following year Bartram sent to his English patrons a "Journal of the Five Nations and the Lake Ontario," containing accounts of the area's soil, mountains, lakes, vegetation, and wildlife, as well as the proceedings of an assembly of Indian chiefs gathered to treat with an agent from the Province of Pennsylvania. A full account—the elder Bartram's best journal— was published in London in 1751 under the copious title: *Observations on the inhabitants, climate, soil, rivers, productions, animals, and other matters worthy of notice. Made by Mr. John Bartram, in his travels from Pensilvania to Onondago, Oswego and the Lake Ontario, in Canada. To which is annex'd, a curious account of the cataracts at Niagara. By Mr. Peter Kalm.* An adept naturalist and one of Linnaeus's favorite students, Kalm was now a correspondent and collaborator. He had toured the American Colonies from 1748 to 1751 and afterward published his *Travels.* Although he has been accused of appropriating some of Bartram's discoveries, he gave Bartram much credit in print and described his visit to the botanical garden at Kingsessing as a "pilgrimage."

The expedition to Lake Ontario had been a mission on which Conrad Weiser, serving as agent for the government of Pennsylvania, met with the Iroquois to arbitrate a dispute between the Indians and the Colony of Virginia. Bartram had accompanied the official party in order to explore and gather specimens. It was possibly—indeed, probably—this experience that resulted in a suggestion of major historical importance which Bartram later made to Benjamin Franklin: a proposal for an ambitious western survey expedition. After listening to Bartram's ideas for such an exploration, Franklin conveyed the suggestion to Thomas Jefferson. And Jefferson's instructions to Lewis and Clark closely resembled Bartram's proposals to Franklin.

In 1751, Franklin and a business partner published an American edition of Dr. Thomas Short's *Medicina Britannica,* with a preface "by Mr. John Bartram, Botanist of Philadelphia." Although Bartram kept journals that were of immense help to other naturalists, he did not enjoy writing for publication. His total published writings were relatively meager and would have been more so had it not been for the urging of men like Franklin. Even the coaxing of such valued friends was not always successful, but many years later Franklin was still trying. On January 9, 1769, he wrote to Bartram from London with enthusiastic advice: "I wish you would . . . employ your leisure hours in a work that is much wanted, and which no one besides is so capable of performing. I mean the writing of a Natural History of our Country. I imagine it would prove profitable to you, and I am sure it would do you honor."

When the comprehensive natural history eventually appeared, the country was no longer a cluster of British colonies but a confederation of states, and the author was not John Bartram but his son William.

In 1753, Franklin had offered another piece of advice, to the effect that John Bartram's fourteen-year-old son Billy, who was already showing artistic aptitude and an interest in natural history, ought to be trained in printing and engraving. Franklin himself volunteered to teach him printing and found another craftsman to teach him engraving. Thus, he reasoned, Billy could capitalize on his drawing skill and would eventually earn a good livelihood even if he did not match his father's success in the natural sciences. Never would he have to depend on patrons as his father did. Evidently the boy dabbled in printing and engraving but certainly did not persist in learning these crafts. That same year he accompanied his father on a tour of the Catskills and a visit to the Newburgh, New York, home of Jane Colden, an American-born caricaturist who collected and sketched natural specimens. It was here that the Bartrams first met Alexander Garden. Billy Bartram seems to have been impressed by Jane Colden's collecting but not by her illustrations. In fact, the crudity of her renderings may have sparked his ambition, for he was aware that his own drawings were better. He had been sketching birds and was soon trying his hand at depicting vegetation accurately. His father proudly described him as "my little botanist."

The following year John Bartram wrote to Jane Colden that "little Billy's" illustrations were already "far beyond Catesby's." He sent samples to Peter Collinson, and through Collinson, he sent a letter to Dr. Gronovius at Leiden, telling him, "I have a little son about fifteen years of age that has traveled with me now three years; & ready he knows most of ye plants that grows in our four governments [;] he hath drawn most of our oaks & birches . . . this is his first essay in drawing plants . . . he hath drawn several birds before." On the back of the letter Collinson added a note: "His sons Drawings are very fine."

That year and the next, young William Bartram attended school in Philadelphia, but there was time enough in the autumn of 1755 for him to accompany his father on another exploration into the Catskills. Thereafter, the two often traveled together. It was also in 1755 that John Bartram suggested to Alexander Garden the possibility of a series of borings to search for minerals, learn the "composition of the earth," and "compose a curious subterranean map." Out of this growing interest in geology came his declaration to Peter Collinson the following year regarding his unshakable "notion that limestone and marble were originally mud, impregnated by a marine salt."

During this period, William Bartram, too, was progressing in his efforts to delineate nature. In 1756, Collinson sent the boy a request, in a letter to his father, for drawings of all species of turtles he could find. In the same letter he praised an illustration the seventeen-year-old William had sent him showing the tupelo, or wild lemon, tree: "His drawing and painting of the Tupelo is fine. . . . There is a natural freedom through the whole, and no particular omitted—the insects on the leaves &c." At about this time William also shipped dried specimens and descriptions of fourteen Pennsylvania birds to George Edwards. Several artists of nature were influenced and helped by Edwards, one of whose simple but very useful suggestions to them was to wash and dry all bird specimens before painting them, as he was receiving some faultily colored portraits that faithfully mirrored the hues of plumage as it appeared in preservative spirits. William Bartram's early work was imitative of Catesby and Edwards, and subsequently he was influenced by George Dionysius Ehret, a Danish-born botanical illustrator in England, who was among the finest of such artists. But Bartram was already showing an accuracy and independence of perception that would mark his best work. Soon Collinson showed the young man's specimens and paintings to another Quaker gardener, Dr. John Fothergill, who had introduced ninety-six foreign species into English horticulture and maintained one of England's largest private botanical gardens. Fothergill urged young Bartram to "preserve seeds from some of the most beautiful flowering plants, as well as those which may be useful in Medicine," and to "observe and draw plants and all varieties of creatures."

This new English friend would later be a major patron, but in the 1750s the elder Bartram foresaw no such prospects for his son. Therefore, when William was eighteen, he was apprenticed to a Philadelphia merchant. He would have had much in common with that later artist-naturalist John James Audubon, who also delved somewhat indolently and more than somewhat ineptly into commerce and farming. Fortunately, young Bartram continued to draw and study nature in his spare time. Collinson published his drawings of a dove, and Edwards based a dozen of his own illustrations and descriptions on specimens and drawings sent by Bartram.

With William engaged in trade, John Bartram again set out on lone explorations—through the Carolinas in 1760, and the following year to the newly settled frontier village at Fort Pitt. As usual, detailed journals of the expeditions went to his English patrons for the benefit of science.

During his 1761 journey to the future site of Pittsburgh, he encountered a group of Indians, one of whom snatched his hat "in a great passion, and chawed it all round," a strange action which Bartram precipitately interpreted as a cannibalistic threat. Bartram's anthropological notions mixed bigoted ignorance with enlightenment in a peculiar blend. He had held slaves but had freed them, and they sat at table with him and some of his distinguished guests at Kingsessing. This could hardly have rested well with some of his fellow Quakers who kept slaves and made no secret of their scorn for blacks. The former slaves, now salaried servants, gratefully kept the farm thriving during Bartram's absences, thus vindicating his attitude toward them.

His attitude toward Indians was another matter. Again unlike his fellow Quakers, he doubted that they could be "civilized" and saw no reason to treat them gently. Resentful that the French and Indian Wars had hindered his explorations, he declared that the only way to deal with Indians was to "bang them stoutly" and he was evidently not much disturbed when Governor John Penn acceded to the demands of non-Quaker constituents and offered bounties for the scalps of all Indians above the age of ten. William Bartram, on the other hand, was to observe and study the Indians with greater objectivity and arrive at rather enlightened conclusions for his time. It is ironic that when both men were given Indian names the father's had the more impressive ring. The Seminoles named William Bartram the Flower Hunter, while among the Delawares his irascible father was reverently called the Truth Teller.

There were additional reasons for friction between John Bartram and the Society of Friends. His field studies had awakened in him a very personal variety of deism, in his case a belief in God on the evidence of reason and nature alone, with little use for supernatural revelation, and coupled with a conviction of a "Unifying Principle" or set of principles—in essence, that plants, animals, and man all operated on the same God-given principles and were thus intertwined, and that the omniscient Creator provided a balance of animal and plant life. These beliefs, together with his son's later perceptions of the interdependence among living things, have led some commentators to credit the Bartrams with a mystical glimmering of the interrelationships and diversity among organisms—the study that lacked even a specific name until the 1860s when the German evolutionist Ernst Haeckel coined the word "ecology."

John Bartram's ideas regarding animal behavior and psychology were similarly ahead of his time. He held that "brutes possess higher qualifications and more exalted ideas than our traditional mystery mongers are willing to allow." The term "mystery mongers" was Bartram's name for preachers. Although the Quakers held their meetings without an officiating parson, they were embarrassed by Bartram's anticlerical castigations and shocked by his ideas about animals, nature in general, and God. John Bartram's convictions prompted him to make statements that occasionally shocked even his friend Peter Collinson. He said in one of his letters, "Living in Love and innocency, we may die in hope. . . . If we don't go to heaven, I believe we shan't go to hell."

At one point, the Darby Meeting of the Society of Friends charged him with "disbelieving in Christ as the Son of God," although the final charges gently avoided mention of outright heresy and vaguely substituted mention of "Dark notions." In 1758, the Darby group finally disowned him—verbally cast him out. Characteristically, he continued to regard himself as a Quaker, continued to attend meetings when the spirit moved him, but also continued to be defiant in his theology. He later expressed an aspect of that theological defiance by carving an inscription into the stone lintel above his study window at Kingsessing: "It is God alone, Almighty Lord, The Holy One, By me Adord. John Bartram, 1770."

William Bartram strove a little harder to conform, both to the tenets of Quakerism and to his father's wishes. In an effort to become a trader, he went to Cape Fear, North Carolina, in 1761 to live with an uncle who had good connections. But neither his heart nor his mind was in trade. In 1762, after his father arrived in the area on another of his explorations, William gave up the effort at least temporarily and returned to Philadelphia with new specimens and drawings. Among the curiosities John Bartram brought back from his Carolinean explorations was that "most wondrous plant," an insectivorous member of the sundew family that William dubbed the Tipitiwichit—the Venus's-flytrap (*Dionaea muscipula*). This new discovery was (and is) the only known species of its genus, growing wild nowhere in the world but on the coast of the Carolinas.

John Bartram's obligation to send Collinson boxes of seeds at five guineas a box had terminated in 1760, but the friendship continued, as did occasional shipments of seeds, and in 1765 Collinson obtained for him an appointment as Botanist to the King (George III) with a stipend of fifty pounds per year. There was more honor than financial profit in the appointment, since the Crown did not pay shipping costs or other expenses, and a new horse alone cost Bartram forty pounds. Still, the prestige assured him of continued patronage. Evidently feeling more than usually secure and perhaps convinced that his son's security lay in the study and illustration of natural history, he now took

William as assistant on a most ambitious expedition. Seeking new rarities for His Majesty and other patrons, father and son sailed from Philadelphia to Charleston and then traveled overland through Georgia and Florida. Once in Florida, their mission for the Crown was to be enlarged; they were to search for the sources of the "San Juan" (St. Johns River).

On September 20, 1765, in the highlands of lower Georgia, they reached the Altamaha River. At that time the river was Georgia's southern frontier and its name was a syllable longer— Alatamaha. They lingered there, intrigued by the flora. A week later John Bartram wrote to Collinson of seeing magnolias "100 feet high, and 3 or 4 feet in diam. What a noble sight!" Briefly they lost their bearings although they were only about four miles from Fort Barrington, and then, while heading toward the fort on October 1, they came upon a small, handsome tree—no more than a tall shrub, really—which they correctly assumed to be a new species. Though it was no longer in flower at that time of year in that latitude, they recognized it as a species of Gordonia (a member of the tea family, related to the Asiatic teas and named after the London nurseryman James Gordon). To honor their friend Benjamin Franklin, they named it *Gordonia pubescens Franklinia*—the Franklinia tree.

Credit for first reporting and describing this new species has sometimes been attributed to the naturalist Humphrey Marshall, John Bartram's first cousin. In 1785, Marshall published *Arbustum Americanum*. The book contained many descriptions—including that of the Franklinia—contributed by William Bartram. The species was now renamed *Franklinia alatamaha,* a classification still accepted although it is popularly called the Gordonia as well as the Franklinia.

The description in Marshall exemplified Bartram's attention to detail and, toward the end, his associative powers and occasional inclination toward subtle lyricism:

> This beautiful flowering, tree-like shrub rises . . . about twenty feet. . . . The leaves are oblong, narrowed towards the base, sawed on their edges, placed alternately. . . .
>
> The flowers . . . are often five inches in diameter . . . composed of five large, roundish, spreading petals, ornamented in the center with a tuft or crown of gold coloured stamina; and possessed with the fragrance of a China Orange.

The Bartrams described their discovery but could not provide a specimen in bloom during the 1765 expedition. Eight years later, in the spring of '73, William Bartram was in the same area again, conducting an exploration financed by John Fothergill. This time he found the plant festooned with beautiful creamy white blossoms, and he collected specimens from which he later grew Franklinias at the famous botanical garden on the Schuylkill. He did not realize at the time how rare the plant was or that his garden alone was to save it from extinction.

After that, the tree was seldom seen in the wild, but William Bartram painted an elegantly detailed portrait of the Franklinia in bloom for Dr. Fothergill, and for many years this picture served in lieu of a type specimen, as the only graphic evidence of the existence of a rare and magnificent flower. The legend beneath the painting reads:

> *Franklinia alatamaha.*   *A beautiful flowering Tree.*
> *discovered growing near the banks of the R. Alatamaha in Georgia.*
> *Willm Bartram. Delin.*
> *1788*

Like many a plant doomed to extinction (and, for that matter, like the dinosaur and the mastodon in earlier epochs), the Franklinia was no longer competing successfully with other denizens of its environment, nor colonizing new habitat. No one has seen a wild Franklinia on the banks of the Altamaha or anywhere else since 1790, yet it has survived to become a popular American ornamental, thriving almost everywhere except in the northernmost states. Every living Franklinia tree is a descendant of those grown by William Bartram in his botanical garden on the west bank of the Schuylkill.

Bartram found that the Franklinias he planted there exhibited a curious adaptation to the Pennsylvania habitat. They no longer bloomed in the spring as their wild southern forebears had; instead they began to bloom in late summer and sometimes continued until the first frost. Evidently this man-induced evolutionary change was advantageous, for now all Franklinias everywhere bloom in summer and autumn.

When the Bartrams set out on their 1765 expedition, William was only twenty-six years old but his father was sixty-six, a venerable age for a man of the eighteenth century. Nonetheless, John Bartram was still strong, confident that he could withstand the rigors of wilderness travel, and eager for new discoveries. That of the *Franklinia* was followed by another a few months later, on January 24, 1766, when John Bartram found and recorded *Illicium parviflorum,* a large, new, yellow-flowered species of anise shrub. And later that year he also found a purple-flowered variety whose discovery has sometimes been mistakenly attributed to John Ellis a decade later.

Upon reaching St. Augustine, the Bartrams began a new phase of their mission, the exploration of the St. Johns River. They traveled nearly four hundred miles by canoe, surveying both the mainstream and its branches and connected lakes. They made the first maps and charts of the waterway's course, widths, depths, distances, and even currents. John Bartram returned to Philadelphia in June with a "fine collection of strange Florida plants," while William remained on the St. Johns, where he acquired a plantation and once more tried his hand as an entrepreneur, this time raising indigo and rice. The next year, 1767, John Bartram's *Account of East Florida* was published in London, followed two years later by the *Description of East Florida* [by William Stork] *with a Journal by John Bartram.*

William Bartram, meanwhile, was enjoying somewhat less success. The indigo plantation was poorly located and financially disastrous. Misfortune seemed to dog him, for when he admitted failure and took passage for Charleston he was shipwrecked a short distance from St. Augustine. But by 1767, he was home, living near his birthplace and humbly working on a farm. He was not sufficiently discouraged to seek obscurity very enthusiastically, however, and apparently he welcomed rescue when, in the summer of '68, Peter Collinson wrote to his father with news of commissions for William. For the Duchess of Portland he was to draw "all Land, River and your Sea Shells, from the very least to the greatest," and for John Fothergill, fellow Quaker and collector of American curiosa, he was to draw mollusks and turtles. Other patrons occasionally helped, but Fothergill became a permanent mainstay and the Duchess probably remained the second most important benefactor. In a bound album at the Botanical Library of the British Museum is the largest collection of

Bartram originals, fifty-nine drawings and paintings executed for Dr. Fothergill. Nearly two dozen of them represent species that were new to science when Bartram illustrated them.

Not all of the news was heartening in 1768. Peter Collinson, the treasured colleague John Bartram never met, died that summer. Bereft of his old friend and feeling lonely even while surrounded by his family, Bartram found some solace in his equally close friendship with Benjamin Franklin, who had been in London for several years. "I have no friend as intimate or capable as my dear Benjamin," he wrote to him. "Although I have been deprived of thy agreeable conversation for several years, I have thy pretty exact picture hanging by my bed which gives a dayly fresh remembrance. . . ." That year Franklin and Bartram became regular members of the reorganized American Philosophical Society, while young William was elected corresponding member, and in 1770 Fothergill was elected to foreign membership. For Bartram the father, Franklin replaced Collinson to some extent, while Fothergill did so for Bartram the son. Not long afterward, when John Bartram's eyesight began to fail, Franklin sent thirteen pairs of lenses from London so that Bartram could select the most effective spectacles. Franklin also sent exotic seeds for the garden and later, when the War for Independence ended sales of Bartram's seeds in England, he offered to sell them in France.

William Bartram once again sustained a battering in the arena of commerce in 1769 and '70, this last time in Philadelphia, but he quickly extricated himself from the near certainty of bankruptcy and, supported by his new English patronage, retired to his Uncle William's Cape Fear home to continue drawing. He was summoned home two years later, when his father's vision was failing and the family wanted help in maintaining and enlarging the garden, but he did not stay long, for John Fothergill now proposed to finance him in an extended expedition through the South and Inland to the Mississippi. Planned as a two-year journey, it lasted five and resulted in descriptions, drawings, and specimens of many new plants as well as reports on Indian culture, soil, topography, birds, mammals, reptiles, amphibians, fishes, and animal behavior.

In the spring of 1773, William Bartram sailed for Charleston and thence to Savannah. He was somewhere in upland Georgia when he received the news that his early mentor and patron, George Edwards, had died at the age of eighty on July 23. He continued to explore Georgia and then, in 1774, he again explored eastern Florida. In '75 he traveled back into Georgia, sailed to Charleston, and in the spring made an excursion into Cherokee country, through the Carolinas, Georgia, and Alabama. It is believed that he received news of the Battle of Lexington while on this journey. That summer one of his reports to Fothergill exemplified his exceptional sharpness of observation. In "a swamp at the head of a bay or lagoon" on the Tombigbee River in southern Alabama, he perceived that the white cedars differed subtly from those in Pennsylvania. At the time little attention was paid to such subtleties, but one hundred and eighty-seven years later white cedars were reclassified taxonomically, and the southern tree he had noticed was recognized as a separate species.

Though the long wilderness treks were beginning to undermine his health, he continued, reaching the area of Baton Rouge in late October, 1775. Shortly before this he had made one of his rare rest stops, remaining on an island in western Florida for more than a month while recuperating from an illness that affected his eyes and therefore must have given him great anxiety. He spent most of the next year in Georgia and Florida, and that summer joined a group of volunteers under General Lachlan McIntosh to repel a rumored British invasion, to be launched from St. Augustine. When the invasion failed to materialize, he resumed his explorations and in the fall turned northward, toward home. During these years of adventure, he prepared a journal for John Fothergill. The journal remained in manuscript until 1943, when Francis Harper published a carefully annotated edition, but it had served a worthy purpose during Bartram's lifetime, for he drew heavily on it in writing his *Travels*, a classic book of American natural history.

He reached home early in 1777 to find his father showing the symptoms of age and frailty that portend death. The old man passed his last days amid mementos of recognition—a silver cup from Sir Hans Sloane, a letter from Queen Ulrica, documents regarding his membership in the Royal Academy of Sciences at Stockholm, a gold medal from the scholarly gentlemen of Edinburgh, and so on. But most of his friends and patrons were gone. He was more apprehensive that the British might dese-crate his garden than he was of death, and it is believed that the unwarranted fear of vandalism hastened the end. He fell ill on September 22, 1777, and died only a few hours later. Linnaeus died less than four months after that; Peter Kalm died in 1779, and John Fothergill died in 1780. Many of William Bartram's friends and old mentors were either gone or too old to be active, and he himself no longer had the stamina for exploration.

He kept busy tending and improving the garden, writing his *Travels,* exchanging information with colleagues, and entertaining distinguished friends. Though he had never married, he was surrounded by his brothers' families and appeared to be content. There were many visitors to stimulate him intellectually: Benjamin Franklin and George Washington; the estimable French botanist André Michaux; the Welsh naturalist and writer Thomas Pennant, who quoted the Bartrams on the zoology of half a dozen American mammals and remarked in 1785 that John Bartram had been the first scientist to describe Pennsylvania's ruffed grouse; Dr. Jacob Gilliams, the dentist who founded the Academy of Natural Sciences of Philadelphia; Gilliams' friend and William Bartram's grandnephew, Thomas Say, who was to become a leading entomologist and malacologist; George Ord, a capable early zoologist; Thomas Nuttall, whose valuable works were to include the *Genera of North American Plants* in 1818 and *Sylva* nearly thirty years later.

Among the most promising of the later visitors was Alexander Wilson, a friend of Gilliams and Ord. He first came to the garden in 1802. At that time, he felt insecure about his ability and future, just as Bartram once had, and Bartram inspired him to become more serious—more dedicated—in his study of ornithology and to master ornithological illustration. Some of Wilson's great *American Ornithology* was written with a quill given to him by Bartram. Wilson invited Bartram to accompany him on an expedition to New Orleans, an invitation sadly declined because of age, poor health, and eye trouble, but Wilson later honored his friend in another way. He named a new species of bird the Bartram's tattler. The bird has since come to be known as the upland plover but it still memorializes Bartram since it is also called Bartram's plover and its scientific name remains *Bartramia longicauda.*

In 1782, the trustees of the University of the State of Pennsylvania elected William Bartram Professor of Botany. His genius for teaching visitors notwithstanding, as a lecturer he was untrained, unsuited, and unwilling. Never once did he lecture. Seven years later he was replaced in title (as he had been long ago in fact) by his friend Benjamin Smith Barton, who held botany classes in the Bartram garden. In 1789, at Barton's urging, Bartram wrote *Observations on the Creek and Cherokee Indians,* an estimably rational ethnological report for its time but one that, unfortunately, remained unpublished until 1853. By the time Barton died in 1815, he had used many of Bartram's descriptions—as well as a few illustrations Bartram made for him—in his own botanical works, such as *Elements of Botany.* He has been unfairly accused of minor scientific plagiarism, for he acknowledged the source of his material and the two naturalists remained close friends. In a letter to Barton in 1803, Bartram revealed the kind of biological insight that characterizes a gifted naturalist:

> I send thee a beautiful specimen of a Jumping Mouse. . . . Its beautifull robe cant escape thy notice but I perceive it is faded since deprived of Life. Which to me is a convincing proof that there is a continual circulation of animal juices even [in] the Hairs, feathers & scales of fishes whilst alive.

An angler sadly watching the glow of a trout fade away would understand precisely what Bartram saw. His conclusion regarding "animal juices," if simplistic in the light of later investigation, was not very wide of the mark.

By 1790, Bartram was seeking subscribers to his forthcoming book *Travels* (an ancient marketing strategy that is still undergoing refinement by publishers who advertise for prepublication sales and subscriptions to series of books). One of those who paid for a subscription was a seed customer, Thomas Jefferson. In the autumn of 1791 the work was published by James and Johnson of Philadelphia. The following year it was published in London, and then again in Philadelphia, and then in Dublin. An immediate success in spite of detractors who questioned its accuracy, it was translated within the decade into German, Dutch, and French. Its full original title was *Travels through North and South Carolina, Georgia, East and West Florida, the Cherokee country, the ex-*

tensive territories of the Muscogulges, or Creek confederacy, and the country of the Chactaws; Containing an account of the soil and natural productions of those regions, together with observations on the manners of the indians.

The title page proclaimed that the book was "Embellished with copper-plates." Unfortunately, the originals of these illustrations have been lost, but many other Bartram portraits of nature have survived in repositories such as that at the British Museum. They were arranged in no more systematic order than the later bird and mammal portraits by Audubon, for they were executed and shipped to patrons on order or when the discoveries were made. But this did not detract from their scientific or artistic value. Bartram's painting of the great yellow bream, or warmouth, served as a type specimen, as did the painstaking portrait of the Florida sandhill crane which eventually came to the Museum. Bartram had counted on supplying a type specimen of the crane, for his hunting companions in Florida shot one. Unfortunately, they misconstrued his reason for wanting the bird, which was for science rather than sustenance, and they ate it. His drawing was therefore the nearest approximation to a type specimen and was so regarded. Moreover, he carefully described the bird in *Travels.* Thus he was credited with its discovery. Its full scientific designation is *Grus canadensis pratensis* Bartram.

Not all of his paintings have the appeal of his crane or the exquisite delicacy of his Franklinia, and some include irrelevant objects—freshwater animals or plants in a marine environment or vice versa—but many are beautiful and quite a few show the subject in its natural environment. Like Catesby before him and Wilson and Audubon later, he was foreshadowing insights into the importance of the biome.

This was again evident in the pictures and text of *Travels,* wherein he presented a number of interesting interrelationships: a spider preying on a bee, which had landed to feed on a leaf; a snake fighting an injured hawk; alligators gathered in the shallows to feed on a swarm of fish.

Literature as well as science benefited, for there are indications that Shelley and Wordsworth were influenced by his descriptions, particularly of flora, and made poetic use of some of them. Well they might. *Travels* revealed Bartram to be a writer who could create images of great detail and beauty from something

as unprepossessing as a sunfish "as large as a man's hand. Nearly
oval and thin," he noted, "being compressed on each side . . .

> the top of the head and back of an olive-green, be-sprinkled with
> russet specks; the sides of a sea-green, inclining to azure, insensi-
> bly blended with the olive above, and beneath . . . a silvery white,
> or pearl . . . powdered with specks of the finest green, russet and
> gold; the belly is of a bright scarlet-red, or vermillion, darting up
> rays or fiery streaks into the pearl. . . . The eyes are large, en-
> circled with a fiery iris; they are a voracious fish, and are easily
> caught with a suitable bait.

He had a similarly fine touch with larger subjects, as in his
description of aquatic life at Salt Springs, Florida:

> Innumerable bands of fish are seen, some cloathed in the most
> brilliant colours; the voracious crocodile stretched along at full
> length, as the great trunk of a tree in size, the devouring garfish,
> inimical trout, and all the varieties of gilded painted bream, the
> barbed catfish, dreaded sting-ray, skate and flounder, spotted
> bass, sheeps head and ominous drum; all in their separate bands
> and communities, with free and unsuspicious intercourse per-
> forming their evolutions. . . .

But there were flaws in the book. Bartram is believed never to
have seen proofs before publication, and there were numerous
misspellings and garbled names. There were also descriptions of
unknown plants which, at first, could not be found again. His
most controversial report concerned the alligators he had observed on the St. Johns River. He described them as being more
aggressive than they seemed to be in areas where men could observe them. This was because alligators become less aggressive
when men frequently invade their habitat. Those seen by Bartram had encountered few if any human beings and perhaps
showed more appetite than fear. More important, he described
them as bellowing: "At the approach of day, the dreaded voice
of the alligators shook the isle, and resounded along the neighboring coasts." Unfortunately, alligators bellow only on appropriate occasions, and few white men had ever heard the sound.
The veracity of his reports was not fully confirmed until 1822,
when Major John Eatton Le Conte explored the same area. Bartram had been the first to publish a full description of the Amer-

ican alligator but because he neglected to christen it with a binomial, taxonomic listings recognized a later investigator as discoverer of the species.

The criticisms of his book caused him to withdraw into his garden and himself. He supplied illustrations and descriptions for Barton, and encouraged scholarly visitors to study natural history, but he spent his late years in a state approaching retirement. Circa 1800, Jefferson offered him the position of botanist on the Lewis and Clark Expedition. He must have been pleased, remembering that the original idea for such an expedition had been his father's, but he was past sixty and did not feel he had the stamina for another trip into the unknown wilderness. He was no longer even confident of his dexterity in the garden. He lacked his father's love of physical labor, and he had broken a leg some years earlier in a fall from his cypress tree while gathering seeds. He had been incapacitated for months, and the recollection remained painful.

Yet he was healthier than he realized, for he lived to be eighty-four. Death came suddenly and easily, the result of a ruptured vessel in a lung, on July 22, 1823. By then the accuracy of his reports was again being accepted. His scientific stature was assured, and not in the study of botany alone.

Though his anthropological views showed an understandable Quaker bias, he is considered to have been a writer of "rational restraint" on the culture of Indians, and passages in his *Travels* are among the best early works on mound-building. Still more advanced was his effort in the book to use comparative linguistics to speculate on the origin of various Indian groups. And in 1956, Frances Densmore, writing about Seminole music, quoted a *Travels* passage about the playing of the cane flute—a most valuable description of an art and ethnological tradition that has long been lost.

He made still more significant contributions to zoology, despite occasional inaccuracies. He was the first naturalist to provide reliable descriptions of the reptiles and amphibians of Florida, and in ornithology he prepared the way for Wilson by including in the *Travels* his "Catalogue" of two hundred and fifteen native birds. In 1875, the eminent ornithologist Elliott Coues reproduced the Catalogue and provided commentary on each species named. Fifty-two of Bartram's classifications were too dubious to be matched with known birds, but even a few of these have since been identified. For example, Bartram described a "little brownish spotted bittern" which he named *Ardea subfusca,* evidently having been misled by an immature night heron.

After subtracting such inevitable errors from the list, the achievement remains astonishing. An estimate of its importance was succinctly expressed by Coues as the "starting-point of a distinctively American school of ornithology."

Chapter 4
ALEXANDER WILSON

Formal education ended for Alexander Wilson in his tenth year
He was the son of a smuggler, and in the vicinity of Lochwin
noch, Scotland, he was known as "the smuggler's callan"—a term
which, in the Scottish vernacular of the late eighteenth century
signified not merely a smuggler's son but a smuggler's appren
tice. In his biography *Alexander Wilson: Naturalist and Pioneer*
Robert Cantwell notes that when young Wilson was not perform
ing chores for his father or his father's revenue-dodging associ
ates, he was often occupied in poaching the game lands of the
gentry. Another commentator, Alexander B. Adams, declares in
Eternal Quest that Wilson "certainly helped his father from time
to time" in "a battle of wits with the Crown's revenue officers."
Reminiscences of contemporaries and Wilson's own guarded ref
erences to his youth confirm that he was a smuggler and
poacher.

Other primary sources are yet more damaging. Court records
show that he was guilty of sedition. The laws he broke in this in
stance were tyrannically repressive, but the same court records
prove that he also was a convicted and self-confessed black
mailer. Perhaps the mildest of his offenses was what he would
have called licentiousness. Contemporary accounts and his own
letters indicate that he was twice a fugitive from sexual scandal
The first of these episodes was both tawdry and laughable. The
second may have taken place chiefly in Wilson's mind; it bore no
consequences beyond clues that early misfortunes may have
scarred him with a mild paranoia.

48

Paradoxically, this ill-educated miscreant was a scholarly man of high and unswerving moral principle. A talented minor poet and painter, he brought a unique sensitivity to the study of nature as well as to scientific reportage and illustration. His genius for close observation and deduction gave new depth as well as accuracy to field investigation. In less than a decade he completed most of a nine-volume work, *American Ornithology,* which may well stand as the single most important pioneering contribution to natural history in this country. Later ornithologists have called him the father of the science.

Biographers, in dwelling on the courageous determination that made possible such a massive achievement before his death at the age of forty-seven, have perhaps underemphasized a subtler facet of his scientific greatness. This was an attention to detail that influenced investigation by means of dissection and the observation of captive specimens as well as field study. For example, his analyses of contents in the crops and stomachs of birds modified common beliefs and provided new information regarding food preferences and requirements. And his observation of wild birds, captured alive for extended study, swept away much confusion about plumage coloration as a basis for distinguishing species and gender. Such revelations often altered conclusions made from field observations alone.

His dissections and study of captive specimens also illustrated dramatically the linkage of discoveries from one naturalist to the next. Investigation by dissection was hardly new. For two successive years Mark Catesby had dissected large numbers of bobolinks as they arrived in the Carolinas on their fall migration. Because the autumn plumage of the male resembles that of the female, some observers had concluded that only females visited the Carolinas at this season. To the skeptical and inquisitive Catesby this seemed unlikely, but upon dissection the birds did, indeed, all appear to be females. While failing to solve the puzzle (and noting that the males and females of some species do tend to migrate at slightly different times) he awakened the interest of other naturalists. The next to investigate was William Bartram. He, too, failed, mistaking the male and female for separate species—a not unlikely postulation in view of the evidence and the state of the science at that time. Even for as keen an observer as Bartram, who had recognized the Florida cardinal (*Richmondena cardinalis floridana*) to be a distinct subspecies, the common bobolink was an enigma.

Alexander Wilson's delicate dissections and minute examinations of various birds evidently led him to suspect the truth, easily verified by collecting bobolinks alive and keeping them as pets—that is, laboratory subjects. When he kept the birds long enough to molt, the changing plumage revealed some of the supposed females to be males. In many birds, the male gonads shrink drastically after the breeding season. Among bobolinks he found that the male reproductive organs were so reduced as to be indistinguishable from those of the female in autumn, though evident upon dissection during the breeding season. Thus the puzzle was solved: male and female "ricebirds" were visiting the Carolina ricefields in roughly equal numbers.

Wilson was born on July 6, 1766, in Paisley, the Scottish center of the weaving industry. There were two older sisters, a third having died in infancy. His father (also named Alexander but known to his peers as Saunders) was then a relatively prosperous weaver who had once been a soldier and more recently a smuggler. Smuggling was a common and not altogether unrespected occupation among Scots resentful of British rule and able to make a precarious living (and occasionally a fortune) in illicitly imported silk, sugar, tea, tobacco, and other items subject to exorbitant English tariffs. A famous smuggling route stretched all the way from Chesapeake Bay to the cliffs at the Firth of Clyde on Scotland's western coast and thence along the Great Road through Paisley to Glasgow.

During the American Revolution the trade was expanded to include arms and gunpowder traveling in the opposite direction, and the Earl of Pembroke asked rhetorically, "Will Washington take America, or will the smugglers take England first? The bett would be a fair, even one."

But Alexander Wilson's mother, Mary M'Nab Wilson, like many women who had grown up among smugglers, disliked the dangers of the trade and the absences of a husband who undertook clandestine journeys. She induced Saunders Wilson to stay at his loom and she sent young Alexander—Sandy, as he was known—to Paisley Grammar School. Shortly before Sandy Wilson's tenth birthday his mother died of tuberculosis. His father soon returned to smuggling and almost as soon married a widow, Mrs. Catherine Brown Urie, who already had two children and soon added more to the Wilson clan.

England was at war with her colonies. Trade was disrupted, and a Scottish working man was poverty-stricken almost by definition. Sandy, whose parents had intended to train him for the ministry despite his somewhat rebelliously expressed boredom with theological tutoring, was taken from school and sent as a cowherd to a farm a dozen miles away. When he was thirteen he came home to be apprenticed to a brother-in-law, William Duncan, a weaver.

The appointment of a new "sheriff-substitute" (a deputy, or undersheriff) named James Orr was making smuggling a more than usually hazardous offense at Paisley, and the family now moved to nearby Beith, where Saunders Wilson was almost immediately fined for the same offense. The boy remained with Duncan, while his family moved another few miles to Lochwinnoch. There Saunders Wilson rented an ancient, partially ruined castle known as the Tower of Auchinbathie. Just down the slope from the Tower, conveniently close, lived six journeymen who wove smuggled silk.

Each summer Saturday until his apprenticeship ended in 1782, Sandy Wilson walked the ten miles from the Duncan home to the Tower, and then he moved there. At first he spent his time weaving, running errands for the weavers and smugglers, loafing, reading, writing ballads, and hunting. When he was sixteen he became a journeyman weaver at Lochwinnoch, but he continued to live at the Tower until his stepmother sent him away—for reasons of loving discretion rather than cruelty. A fifteen-year-old girl named Meg Duncan had become the bride of a tyrannical and eccentric seventy-five-year-old landlord named John Craig. In view of her energetic attentions to the weavers—and particularly to Alexander Wilson—no one entertained the notion that Craig had fathered the child she was expecting.

Wilson departed without protest and worked again for Duncan, now near Edinburgh, weaving and peddling the woven goods. For nearly four years he spent most of his time roaming Scotland, selling handkerchiefs, flags, lengths of muslin and silk, and the like. He distrusted Duncan (who proved to be unreliable in all his relations) and sometimes lied to him about the direction of his journeys. As he occasionally stopped at the Tower of Auchinbathie, perhaps he was still working with the smugglers. But during this period he was also educating himself and attempting to become a poet. He read Milton and Goldsmith, and he knew much of Pope by heart (though he was so fond of intermingling his own words and lines with Pope's that in later years he mis-quoted that poet by inadvertently adding what he himself had composed in youth). And he wrote verse, occasionally enriched by such apt descriptions as that of a peddler "beneath a load of silks and sorrows bent," but usually more doleful or sentimen-tally lyrical than impressive.

During the long peddling trips he also spent much time col-lecting curios, fossils, and tombstone inscriptions, and visiting rural poets, musicians, philosophers, and botanists. His inquisi-tive inclination was beginning to emerge even while, without knowing it, he was perfecting the craft of describing nature. By sketching some of his own designs for woven goods, he was also improving his drawing ability, though without any particular goal.

By the mid-eighties he had set himself up as a semi-indepen-dent weaver in Paisley and then, when he was twenty, the first book of poetry by Robert Burns appeared. The inspiration of Burns, who lived not far away, made Paisley a center of poetry, gave Scotland a truly native poetic literature, and encouraged a rash of dialect verse of inevitably uneven quality. Wilson's own verse showed marked improvement. Burns wrote poetry based on his personal experience, of rural and farm life. Wilson now wrote about weavers, and when a watermill-driven cottonworks was erected—one of the early mechanical marvels of the indus-trial revolution—he composed verse about the "wheels turning wheels in mystic throng." When a second factory opened, with mechanical contrivances to ease the toil of weaving and facilitate creativity at the loom, his lines were exultant: "To bid beneath our hands, gay blossoms rise, In all the colours of the changing skies." Sometimes, too, he wrote in Burnsian dialect, and such verses were among his most successful.

In 1788, after the death of a friend named William Wither-spoon, Wilson called on Thomas Crichton, a local man of letters. He did not know Crichton but Witherspoon had known and ad-mired him. Wilson and Crichton exchanged condolences and talked of literature. Then Wilson showed some poetry to his new acquaintance and Crichton soon afterward persuaded a local printer named John Neilson to publish a volume of Wilson's work.

The following September, Wilson set out on a six-week peddling trip. He had reluctantly agreed to sell subscriptions—take orders for the forthcoming book—during this trip. But Scottish householders had little money for cloth, much less for poetry. When he returned he was able to pay neither his printer nor the manufacturer who supplied the cloth he was selling. The manufacturer threatened to have him jailed. Neilson, however, suggested that Wilson apply for assistance to William M'Dowell, a wealthy landowner, member of the House of Commons, social reformer, and a friend to the weavers and other poor workingmen. It was M'Dowell's land that Wilson had most often poached, for Mr. M'Dowell had no objection to a bit of harmless trespassing by a hungry boy with a fowling piece, whereas other landlords might set the dogs or the sheriff on anyone who accidentally set foot on their property. William M'Dowell was to commit suicide in 1810, after the West Indian trade collapsed and his companies went bankrupt, but in 1789 he was a wealthy merchant, banker, and philanthropist. When he purchased two subscriptions and promised additional orders, the cloth manufacturer withdrew his threat and the printer published the book, which included lyrical nature poems, character sketches, a comic Hogarthian narrative based on old John Craig and young Meg Duncan, and chaste love poems to an anonymous lady—Martha M'Lean, Wilson's first and greatest love.

But the effort to prepare the book, sell it, and pay some of his debts ruined his health. Bedridden for months with an ailment described as an "inflammation of the lungs," he was expected to die. When he was able to travel again he made another peddling trip for his brother-in-law and then returned to work as a weaver in Paisley.

Shortly afterward, in February of 1791, he and six other writers were invited to enter a poetry contest in Edinburgh. Each entrant was to compose and recite a poem championing one of two fine Scottish poets—Allan Ramsay (who had written chiefly in conventional English) or Robert Fergusson (Burns's favorite poet, who had written only in the Scottish vernacular and some of whose work was unintelligible beyond the border). At first indecisive about competing, Wilson gave himself little time to prepare. In one week he wove forty ells of cloth to earn sustenance, wrote a 210-line poem for the contest, and walked the fifty-two miles to Edinburgh. Of the seven contestants, he alone favored Fergusson. Each member of the audience of five hundred paid sixpence for admission and a vote. The man for whom they voted would receive all the admission money. Wilson lost by seventeen votes because Robert Cumming, a good poet and an aristocrat with more money than scruples, brought with him a claque of forty friends. But Wilson won an ovation and the opportunity to contribute to a new literary magazine, *The Bee*.

While continuing to weave, he published a second edition of his poetry collection, paid some of his debts, and wrote bad verses for hymns as well as somewhat better though anonymous erotic poetry to an anonymous lady. The lady was, of course, Martha M'Lean. Her social status was much above his, and he could not support a wife, but she loved him, evidently bedded with him, and probably would have married him if further calamity had not intervened.

During this period Wilson also wrote a minor masterpiece, a comic ballad entitled "Watty and Meg" about a quarrel and reconciliation of a husband and wife. Its sales, said to total a hundred-thousand, canceled his remaining obligation to Neilson and raised his station from indebted to merely poor. But now trade was again disrupted and the weavers were suffering through another severe economic depression, this time chiefly occasioned by the French Revolution. In 1792, Wilson began writing anonymous poetic satires in behalf of the weavers, berating mill owners and other members of the privileged classes. One of the poems—concerning exaggerated property rights and oppression—made its point in terms of a landowner who was infuriated when a peddler stepped from the road into his woods just long enough to defecate in private. Another ridiculed two unnamed but identifiable Paisley employers who cheated on payments to their weavers. A third proved to be his undoing.

It was entitled "The Shark, or Lang Mills Detected," and it was an obvious satire on William Sharp and his establishment, Long Mills. The poem was couched in dialect so crammed with technical weaving terms as to be partly indecipherable to anyone unfamiliar with the industry's jargon. Thus it appeared to be little more than a scolding doggerel satire to laymen—but not to the weavers or their employers. The crux of a charge of libel rested in a few lines, following a stanza in which The Shark had summarily evicted "His ghastly conscience, pale and spent":

> This done, trade snoovt awa wi' skill
> And wonderfu' extention;
> And widen't soon was every mill,
> (A dexterous invention!).
> Groat after groat was clippet aff
> Frae ae thing and anither;
> Till fouk began to think on draff
> To help to haud thegither
> Their banes that day.

Those who grasped only a smattering of the vernacular understood that, somehow, bit after bit was being snipped from the weavers' piecework pay, until impoverished folk had to consider eating chaff ("draff" in the Scottish vernacular) to hold their starving bones together. Those who grasped more realized that the entrepreneur, with his conscience exiled, had immediately devised some "dexterous invention" to lengthen every measurement of woven cloth. And those familiar with mill owners' practices realized that this "wonderfu' extention" was a furtive lengthening of the measuring devices used for determining the amount of work that was done and must be paid for. The stretching of measurements by even a fraction of an inch could be multiplied by length after length of piecework done each long day by each weaver. And if one employer did this and was not exposed, soon they all would. The underpayment could be multiplied by the ten thousand weavers of the entire region. The versifier was accusing The Shark of initiating an incredibly massive swindle of the poor.

But when William Sharp and his attorney appeared at Sheriff Orr's office it was to charge Wilson with blackmail as well as libel. Sharp had received a manuscript copy of the poem in Wilson's handwriting. It had been delivered the previous day, May 22, 1792, with an accompanying note, also in Wilson's handwriting:

Sir,
    The enclosed poem, by particular circumstances, has fallen into my hands. The author, I can certainly assure you, is on the eve of

concluding a bargain for the MMS. The offered price is five pounds.

If you know of any person who will advance *five guineas,* the manuscript from which I copied the enclosed, shall, with the most solemn regard to justice and secrecy, be immediately destroyed and buried in perpetual oblivion. If not, three days shall publish it to the world.

I give you *three hours* to deliberate on the offer, by which time I expect a final and determined answer, addressed to A.B., to lie in J. Nelson's, bookseller, Paisley, till called for. If the *price* or *copy* is not received by four o'clock this present afternoon, I can no longer prevent the author from proceeding with his production as he may think proper.——I am, Sir, your wellwisher,

A.B.

Tuesday
Half-past 11 o'clock, A.M.

On Wednesday, when the complaint was lodged, Wilson was in Glasgow. He returned that night and was outside Neilson's shop when he was seized by five men, evidently constables. The constables may, however, have been in Sharp's employ and they may also have been British agents. At this time the Crown was brutally supressing a growing labor-reform movement. Henry Dundas, Home Secretary and chief of British Intelligence, was hiring throngs of agents—informers who filed secret reports concerning anyone who wrote, spoke, or acted in any way that might be construed as "disloyal." Among the targets of the repressive campaign were workingmen's clubs and associations—forerunners of organized unions—many of which were politically radical, and these certainly included the Scottish weavers' clubs. The government was preparing to classify the weavers' meetings as seditious acts, and Wilson had served as secretary at more than one such meeting. Two of Wilson's close associates were the brothers James and William Mitchell, both radical leaders of the weavers. After it was discovered that at least one of them, James, was a government agent, they fled to America. When Wilson was brought before Sheriff Orr, he confessed that the manuscript and extortion note were in his handwriting, but insisted he had copied the poem from another manuscript and he refused to divulge its authorship. Someone, probably James Mitchell, denounced him as the anonymous poet. It really mattered little, since neither the weavers, the employers, or the authorities doubted that Wilson himself was the libelous writer.

Scotland then had no criminal libel law, and Sharp, to the obvious relief of the government, had no intention of pressing his civil suit. A libel case would have required evidence of the truth or falsity of the accusation contained in the poem. Contemporary commentators later averred that the charge in the poem was probably quite true. Therefore a libel suit would have been exceedingly embarrassing for Sharp, for industrialists in general, and for the government. Even if Wilson were convicted, he might well emerge as a martyred hero of labor, and there was a constant possibility of rioting. Hence, Wilson was tried only for the criminal act of extortion, not for libel, yet one of his penalties was to burn several copies of the poem in public.

There was no question about the handwriting, and Wilson could not have retracted his confession even if he had thought such a tactic might aid him. Speaking lamely in his own defense, he admitted the attempted extortion, "from what motive, the defender acknowledges himself unable to comprehend."

Scots in the 1790s regarded smugglers in roughly the same light that Americans regarded bootleggers during the era of Prohibition. By the accounts of Wilson's peers and on the basis of all other evidence, the "smuggler's callan" had become a righteous young man who could not possibly stoop to extortion. Moreover, he was very intelligent—far too intelligent to extort money so openly that he was bound to be caught. Yet he had done precisely that, and no one has ever unearthed his reasons. Perhaps he wished to make himself a martyr, thereby publicizing the dishonesty of the mill owners and dramatically aiding both the local weavers and the national reform movement. Perhaps he committed extortion at the urging of the most radical weavers, particularly the Mitchells, in the quixotic hope that Sharp would make payment and in so doing would tacitly admit the charges in the poem. Years later he spoke with revulsion of the Mitchells and on one occasion met with them in New York, apparently for no other reason than to confirm that they had become near-derelicts (and perhaps to tell William Mitchell—who arrived at Wilson's hotel room drunk—what he thought of someone whose loyalty was for hire).

Wilson was fined ten pounds and ordered to pay Sharp damages of fifty pounds; he was to remain in jail until the entire sums were paid (a life sentence since there was no hope of raising so much) and then he was to beg pardon of God and William Sharp in open court.

The court records are vague with regard to the time Wilson served, but evidently he was imprisoned for many months between the spring of 1792 and the first week of 1794. The sheriff released him several times (perhaps out of compassion, perhaps when the mood of the populace threatened rioting) and then jailed him again. In January, 1793, Sheriff Orr announced that he must serve a two-week sentence (as if he had not already been imprisoned for much longer) after which he would be released if someone would put up a two-year bond for his good behavior. The bond was furnished by Thomas Witherspoon, brother of the close friend who had died five years before. Wilson was led from jail on February 6, made to burn two copies of the poem in public, and released. Finally, in May, the still unpaid fine and damages were reduced. Wilson was to pay Sharp five pounds and five shillings, and he was to pay a fine of two pounds, twelve shillings, sixpence, plus costs of three pounds, ten shillings.

Wilson's relief must have been extreme. Under the terms of a royal proclamation against seditious writing, any work defined as disloyal by the authorities qualified as a "revolutionary document." Authorship of such a poem as he had written was punishable by death or transportation to the penal colonies. Indeed, for offenses of even less magnitude the Crown shipped reformers to the Australian penal colony, and the hardships at Botany Bay killed several of them. The sheriff may have suddenly reduced the penalties and settled the case out of pity for Wilson or out of fear that the Home Office might press further charges and turn him into a Scottish martyr.

Wilson lived with Thomas Witherspoon that fall and winter, while working to pay his debt. But the authorities were not yet satisfied that he was cowed. In January, 1794, he was brought back to court on a charge of having written and circulated a call for a meeting of the Friends of Liberty and Reform six months previously. After pleading not guilty, he was released on low bail. The charge—a threat, really—was not prosecuted.

By now, Wilson was convinced that he would never prosper or be left in peace if he remained in Scotland. After months of weaving, peddling, and living in total austerity to save money, he planned to sail for America with William Duncan's family. At the last moment Duncan changed his mind and refused to go, but his son, also named William, decided to accompany Wilson. The *Swift,* an American ship, was loading at Belfast, carrying three hundred and fifty emigrants. Wilson and his nephew were able to secure deck space. They arrived at New Castle, Delaware, on July 14, 1794.

With only a few shillings borrowed from a fellow passenger, they set out for Wilmington to seek work. There was none. They left the next day, walking toward Philadelphia. Wilson carried his fowling piece and a pack; Duncan's only possessions were his clothing. Along the way, Wilson found that the green summer of this New World was reawakening the curiosity he had indulged as a roaming Scottish peddler. He saw a red-headed woodpecker (*Picus erythrocephalus*)—a species found only in America. He shot the strange bird in order to have a closer look at it. He recalled later that he had regretted killing it, for it seemed the most beautiful bird he had ever encountered. As casually as that, without a conscious goal, he began collecting and studying specimens.

There was no demand for weavers, but in Philadelphia the immigrants found work. "After we had spent every farthing we had," Wilson wrote to his father, "and saw no hopes of anything being done that way, we took the first offer of employment we could find." At the shop of John Aitkin, Wilson became a copperplate engraver, and the experience was to prove valuable years later. There were several more jobs, several other residences. Wilson taught school at Bustleton, Pennsylvania, for one term in 1795, and in 1796 moved to a better school at Milestown, some twenty miles from Philadelphia. There he taught for five years—a schoolmaster who had left school at the age of ten—studying diligently to keep ahead of his students, learning German so that he could converse with his students' parents, learning mathematics well enough to perform surveying work for local farmers. While hunting upland birds and ducks (and studying them but with no intention yet of becoming the first naturalist to describe and paint such species as the canvasback and the American widgeon) he felt a growing sense of awe at the number and variety of American birds. He began to keep wild pets—a bluejay, a yellow-shafted flicker, an orchard oriole, robins, a pine grosbeak, a pair of purple finches, tanagers and humming-birds, thrushes and wrens, and others. Ever since his arrest in 1792 (and his consequent realization that to marry Martha M'Lean would be to ruin her) he had suffered from chronic despondency. Now his despair began to evaporate. He and his nephew considered the possibility of clearing farmland and sending for the Duncan family. In 1798, young William Duncan traveled north to see land that they had heard about, and that year they bought a hundred and fifty acres, situated between Cayuga and Seneca Lake, in western New York. Duncan was to clear it and establish a farm, while Wilson continued teaching.

Wilson had vowed never again to be enmeshed in radical reform movements or in politics of any kind. "While the world remains," he declared in a letter to his father, "there will be tyrants and freemen, reformers and revolutionists, peace and war . . . and he is only the wise and happy man who, in following a peaceful employment through private life, intermeddles with politics as little as possible." But he was already feeling a strong patriotic enthusiasm for his new country, accompanied by an attraction to the Jeffersonian form of democracy. His Milestown neighbors asked him to deliver an address on Jefferson's inauguration day in 1801, and he did so, to stirring applause. The speech was quoted in Jeffersonian newspapers and then published by a Philadelphia printer. Wilson was enjoying a new reputation and bright prospects when, on May 1, 1801, he wrote a strange letter to a friend named Charles Orr, a fellow Scot living in Philadelphia. "I have matters to lay before you that have almost distracted me," he said. "Do come. . . . I shall not remain here long. It is impossible that I can. I have no friend but yourself, and *one* whose friendship has involved us both in ruin or threatens to do so. . . ."

When Orr arrived, Wilson spoke almost incoherently of an inevitable scandal involving "her who loved me." Biographers have suggested that Wilson was having an affair with a married woman and suddenly found some reason to fear discovery. The identity of the woman has never been learned, or the nature of the scandal confirmed. In some of his subsequent letters Wilson spoke of having humiliated his love, of considering himself disgraced, of being a failure. Years later he made no secret of his love for Sarah Miller, who had been a sixteen-year-old neighbor at Milestown. At the time of his death he probably planned to marry her. But there is no evidence that she was the "humiliated love" of 1801. And there are little incoherencies and contradictions in the correspondence of the time, false notes indicating that perhaps Wilson was cloaking something other than adultery. It may have been something as innocuous as unrequited love or something as disturbing as impotence. Not even Benjamin Franklin had made adultery quite fashionable in rural America, but the revelation of impotence would have been a deeper disgrace, and one biographer, Robert Cantwell, has theorized that much of Wilson's life after his imprisonment "might be characterized as dominated by a fear of impotence."

Whatever the cause, Wilson abandoned his possessions and fled from Milestown on the night of Orr's visit. He never returned. Riding a recently acquired horse, he traveled fifteen miles to Wrightstown, New Jersey, where he stayed briefly with a friend, and then rode to New York. That fall, after writing to friends that he was staying in New York City, he began teaching school in a century-old cabin at Bloomfield, New Jersey. He lived there in secrecy and despair until that winter, then returned to Philadelphia looking for employment.

Having decided that teaching was no profession for him, he accepted with some misgivings the offer of a position as teacher at the Union School of Kingsessing, near Gray's Ferry, almost next door to William Bartram's botanical garden. The salary was to be one hundred dollars per quarter-year, more than he had ever earned. Still doubting whether he was worthy of the post, he held his first class on Monday, March 1, 1802.

That year he visited the famous garden and met William Bartram, but he was too diffident in the beginning to discuss with the great botanist and ornithologist his inquisitive passion for American birds. Streams flowed on both sides of the house where Wilson now lodged. He rambled through the woods and rested on the banks, observing birds, noting oddities such as the fact that male towhees arrive earlier in the spring than females, and recording his impressions of birds—the woodpeckers "thumping like carpenters" and the owls, "these grave and antiquated wanderers of the night." Examining the nests of orchard orioles, he recorded with wonder that in one he found a single thirteen-inch blade of tough grass hooked or woven into the structure at thirty-four different points. This enthusiastic noting of small but significant detail was to mark all his work. Orioles are master builders, and the former journeyman weaver was delighted by the ingenuity of their basketlike nests.

In the summer of 1802, Wilson received word that the Duncan family was coming over from Scotland. He walked all the way to the little farm, near where the town of Ovid, New York, would later be founded, to help his nephew prepare it for them. When he returned to Kingsessing he found his sister Mary and six children awaiting him; the elder William Duncan had drunk away his passage money and abandoned them in Belfast. Wilson managed to establish the clan—and his niece Isabel—at the farm before school opened. Then he added night classes to his teaching curriculum to help support them.

Despite these added responsibilities, life at Kingsessing was again lifting him out of despondency. He was beginning to sketch the birds he saw, and he practiced drawing an owl which he had shot, mounted on a miniature stump, and placed on his desk. He found it sometimes frustratingly difficult. In fact, he wrote, "I declare the face of an owl, and the back of a lark, have put me to a nonplus." Finding the delineation of breast feathers particularly baffling, he confined most of his efforts to profiles. But the frustration of failures was more than offset by the elation of successes. Each day his fascination with birdlife increased, until an idea as strong as a missionary's "call" began to form. In June, 1803, he wrote to Thomas Crichton in Paisley that he was beginning the project of drawing "all the finest birds of America."

That summer a nest of nearly fledged hummingbirds was brought to him. He kept them in his room, sustaining them with a supply of flowers sprinkled with sugar water. He kept one of them through the next winter in a gauze enclosure, and would have kept it longer but the bird got out, injured itself against a wall, and died. He visited the Philadelphia museum of the artist and naturalist Charles Wilson Peale, who had raised a pair of hummingbirds. Peale encouraged him, not merely in observing captive birds but in the purposeful study of nature. At last he had the confidence to approach William Bartram for advice, criticism, and, if fortune held, encouragement.

He began by sending Bartram notes asking for criticism of sketches he had made of plants and birds. "I am quite delighted with the anemone," Wilson wrote, "but fear I have made but bungling work of it. . . . Chief part of what I do is done by candle light." That was November, 1803. The following March he sent "a few attempts at some of our indigenous birds, hoping that your good nature will excuse their deficiencies, while you point them out to me. . . . I am almost ashamed to send you these drawings. . . . They were chiefly coloured by candle-light."

That month he also wrote to Alexander Lawson, a friendly and skillful Philadelphia engraver, "I am most earnestly bent on pursuing my plan of making a collection of all the birds of this part of North America." Wilson felt certain there were far more birds than the 215 species catalogued by Bartram, and there is no evidence that Bartram disagreed. The expense of such a project—the expense of the colored plates alone—would be staggering. Lawson advised against it. But Bartram, who had been astonishingly generous in his corrections, criticisms, instruction, and encouragement, thought Wilson might have the fortitude and skill to carry the project through if he kept improving his portraits and his scientific knowledge.

Help was now coming from an unexpected source: his students. One of them brought him a live mouse caught in the classroom and suggested that he mount it in a natural pose for a small prey species—clutched in the talons of Wilson's mounted owl. Wilson observed the mouse for a while, began sketching it, and discovered that he could draw an animal in a more lifelike way by using a live model. After drawing the creature he freed it, and then he began paying his students small sums for live specimens. Bartram must have been amused and pleased by Wilson's account of his progress:

> While others are hoarding up their bags of money, without the power of enjoying it, I am collecting, without injuring my conscience, or wounding my peace of mind, those beautiful specimens of Nature's works that are forever pleasing. I have live crows, hawks, and owls—opossums, squirrels, snakes, lizards, &c, so that my room has sometimes reminded me of Noah's ark. . . . A boy, not long ago, brought me a large basket full of crows. I expect his next load will be bull-frogs, if I don't issue orders to the contrary.

In June, 1804, he appeared at the Court of Common Pleas in Philadelphia, where he petitioned for and was granted citizenship. The family on the New York farm was prospering, and so was he. And now he was an American artist and naturalist, prepared to explore his country and record its natural treasures. That fall he went on a walking trip to Niagara Falls with William Duncan and a young man named Isaac Leech, a former Milestown neighbor. Along the way they slept at hunters' cabins, farms, and village taverns, and they shot game for sport, food, and specimens. On a couple of occasions they were nearly drowned and on a couple of others nearly frozen. Leech and Duncan did not make the entire trip to Niagara and back, but the thirty-eight-year-old Wilson did, covering nearly thirteen hundred miles in two months. And then he described the journey in a 2,219-line verse narrative, *The Foresters.*

By now, however, he was not much concerned with the minor literary successes that seemed to come so easily to him. He was more interested in a strange little specimen he had shot near the Mohawk River, a bluish-gray and white bird with some features resembling those of the bluejay. Bartram could not identify it. In March, 1805, Wilson sent pictures of it to President Jefferson as a mark of esteem, having been made bold enough to do so by Bartram's friendship with Jefferson. The President sent Wilson a friendly letter of encouragement, in which he remarked that the bird was unfamiliar to him too. Wilson let it be displayed as a new specimen at Peale's Museum, only to learn afterward that it was the Canada jay (*Perisoreus canadensis*)—quite familiar in the northern part of the country and already known to science. The experience increased his caution in subsequent ornithological studies.

At about this time, he borrowed tools from Alexander Lawson and began making a copperplate engraving of a bluejay. He planned to complete a few engravings and colored plates without any help and use these samples to obtain subscriptions that would finance his first volume. He would use the profits to advertise for more subscriptions, to finance a second volume, and to support himself while he traveled to collect still more subscriptions and discover the birds indigenous to other parts of the country. By February, 1806, he had finished a hundred drawings and had made copperplates of a jay and an eagle. Then, with Bartram's endorsement, he wrote to Jefferson and enclosed an application for a post as naturalist on Zebulon Pike's expedition into the West. Even without the profits from a first volume, this would enable him to search for unfamiliar birds in a vast wilderness. The route was to penetrate Spanish territory, and there was a possibility of Spanish resistance. Therefore the expedition was a state secret (perhaps one of the worst-kept military secrets of American history). Jefferson did not acknowledge Wilson's application. Years later he said he had never received it. Perhaps one of his aides, appalled to learn that the expedition was becoming common knowledge and worried about the President's reaction, had removed it from the letter.

Within a month, however, a new avenue of finance was opened to Wilson. Two of his students were the sons of the prominent publisher, Samuel Bradford, who was planning a twenty-two-volume American edition of *Rees's Cyclopaedia*. Bradford offered to pay Wilson nine hundred dollars a year to edit the *Cyclopaedia* while gathering material for the ornithological work. And Bradford would publish that as well. It was to be completed in five years, it was to be called *American Ornithology*, and it was to consist of ten volumes, each containing ten plates with several birds to a plate, and each also containing a text describing the birds and detailing the life histories of those species which were familiar to Wilson or could be adequately investigated. As Wilson's explorations and subscription-gathering journeys consumed more and more time, he devoted less and less attention to the *Cyclopaedia*, though he did, indeed, edit some articles and contribute a few of his own.

Wilson proceeded with a fervor only partly explicable in terms of his conviction that he was contributing to science and art. He also had a somewhat mystical belief, expressed on several occasions, that the living riches of America's wilderness formed a common heritage—a kind of natural unifying fabric—linking all the peoples of diverse ancestry and background to a single destiny in a young, vigorous nation. His opus, then, would be a labor of patriotism as well as science.

Not even imprisonment had quite cured Wilson of his passion to be a civic activist, evident in this patriotic elan and occasionally in more concrete (though now harmless) remarks and actions. In 1807, when robins were being shot by the cartload for the Philadelphia market, he planted an anonymous story in the newspapers alleging that the pokeberries on which the robins were gorging themselves in autumn made their flesh unwholesome.

He knew quite well that pokeberries had no effect on the edibility or tastiness of robins, but he was still mildly inclined to subterfuge and he felt that the welfare of mankind was bound to the welfare of wildlife. He was righteously elated by the effect of the story, which reduced the demand for robins and thus curtailed the slaughter. In 1812, he was to write that one day "the population of this immense Western Republic will have diffused itself over every acre of ground fit for the comfortable habitation of man—when farms, villages and glittering cities, thick as the stars in a winter's evening—overspread the face of our beloved country." His concern about a decline of wildlife and about the blanketing of the natural environment with human habitation must strike a modern reader as astonishingly farsighted. It was, but so was that of many other early naturalists, in whose work Wilson was immersing himself. As early as 1770, John Fothergill had written to John Bartram, stressing the importance of obtaining from young William Bartram accurate drawings of American tortoises because, "as the inhabitants increase, the species of this and some other animals, as well as vegetables, will, perhaps, be extinguished, or exist only in some still more distant parts."

Wilson planned to include familiar local birds in the first couple of volumes of his work so that those volumes could be completed quickly, their proceeds to subsidize more distant explorations. But he could not always adhere to the planned order of work. In 1807, Meriwether Lewis came to Philadelphia to prepare a two-volume account of the Lewis and Clark Expedition. He gave Frederick Pursh 150 plant specimens to draw for the work. Most of the bird specimens had been lost on the return trip from the Pacific, but he had three new species and he asked Wilson to draw and describe them. Wilson named them the Louisiana tanager (later renamed the western tanager), the Clark's crow (Clark's nutcracker), and Lewis's woodpecker. Thus Wilson became the first ornithologist to record western birdlife. He was able to include these species in his *Ornithology,* and he also made use of information furnished by Lewis and by John Ordway, a hunter on the expedition, regarding other western findings such as the feeding behavior of magpies. Wilson made some of his own discoveries much closer to home. For instance, he was the first to describe the sharp-shinned hawk (*Accipiter striatus velox*). He discovered this new species soaring over Bartram's garden one day while he was hunting for new birds to be included in an early volume. He was also the first naturalist to furnish good descriptions of the calls of many birds, ranging from the rough-legged hawk to the wood thrush and the Baltimore oriole. In his intense effort to paint birds accurately, he counted the scales on their legs and feet, and in his effort to communicate the intricacies of life cycles he sought still other details—for example, checking the average number of eggs in a goldfinch nest (five).

In the spring of 1807, he shot a summer redbird (tanager) that had greenish wings. He painted it, but identified it only tentatively, putting it aside pending further investigation. That summer he wandered alone into the Blue Mountains. There he shot another, somewhat redder specimen and he began to suspect that European naturalists were mistaken in listing four separate species. They had worked from dead specimens of various ages. And so he raised one in captivity, observing the change from juvenile coloration to mature plumage. The four species were one. Throughout *American Ornithology* he corrected such errors—but gently, for his own experience had made him sympathetic toward the problems of earlier naturalists. At the same time, he noted many behavioral changes exhibited by wild birds when kept in captivity. These and other observations constituted a previously unrecorded wealth of ornithological lore.

In the autumn of 1807, he journeyed to New York to sell subscriptions to his work. There he met with Robert Fulton, to discuss a *Cyclopaedia* article on canals and the use of steamboats on canals, and he sold Fulton a subscription to the *Ornithology*. Armed with an impressive prospectus, he hoped to take orders from other prominent citizens, whose names would serve as testimonials. He fared poorly in New York and Albany, though while he was away Jefferson ordered a set of the books. He was soon home again, painting and writing in the winter, dissecting creepers in the spring, completing the first volume, opening the second with a plate and essay devoted to the red-headed woodpecker—the first American bird he had ever collected. Volume 1 was published in September, and he left again, to tour "the Eastern States," as he told Bartram, "through Boston to Maine, and

back through the State of Vermont, in search of birds and subscribers." In the next few years he was to travel more than ten
thousand miles.

He failed to obtain an order from the faculty or library at
Princeton and again at Rutgers, but in New York he was introduced to a number of subscribers by Dr. Samuel Mitchill, an
amateur ichthyologist who was also helpful to Audubon. In
Greenwich Village he took an order from Tom Paine, who died
before the second volume was published. And in Albany and
Dartmouth he found still more subscribers, some of them sufficiently prominent to attract others. Then he turned southward.

In Baltimore, the state legislature voted unanimously against a
resolution advising Maryland to subscribe. Wilson was somewhat
daunted but he recuperated quickly. On December 17, he called
on the President, whose influence quickly brought seventeen
more subscriptions. Wilson's relations with his publisher, Bradford, slowly deteriorated as engraving, printing, and coloring
costs mounted, but Wilson had promised him only two hundred
subscribers for the first volume, and now that number seemed
assured. In Virginia he found more subscribers and more birds
to study. Near Petersburg he shot a grackle, chiefly to satisfy
himself that he was right in his classification; he was. Other naturalists had listed five species, all of which have proved to be the
same purple grackle (*Quiscalus quiscula*) though there are quite a
few subspecies.

Near Wilmington, North Carolina, he became exultant at the
sight of ivory-billed woodpeckers (*Campephilus principalis*). Catesby had first described them less than a century before, but
Wilson knew that they were already becoming scarce as forests
were cut and their principal food—the larvae of wood-boring insects—steadily diminished. He killed two of the birds for study,
but what he wanted was a live specimen. He winged one, captured it, and rode into Wilmington carrying it, though its
screams at first made his horse bolt and later brought concerned
women to their doors, for it sounded like a child crying. He left
the bird in his room at an inn while he tended his horse. When
he returned, it had chipped away the plaster near the window
and was boring through the outer wall. Next he tethered it to a
mahogany table, which it nearly demolished. When he tried to
handle the bird, it cut him severely. He had difficulty calming

the big, powerful woodpecker, and he did not know what to feed it. He drew it quickly, and on the same plate showed a red-headed woodpecker to illustrate comparative sizes. The ivory-bill was the largest of woodpeckers, a magnificent red-crested black and white bird averaging twenty-one inches in length. He wanted to release this marvelous creature, which now seemed to be weakening. He kept it with him as he rode south from Wilmington, trying to nurse it, but he still could not find any food it would accept. Inevitably, the bird died.

Perhaps he was somewhat cheered by the discovery of another woodpecker at about this time, a new species, a little ladder-backed black and white bird with a red streak above its white cheek. The discovery made him the first to name, describe, and furnish a type specimen of the red-cockaded woodpecker (*Dendrocopus borealis*). The specimen was added to the growing collection at Peale's Museum.

On February 10, he watched whooping cranes flying over the Waccamaw River in North Carolina. Even in 1809, when neither their western and northern breeding grounds nor their remote southern marshes had been desecrated by human intrusion, these great white birds were becoming rare along the migratory flyway Wilson now explored. It is true that two years later Thomas Nuttall recorded immense flights of whooping cranes as they made their way up the Mississippi Valley; "the bustle of their great migrations and the passage of their mighty armies fills the mind with wonder," he declared. But they were disappearing from the Atlantic Seaboard and Wilson predicted that they would ultimately vanish. There was a trace of wistful elegy in his notation of "the tallest and most stately species of all the feathered tribes of the United States."

The interludes of pensive exploration in woodlands and meadows, marshes and swamps, along stream banks and over wide savannas were a curative respite from bouts of salesmanship in towns. According to Bradford's subscription agreement, each purchaser of the *Ornithology* was to pay twelve dollars a volume. After seeing Wilson's samples, few prospective customers quarreled with the interest or quality of the books but many were reluctant to assume an eventual obligation of one hundred and twenty dollars for the projected ten volumes. A purchaser was to pay for a volume at a time, his twelve-dollar installment to be due by the end of the year in which he received one of the volumes from the nearest book-selling agent, from Wilson himself, or by direct shipment from Philadelphia. Thus, even Wilson's successes in finding subscribers had so far produced only agreements—promises—not a dollar in cash.

When he reached Charleston he received his first cash payment. Upon seeing Volume 1, General James Wilkinson was so intrigued that he paid twelve dollars on the spot and kept the sample copy instead of waiting for shipment of the book.

Wilson was elated, but elation gave way to bewilderment in Charleston and elsewhere as he encountered a strangely cold reserve among some of the prominent residents. With his writing, painting, selling, and field studies consuming all his energy, he had once again lost interest in politics. He was unaware that any friend of General Wilkinson was suspect to many well-informed citizens. He was not even fully aware of the controversy and distrust attached to the General's name. Wilkinson was the man whose denunciation had led to the trial of Aaron Burr. But now, and with good reason, this general in command of the United States Army was himself suspected of being a paid secret agent in the service of Spain. Wilkinson supplied small bits of ornithological information based on his hunting experiences in the West; for example, he enabled Wilson to report that rails, considered to be coastal birds, were plentiful on the waters of the deep interior. But it was fortunate for Wilson that his visit with the General was brief and their association not close enough to produce still another serious scandal.

By now he had sold a hundred and twenty-five subscriptions. As he proceeded southward, hospitality and the weather grew agreeably warmer, orders mounted, and there were new aspects of nature to be investigated. Near Beaufort, South Carolina, his horse took fright and leaped from a ferry. Wilson had to dive into the river and swim the animal ashore. The incident did not darken his mood, for the area of Beaufort was a vast watershed of species where northern and southern flora and fauna overlapped. "I am utterly at a loss in my wood rambles," he wrote to Bartram, "for there are so many trees, plants, shrubs, and insects that I know nothing of."

Here Wilson was befriended by Stephen Elliot, an amateur

botanist who had a residence in South Carolina and a plantation in Georgia. Wilson used both homes as headquarters for ornithological hunts, and he was also indebted to Elliot for the partial solution to a mystery concerning the towhee. In Pennsylvania, Wilson had noted, the towhee was a red-eyed bird. In the South, he encountered what appeared to be the same bird but with a white iris. At first uncertain whether the northern and southern birds represented two distinct species, he speculated in the *Ornithology* that they were the same species—that the color of the eye changed, just as the plumage of some birds changed. Elliot, alert for any finding that might help Wilson, seemed to have confirmed this, for he had shot a towhee with one red eye and one white eye.

He and Wilson were wrong in surmising that the iris changed color when the bird migrated, but their conclusion—that the white-eyed and red-eyed birds belonged to the same species— was correct. Both are the towhee (*Pipilo erythrophthalmus*); they are merely two geographic races, subspecies of the same bird.

Another Georgia naturalist who befriended and helped Wilson was John Abbot, primarily a lepidopterist and an excellent painter of insects who had furnished many specimens, drawings, and paintings for the British Museum. Abbot was also interested in ornithology. Wilson has been credited with discovering the black-billed cuckoo (*Coccyzus erythrophthalmus*) but he acknowledged in his description that it was Abbot who first distinguished this species from the better-known yellow-billed variety (*C. americanus*). Abbot also supplied accurate information regarding the habits of soothern birds and their times of arrival from the North or from points farther south. After comparing his own notes with Abbot's, Wilson suggested that changing sunlight, rather than weather, might spur migration. It was a finding confirmed by scientists many years later.

At the end of February, Wilson reached Savannah, and early in March, before sailing for home, he wrote to Bartram that he had taken two hundred and fifty orders for *American Ornithology*. By fall, work was complete on Volume 2, dealing with forty-two birds, and he asked Bartram to go with him on a long birding walk, an expedition to St. Louis. It was at this time that word reached Philadelphia of Meriwether Lewis's death, reported as a suicide. Bartram was growing old, feeling unwell, and saddened by the loss of friend after friend. At first he tentatively agreed to the expedition, but then, quite wisely, withdrew.

Apparently Wilson was no longer certain of his ultimate destination but in February, 1810, having packed sample copies of Volume 2, he set off on a long, circuitous selling and exploring trip. He went first to Lancaster and then walked over the Alleghenies to Pittsburgh, where he bought a skiff, painted *The Ornithologist* on its stern, and when the ice broke headed downriver on the Allegheny for the Ohio and the Mississippi.

On the first day he rowed and drifted fifty-two miles; after that he averaged about thirty-five miles a day. His hands became so sore that he had difficulty drawing, yet his correspondence shows that he thoroughly enjoyed the voyage—an adventure into another unfamiliar region. Near the confluence of the Miami and the Ohio, he shot several Carolina parakeets, then winged and captured one. He kept it in a cage of branches at the stern and fed it cockleburs. It was to be his companion on the remainder of the journey. At Louisville, he sold his skiff, having decided to continue overland. There he saw a newspaper advertisement placed by a local storekeeper, J. J. Audubon, who was offering drawing lessons and painting portraits. He visited Audubon and Audubon's business partner, Ferdinand Rozier. Audubon, though he could hardly afford it, was about to order Wilson's work when Rozier, speaking in French, dissuaded him. Audubon and Wilson hunted together and discussed ornithology before Wilson resumed his journey. There is evidence that they also traded a few sketches, and there is no doubt that Audubon—who was by far the better artist but was not always able to find every species he sought—copied a couple of Wilson's bird portraits.

Years later this led to an absurd dispute between Audubon and George Ord. Ord, an eccentric and quarrelsome man, had completed the ninth volume of the *Ornithology* after Wilson's death. In the sixth volume, published in 1812, there had appeared something that Wilson named a "small-headed green flycatcher" and it reappeared in Audubon's fifth folio in 1838. Ord insisted that Audubon had not seen the bird and drawn it from life or from a specimen but had copied Wilson's representation. Ord was undoubtedly right, since the bird was nonexistent. What

Wilson had taken for a new species had probably been a color phase or stage of development exhibited by a black-throated green warbler. Audubon's Mississippi kite was another bird copied from Wilson, traced and reversed either by Audubon or by an engraver who wished to embellish a plate by adding an extra bird. And there was a third dispute as to the discoverer of the Cape May warbler (*Dendroica tigrina*). Ord himself had discovered this bird in 1812, and Wilson had described it. Audubon pictured it in 1836 and claimed to have discovered it at Henderson, Kentucky, in 1811. Ord, desperate to prevent his single ornithological discovery from being credited to another man, reclaimed priority by changing the date of his Cape May specimen-collecting trip from 1812 to 1811.

But in 1810, Wilson knew Audubon only as a talented, unrecognized amateur, and such concerns would have bored him in any event. With his parakeet riding his shoulder or sometimes in his pocket, he walked on toward Nashville, a strange sight on the backwoods trails: tall, thin, black-haired, solemn, usually clad in city attire but with a fowling piece over his shoulder and a pack on his back. He looked like a cleric on a hunting trip. He named his parakeet Polly and taught it to speak. It came to him when he called. Man and bird must have provided startling entertainment for the other wayfarers they encountered now and then.

Near Shelbyville, Wilson inspected a vast abandoned roosting site of passenger pigeons. It was a stretch of dead beech woods three miles wide and forty miles long. Then he watched an enormous flight of the birds, which took hours to pass overhead and out of sight. He estimated that the flocks stretched through the sky for two hundred and forty miles. Then he took some time to calculate the number of passenger pigeons at three per square yard. Later, in Bartram's garden, he was to make comparable calculations with regard to the number of nests of various species, thus performing one of the earliest bird-census experiments.

In April, in the wilds between Danville and Nashville, he discovered two more new species, the Kentucky warbler (*Oporornis formosus*) and the prairie warbler (*Dendroica discolor*), and a little later near the Cumberland River he discovered yet another, which he named the Tennessee warbler (*Vermivora peregrina*).

In Nashville, as elsewhere in the South, he was appalled by the casual brutality toward slaves, and if he had not retreated from society he might have sold more subscriptions. However, he had a great deal of more important work to complete; for eight days he remained in a hotel room, painting. The following month he set out over the Natchez Trace, covering in reverse the route taken by Meriwether Lewis just before Lewis was supposed to have committed suicide. He discovered glaring discrepancies in the account furnished by one of Lewis's companions, Indian Agent James Neelly. And then, at Grinder's Station, he interviewed the woman who claimed to have found Lewis dying of two self-inflicted bullet wounds. After careful investigation, he concluded that Lewis had been murdered.

Though Lewis was a national hero as well as Governor of the Louisiana Territory, Wilson was the only contemporary ever to investigate the circumstances of his death. To Wilson it seemed to be a combined act of patriotism, friendship, and nature study. He alone paid the innkeeper at Grinder's Station to tend the grave, and then he marshaled his findings in a report entitled "Particulars on the Death of Captain Lewis." At first he was reluctant to have it published—for he was hewing to his vow of shunning politics, and Lewis, at the time of his death, was having difficulties with the Administration over finances and the disorganization caused by the Wilkinson scandal. But Wilson was a contributor to an influential literary magazine, *The Port Folio*, and his account finally appeared in that publication in 1811.

Near Natchez, Wilson stayed for a while at the plantation of William Dunbar, a Scottish-American trader, mathematician, inventor, astronomer, and naturalist. Dunbar supplied some interesting bits of anthropological as well as ornithological lore for Wilson's work. It was he who pointed out that the Choctaws and Chickasaws built birdhouses for purple martins, and that slaves newly arrived from Africa built the same type of birdhouses. He and Wilson were too wise to make any wild surmises about a common heritage among such widely separated peoples; it merely seemed to them worth reporting the common tendencies and attitudes toward nature among diverse human groups.

At Natchez Wilson discovered and described another new species, the Mississippi kite (*Ictinia mississippiensis*). He dissected it and thus confirmed his suspicion—based on prior field observation—that this particular raptor did some of its feeding on the wing, capturing airborne insects. The beautiful silver-white, ash-gray, and chestnut bird provided Wilson with one of his finest plates.

At New Orleans, after selling more subscriptions, he again sailed for home. The ship was becalmed, drifting all the way to Cuba, and then wracked by storms. Wilson unconcernedly remained on deck during the gales to observe stormy petrels, after which he shot and dissected fourteen of them in order to analyze and catalog their crop and stomach contents.

When he arrived in Philadelphia in August, 1810, he was able to tell his publisher that he had sold a total of sixty-thousand dollars' worth of subscriptions, and soon he was able to announce completion of the third volume. Somewhat later, when this volume was criticized because it included less detail than the previous ones regarding bird habits and life histories, Wilson pointed out that there had been no time or opportunity for him or any other naturalist to investigate many of the species thoroughly. What he had done, nevertheless, was to increase man's knowledge of wildlife by a considerable degree, introducing to science a large number of new species. "Nearly half of the whole number of birds [in Volume 3] are such as have never before been taken notice of by naturalists." No one could quarrel with his statement.

That November, he made the first of many trips to Egg Harbor and Cape May, on the New Jersey coast, to obtain specimens for subsequent volumes. At Egg Harbor, he shot a snowy owl, from which he painted one of his most beautiful and famous plates, picturing it on the same page with a small, sprightly sparrow hawk.

He dissected the owl and found that its eyes were sheathed at the rear by a membrane-covered cartilaginous cone. It was obvious that the eyes were immovable in the sockets and that the owl achieved its wide arc of vision through ocular structure and the ability to turn its head almost three hundred and sixty degrees. But the precise function of the conelike sheath was not so quickly apparent. Beneath the membrane he found fifteen plates of cartilage, somewhat like barrel staves, overlapping at the cone's narrow end. He saw that they were movable. The cone could be expanded or contracted by the muscular membrane. He had discovered the secret of the owl's wonderful vision: its eyes can focus telescopically.

Early in 1811, at about the time the third volume was printed and the plates of the fourth were being engraved, Wilson resigned as editor of the *Cyclopaedia*—on which, by now, he was doing almost no work—in order to improve his relations with the publisher, Samuel Bradford, and also to give himself more time for his ornithological work.

The fourth volume began with a lyrical but nonetheless accurate essay on the fish hawk, and a fine plate delineating the eaglelike form and coloration of this big water-haunting bird of prey. He had long ago written a poem that fit appropriately into the essay, a chanty relating how the osprey was regarded by the fishermen at Duck Island, on the Delaware:

> The osprey sails above the Sound,
> The geese are gone, the gulls are flying;
> The herring shoals swarm thick around,
> The nets are launched, the boats are plying. . . .

> She brings us fish, she brings us spring,
> Good times, fair weather, warmth and plenty,
> Fine stores of shad, trout, herring, ling,
> Sheeps-head and drum, and old wives dainty.

> Yo ho, my hearts! let's seek the deep,
> Ply every oar, and clearly wish her
> Still as the bending net we sweep,
> God bless the Fish Hawk and the Fisher!

Volume 5 dealt extensively with shore and water birds seen at Egg Harbor, and subsequent volumes covered waterfowl as well as the less familiar birds of various types which he had seen in his travels. The fifth and sixth volumes were published in 1812, the seventh in 1813. Wilson was working at prodigious speed.

There was another selling trip northward in the spring of 1811, after which he spent much of the summer living at Bartram's home and conducting miniature explorations in the garden. On Bartram's eight acres he made a careful census of actively nesting birds: house wrens, purple grosbeaks, yellow warblers, Baltimore orioles and orchard orioles, chimney swallows and barn swallows, chipping sparrows, catbirds, and so on.

He found fifty-one pairs of nesting migratory birds, and from that figure he computed the probable number of such birds in Pennsylvania. Multiplying Bartram's acreage by four-hundred thousand, he deduced that the various types of habitat in Pennsylvania must support at least a hundred-million. The little exercise in nest-finding and arithmetic was one of the pioneering steps toward bird sampling and extrapolation to estimate wildlife populations.

It was about now that George Ord, a wealthy young Philadelphia sportsman and amateur zoologist, began writing to Wilson about his observations of birds. These observations were not always valuable or even accurate, but Wilson was tired and was occasionally having difficulty with such self-imposed duties as climbing tall trees to examine fledgling hawks and note the defensive behavior of their parents. He therefore welcomed the company of Ord on the trips to Egg Harbor. Moreover, he needed jovial young friends particularly at this time, for he was having serious arguments with Samuel Bradford over money. Malvina Lawson, daughter of the engraver Alexander Lawson, years later attributed Wilson's early death partly to his grief and worry arising from "the dishonesty of his publisher." On the evidence, it seems fairer to state that Bradford was reluctant to go on increasing his already immense investment in a project for which he had lost his enthusiasm and which was not yet bringing any substantial profit. Wilson never accused him of dishonesty, but in his last years he painted and wrote with a hasty desperation, as if in fear that his health would break or his resources melt away before production of the last volume. He was now completing studies and pictures of more than one hundred birds a year, and for a while the shortage of funds forced him to assume additional duties, coloring his own plates when his colorists left him.

He went north again in September, 1812, to collect money from agents in Albany and from the faculty and library of Dartmouth College, at Hanover, New Hampshire. He collected enough to satisfy Bradford, at least for the time being, and on the shore of Lake Champlain he discovered yet another new species, the semipalmated plover (*Charadrius hiaticula semipalmatus*). But the trip was marred by what was perhaps the least important incident of the War of 1812.

Near the Canadian border he was seen wandering the hills and looking over the area from a high ridge. Mistaken for a British spy, he was arrested. Though he was quickly exonerated and released, the episode was understandably depressing to him.

The following spring, he signed the introduction to Volume 7 and by early summer had completed Volume 8, a book largely devoted to ducks seen both locally and in distant regions. He then spent about a month at Cape May. He had intended to pass more time in residence at Bartram's the year before, but was unable to because a half brother, David Wilson, had arrived from Paisley and stayed with him at his lodgings. Now he returned to Kingsessing in the hope of spending the remainder of the summer at the garden. But on August 19, 1813, Dr. Charles Caldwell was summoned to the room where he lodged, in the house of William Jones. Dr. Caldwell found him extremely weak from severe dysentery. After the physician left, Wilson wrote a will bequeathing two sets of *American Ornithology* to his father, one to William Duncan, and everything else he owned to Sarah Miller. She had been his sixteen-year-old neighbor when he left Milestown. For years she had lived near him at Philadelphia, and his many letters to her indicate an abiding love.

Dr. Caldwell ministered to Wilson daily, but there was little he could do. On August 23, 1813, at the age of forty-seven, Alexander Wilson died.

George Ord returned from a trip to find his friend gone. He wrote a long, reverent, somewhat inaccurate obituary and then finished organizing and editing the eighth volume, which Wilson had already completed. It was published the following year. Ten books had been projected, but only a ninth was needed to deal with the remainder of the known birds. And Wilson had finished a great deal of the work for that volume, too, though his descriptive notes were largely missing or in disarray. With the help of the French ornithologist Charles Lucien Bonaparte, Ord completed the ninth volume and it appeared at last in 1829.

Though Ord never became a truly great naturalist, he did produce a worthwhile book of his own on zoology, and he eventually became curator and vice president of the Academy of Natural Sciences and president of the American Philosophical Society—to which Wilson had been elected shortly before his death.

The boundaries of the United States then encompassed a portion of the continent in which three hundred and forty-three species of birds are indigenous. In his *American Ornithology,* Alexander Wilson had presented two hundred and sixty-four of them. If his art was not equal to Audubon's, his text and other essays and poetry exerted an influence on American nature writing that extended to Emily Dickinson. He had provided excellent life histories for ninety-four species, and in his determined explorations had failed to find only seventy-nine of those within America's borders. His books added forty-nine new species to the list of known birds accumulated by the great Bartram. Elliott Coues, the scholarly ornithologist who also paid memorable tribute to Bartram, said of *American Ornithology:* "Probably no other work of ornithology of equal extent is equally free of errors; and its truthfulness is illumined by a spark of divine fire."

Chapter 5
AUDUBON AND COMPANY

Jean Jacques Fougère Audubon, the bastard son of a French slave-trader, was a pampered, foppish wastrel who Americanized his name to John James Audubon, styled himself "an American woodsman," and by dint of fanatic determination transformed himself into something that rather closely conformed to his own description. He was also a genius who revolutionized the study, illustration, and description of birds and mammals.

Before his powers failed, he had grown larger than life in more than one sense, for he was a personage and an institution, an impresario of art and science who gathered about him a large retinue of collaborators so gifted that only an Audubon could overshadow them. Some historians of science have even implied that in his role as impresario he made his greatest contribution to the advancement of zoology.

His work, particularly his ornithological art, has aroused controversy that seems to fledge itself from its own ashes with the regularity of a phoenix. Despite his journals and surviving letters and other documents, much of his early life was generally unknown until 1917, when Francis Hobart Herrick, a professor of biology at Western Reserve University, published a monumental two-volume biography entitled *Audubon the Naturalist*. In this work, which remains definitive, Herrick notes that critics have charged Audubon with a number of sins, but chiefly with accepting credit for the work of colleagues, with being "king of the nature fakirs," and with a superficiality of scientific purpose in that he "never propounded or answered a scientific question." As to the first charge, Audubon printed generous acknowledgments to long lists of associates even while husbanding most of the glory for himself. As to the second and third, Herrick refutes them with factual accounts of Audubon's investigations and is therefore content to understate the case for the defense with the comment that "Audubon's accounts of the birds are copious, interesting, and generally accurate, considering the time and circumstances in which they were produced."

In Audubon's Wildlife, Edwin Way Teale makes clear that some of the criticism stems from the hindsight of increased zoological knowledge. Audubon's painting of a red-eyed vireo was enhanced by the inclusion of a spider building its web. The bodily form of the arachnid and the markings on its back identify it as a jumping spider, *Phidippus audax,* which makes no web. Such errors were common and they continue to occur. Teale's book was published in 1964. Three years later a book about Audubon's paintings of mammals was published by a very able mammalogist who remarked, in a commentary on the nine-banded armadillo, that this North American species (*Dasypus novemcinctus*) cannot roll itself into a defensive ball in the manner of some South American relatives. Audubon portrayed the animal in a standing position but he and his collaborator, John Bachman, reported that it "rolls itself up" when sufficiently alarmed. Actually, though it cannot roll itself up as tightly as some other armadillos, Audubon and Bachman were more accurate in this instance than the modern zoologist.

Teale and his peers concede that there were errors more glaring than that of the spider web—mistaking a sandhill crane for the young of a whooping crane, reporting and naming a new species, the "Bird of Washington," which was probably an immature bald eagle. But neither Wilson nor Audubon nor others could avoid such occasional errors, and Audubon was conscientious in expressing doubt about some of his own findings. Teale might well have added that in 1843 Audubon described a supposedly new species of duck from a specimen that had been shot in Louisiana twenty-one years before. He called it the "Brewer's Duck," explaining that he had named it after his friend Thomas M. Brewer, "as a mark of the estimation in which I hold him as an accomplished ornithologist." However, Audubon stipulated that it might not be a valid species after all, but a cross between the mallard and "some other species, perhaps the Gadwall, to which also it bears a great resemblance." Here was responsible reporting of careful observation. The Brewer's duck has since been recognized as a mallard-gadwall hybrid, just as Audubon suspected.

It cannot be denied that on occasion Audubon let romanticism or expediency jostle realism. Ignoring the fact that the polygamous male turkey wants nothing to do with the female's clutch except perhaps to destroy her eggs or scatter her young, he painted a family portrait with the male proudly leading his timid mate and bustling chicks. Such lapses notwithstanding, he was a keener observer than most of his rivals.

Much of the criticism concerning accuracy was initiated by George Ord, who resented Audubon's competition with Alexander Wilson's work, and by Ord's friend Charles Waterton, an English author and amateur naturalist whose writings for years capitalized on Audubon's alleged shortcomings. Typical was an Ord-Waterton attack on Audubon's famous (and exquisite though melodramatic) painting of mockingbirds defending a nest from a rattlesnake amid a tangle of yellow jessamine vines. Ord and Waterton would have been well advised to criticize the pupils of the snake's eyes, which should not have been round, and its maxillary teeth, which should not have been exposed above the gums. They centered their objections instead on the recurved fangs, which were accurately drawn. Since then, the entire portrayal has been rejected as fanciful because rattlesnakes are not supposed to climb trees. Several years ago another biographer, Alexander Adams, put the question to field biologists in the southern area represented by the painting. They replied that the canebrake rattler common in that region does, indeed, climb shrubs and trees, and that in their study area twelve percent of the snake's diet consists of birds and bird eggs.

For each alleged error refuted, another, sometimes more genuine, is exhumed. In *Audubon's America*, Donald Culross Peattie comments on such an error, again concerning vipers of the genus *Crotalus*—rattlesnakes. In one of his descriptions, Audubon claimed to have observed a rattler killing its prey by constriction. Circumstances forced Audubon to publish many of his descriptions years after the observations were made and, as Peattie theorizes, he must have relied more on memory than on notes in this instance and thereby confused the rattler with the American black snake, which does, indeed, kill prey by constriction. If the controversy had not fed itself on occasional new discoveries, surely the minor errors would be seen in the perspective of the vast achievement—and so they are, by the responsible historians of natural science. They see Audubon as a man both of his time and ahead of it.

He was born at Les Cayes on Saint-Domingue—now Haiti— on April 26, 1785. At first, he may have been called Jean Rabin Fougère but he was baptized Jean Jacques Fougère. His father, Jean Audubon, was a French naval officer engaged in sugar planting and slave trading in the West Indies. Madame Audubon—Anne Moynet—remained at home on the Audubon estates in France, while Lieutenant Audubon sired at least one child with each of two Creole mistresses. Within a year, Jean Jacques Fougère's mother died, and in 1789 his father took him and his infant half-sister Muguet to the United States and then to France, where the childless and tolerant Madame Audubon waited. Five years later, Lieutenant Audubon having legally acknowledged paternity of both children, he and his wife formally adopted them.

They were raised as the children of wealthy aristocrats, and the boy was pampered outrageously by his stepmother. He recalled years later that in the zeal of her love she "hid my faults, boasted . . . of my youthful merits, and said frequently in my presence that I was the handsomest boy in France."

His mathematical ineptitude and dislike of scholarship distressed his father and his tutors, but they were somewhat consoled by his aptitude for more fashionable pursuits such as fencing, dancing, and playing the violin. In adolescence, he was an avid collector of bird nests, eggs, and other natural curiosities. Much of his time was devoted to sketching wild creatures, and he also became an amateur taxidermist. Hoping to interest him in something "useful," his father sent him to a naval school. The boy made quick use of an open window to take what is known among Francophobes as French leave and return to the Audubon estate near Nantes.

In 1802, on the assumption that his artistic inclination might lead to a reasonably respectable career, he was sent to Paris to study at the school of the eminent painter Jacques Louis David. To the seventeen-year old wildlife portraitist, academic instruction remained academic instruction, and stifling, even when the subject was art. He remained in Paris only briefly.

The West Indies having been the recent scene of piracy, warfare, and successful slave rebellion, the sugar plantation was by now lost, as was a large portion of the Audubon wealth. However, Jean Audubon had made an investment that seemed to promise a continued income—a farm called Mill Grove in eastern Pennsylvania, on which was situated a defunct but formerly profitable lead mine. There he sent his ne'er-do-well son in 1803. In America, the young man could learn English and enter some profitable trade while also avoiding conscription into Napoleon's growing army.

He recalled his reaction to this proposal as "indescribable pleasure" and he regarded himself as "master of Mill Grove" at the age of eighteen, despite the presence of his father's American agent, a Philadelphia Quaker named Miers Fisher, who was to supervise the boy's activities as well as the family holdings. Some biographers have implied that Fisher was a Philistine who failed to understand young Audubon's devotion to art and nature. Actually he was a generous and cultured gentleman, one of the early subscribers to Wilson's *Ornithology*, but he was bound to clash with his unruly and irresponsible charge, who neglected the affairs of the farm and of the mercantile world for the affairs of the field and an affair of the heart.

Young Audubon's pleasures as self-styled master of Mill Grove were chiefly the delight of visiting a charming neighbor, Lucy Bakewell, and riding about in dandified new hunting clothes— black satin breeches "with silk stockings," as he later recalled, "and the finest ruffled shirt Philadelphia could afford." But he was not entirely idle. The unfamiliar birds and animals of the countryside quickly sharpened his already enthusiastic curiosity about nature, and in the spring of 1804 he began his first American bird studies.

The accusation of superficiality has not been leveled at Audubon by detractors alone. Dr. Elliott Coues, who believed him to be the most inspired ornithologist of his time, and the greatest popularizer of ornithology, once remarked that Audubon, unlike Wilson, lost interest in a bird once it was drawn. Perhaps even as late as the 1870's, when Coues was writing, the scientific community did not yet grasp the significance of Audubon's pioneering efforts, of which the chief example was the earliest: a birdbanding experiment casually begun in April, 1804. It was the first American birdbanding experiment, perhaps the first successful and fully recorded project of its kind anywhere. Ninety-five years passed before another naturalist, a Danish schoolmaster named H. C. C. Mortensen, was creative enough to repeat and expand Audubon's phoebe-banding investigation with teal, storks, and starlings.

Audubon wondered if fledged birds might not return to their first homes after migrating, and he devised a simple test. As Herrick emphasized in his evaluation of Audubon's idea, "little could he or any one else then have thought that one hundred years later a Bird Banding Society would be formed in America to repeat his test on a much wider scale, in order to gather exact data upon the movements of individuals of all migratory species in every part of the continent."

Audubon published his own account years later in the *Ornithological Biography*, one of his two major text collaborations, as part of his description of the habits of the "Pewee Flycatcher, *Muscicapa fusca*"—now called the eastern phoebe (*Sayornis phoebe*), though confused by some writers with the eastern wood pewee (*Contopus virens*):

> While young, I had a plantation that lay on the sloping declivities of Perkiomen Creek [at Mill Grove, near Philadelphia]. I was extremely fond of rambling along its rocky banks . . . observing the watchful King-fisher perched on some projecting stone over the clear water of the stream. Nay, now and then, the Fish Hawk itself, followed by a White-headed Eagle, would make his appearance, and by his graceful aërial motions, raise my thoughts far above them into the heavens. . . . These impressive, and always delightful, reveries often accompanied my steps to the entrance of a small cave. . . . There it was that I studied the habits of the Pewee; and there I was taught most forcibly, that to destroy the nest of a bird or to deprive it of its eggs or young, is an act of great cruelty.
>
> I had observed the nest of this plain-coloured Flycatcher fastened, as it were, to the rock immediately over the arched entrance. . . . I chanced one morning [April 10, 1804] early to go to

my retreat. . . . A rustling sound over my head attracted my attention, and, on turning, I saw two birds fly off, and alight on a tree close by:—the Pewees had arrived! . . .

On the thirteenth day, the little ones were hatched. One egg was unproductive, and the female, on the second day after the birth of her brood, very deliberately pushed it out of the nest. . . . At last, when they were about to leave the nest, I fixed a light silver thread to the leg of each, loose enough not to hurt the part, but so fastened that no exertions of theirs could remove it.

Sixteen days passed, when the brood took to wing; and the old birds . . . began to arrange the nest anew. A second set of eggs were laid, and in the beginning of August a new brood made its appearance. . . .

At the season when the Pewee returns to Pennsylvania, I had the satisfaction to observe those of the cave in and about it. There again, in the very same nest, two broods were raised. I found several Pewee nests at some distance up the creek. . . . Having caught several of these birds on the nest, I had the pleasure of finding that two of them had the little ring on the leg.

I was now obliged to go to France, where I remained two years. On my return . . . early in August, I had the satisfaction of finding three young Pewees in . . . the cave. . . . One of the parent birds was as shy as possible, while the other allowed me to approach. . . . This was the male bird, and I felt confident that the old female had paid the debt of nature. Having inquired of the miller's son, I found that he had killed the old Pewee and four young ones, to make bait for the purpose of catching fish. Then the male Pewee had brought another female to the cave!

Characteristically, Audubon's report of the experiment took the form of a vivid personal narrative quite unlike modern scientific papers which must be dry, succinct, and replete with tabulations in order to convey great masses of data, but the narrative of the pewees nonetheless included valuable behavioral details in addition to the homing instinct of migratory birds. There was, for example, the notation of the time required for fledging, and there was the observation regarding the ejection from the nest of the unhatched egg. Audubon immediately opened this egg to ascertain that the defective embryo had died before reaching full development. In the manner of modern experimental reports, his full narrative also explained his methods: he frequented the cave and remained there quietly observing until the birds accepted him as a part of their natural surroundings (just as a twentieth-century field biologist does when investigating nesting behavior) and he was soon able to handle the nestlings without causing the adult birds to abandon them. From the first, Audubon seemed to have an instinctive understanding of how to observe birds and mammals very closely without alarming them. Having accustomed the phoebes to his presence, he tried several types of threads and fastening techniques before settling on a material and attachment that would not hinder normal behavior. And in drawing conclusions from limited data, he was more cautious than most naturalists of his time. He found the birds wearing his leg bands again in the spring of 1806, yet he refrained from sweeping generalities, concluding only that birds sometimes, at least, return from migration to their fledging region or site.

By the time of the phoebe experiments, perhaps Audubon felt some vague inkling of his peculiar future vocation, for in 1804 he was also collecting specimens—a fairly easy task for an adept hunter who had mastered the use of a fowling piece during early adolescence—and was drawing details of anatomy and plumage. Quite early he began posing his birds in lifelike attitudes, imparting appropriate actions to them. The same idea occurred independently to Wilson, who portrayed some of his birds flying, but it was an approach that eluded most contemporaries. Their paintings were as lifeless as belled museum exhibits. Though Audubon's work was still quite crude, he was forming an original and naturally conceived basis for later accomplishment.

At this time, Audubon met an English-American sportsman named William Bakewell, whose large farm was located near Mill Grove, and he was soon enamored of Bakewell's fifteen-year-old daughter Lucy. There were, however, impediments to his courtship. His father had ordered the opening of the old Mill Grove lead mine, which had been profitable during the Revolution when lead was in demand for ammunition. Because the expense of opening the mine and beginning its operation was high, and profits were disappointing, the farm had to be mortgaged. In France a mortgage was taken by a wealthy friend, François Rozier, and in Pennsylvania a half-interest in Mill Grove was sold to Francis Dacosta, who was then appointed young Audubon's guardian. Dacosta's opposition to his ward's frivolities surpassed

Fisher's disapproval, and as business difficulties mounted the disputes between guardian and ward were exacerbated.

When Audubon announced in 1804 that he had proposed marriage to Lucy Bakewell, a heated quarrel erupted. Dacosta's prerogatives did not include consent or denial, Audubon declared; he would return to France to obtain parental consent and financial aid. When Dacosta predictably refused money for the voyage, Audubon arranged to secure a loan from a Bakewell relative, Benjamin Bakewell, an importer in New York. In January, 1805, he walked from Mill Grove to New York and there took passage aboard the *Hope* for Nantes, arriving in March.

He remained for a year at a family estate in Couëron, hunting and drawing birds while nearby, at Nantes, his father and François Rozier discussed possible solutions to financial and parental problems. Then, probably on an impulse spawned by impatience or desperation, he joined the French navy but was soon permitted to withdraw. It was decided to bind him and Rozier's son Ferdinand in partnership and send them back to America with instructions to establish themselves in business, preferably at Mill Grove. Ferdinand Rozier was a practical young man; he would doubtlessly exert a steadying influence.

In May, 1806, they arrived in New York aboard the *Polly* and went directly to Mill Grove, where they tried unsuccessfully for four months to operate the lead mine. In mid-September the remaining half-interest in Mill Grove was sold to Dacosta, with the Audubons and Roziers holding a joint mortgage. Ferdinand Rozier suggested to Jean Jacques Audubon (who by now preferred to be called John James although he was still more comfortable speaking French than English) that they join a mercantile establishment for a brief apprenticeship, after which they could open a business of their own. Accordingly, they returned to New York to clerk in Benjamin Bakewell's commission house. First, however, John James Audubon took time to appear before the District Court in Philadelphia, where he was granted a petition to become a naturalized citizen of the United States.

Rozier displayed an aptitude and enthusiasm for the mercantile world while Audubon displayed an equal propensity for absenting himself to continue collecting and drawing specimens. He was soon working and studying taxidermy at a little museum operated by Samuel Mitchill—the same Dr. Mitchill who was to help Alexander Wilson find subscribers two years later. Audubon's mercantile period in New York was premonitory in yet another way, for his single enthusiastic business venture echoed one of William Bartram's commercial misadventures: it was a calamitous speculation in the failing indigo market.

Next Audubon and Rozier purchased a stock of merchandise with their dwindling funds and at the end of August, 1807, set off for the frontier settlement of Louisville to open a general store. This was the year when the British blockade of French trade, having been extended to include American vessels and the impressment of American seamen, led to retaliation in the form of the Embargo Act, a prelude to the War of 1812 as well as a weakening factor in the American economy and a disaster for merchants selling imported goods. But even if there had been no Embargo Act, the store probably would have fared badly, for Audubon was incompetent, Rozier inexperienced, and the settlers of the Louisville area impecunious.

Still, Audubon now considered himself an established businessman, eminently eligible for marriage. He went back to Pennsylvania and on June 12, 1808, at the Bakewell farm, Flatland Ford, he wed Lucy Bakewell, then returned to Louisville with his bride.

Some biographers have treated Lucy Bakewell Audubon almost disapprovingly because in 1820 and the first part of 1821 she refused to leave her employment as a governess in Cincinnati in order to join him in New Orleans, and in 1829 she was reluctant to leave a similar position in Louisiana in order to sail to England with him. Indeed, their correspondence and a few passages in his journals at these times indicate a pained and disappointed coolness on her part and a despairingly remorseful longing on his. Yet she was a remarkably strong, steadfast, compatible wife for an impoverished artist-naturalist who—for all his protestations of selfless love—left her for long periods while he roamed the wilderness in quest of birds and animals or lingered in distant cities to further his publishing ambitions. Apparently she was sustained by a faith in his genius almost matching his own. She endured his squandering of her inheritance as well as his, she labored for years to support their family, gave him money while he earned none, nursed him when he was ill, and on occasion mended rifts of his own making with others who tried to help him.

On their first wedding anniversary, June 12, 1809, Lucy bore his first son, Victor Gifford Audubon. With a wife and infant to support, he still could not bear to be more attentive to what he called "serious storekeeping" than to the sounds of the river and the forest. He augmented their meager income by drawing portraits and giving drawing lessons, but if there were few customers for the store's provisions there were fewer still for art.

It was in March of the following year that Alexander Wilson arrived in Louisville, visited the local portrait painter, and compared wildlife sketches with him. According to Audubon's reminiscences, written many years later, Rozier dissuaded him from ordering Wilson's *Ornithology* by remarking in French, "Your drawings are certainly far better, and again, you must know as much of the habits of American birds as this gentleman." It is possible that even as early as 1810 Audubon's painting was better than Wilson's and he was acquainted with a few western birds not yet familiar to Wilson, but at that time he certainly did not know as much as his visitor about American birds. Evidently it is true that Rozier dissuaded him from buying the work, but Audubon neglected to mention that the firm of Rozier and Audubon was barely surviving and there was no money with which to honor a subscription. In fact, Audubon's entire account of the visit was somewhat self-congratulatory, and it served to feed subsequent controversies about his work. He told of lending Wilson sketches to copy, but not of his own later reliance on a few of Wilson's published plates. Though he took pains in his texts to laud Wilson for several discoveries, charges of artistic plagiarism cannot be definitely refuted. Indeed, one of Audubon's birds was an almost exact duplicate of a Wilson rendering except that it was missing one talon.

Audubon employed assistants in painting his mammals, and probably more than half of those portraits, completed in his later years, were by the hand of his younger son, John Woodhouse Audubon. Herrick and some other biographers have theorized that the bird plagiarism may have been committed without Audubon's knowledge, by one of his associates. The explanation has some credibility in view of Audubon's ego, which was not of the kind to admit any need for dependence on a rival's work. Yet there is evidence that he could stifle both ego and conscience rather than omit a species from his work just because he had not personally seen a specimen. On another occasion—in 1838—he was to publish a picture of a "green flycatcher" that existed only as an inaccurate study by Wilson. What Wilson had assumed to be a new species was probably a color phase of the black-throated green warbler. Audubon's likeness of the nonexistent "flycatcher" was not a precise duplicate of Wilson's but must have been based on it. The case of the bird with too few talons implies a greater degree of larceny, an actual tracing of another man's drawing.

The portrait in question is the lower bird in Audubon's Plate 117, a Mississippi kite. The lines, though not the coloring, constitute an exact duplicate in reverse of Wilson's Plate 25, except that Audubon's version is lacking a toe. Audubon's was engraved in England, probably toward the end of 1831, while the artist was in America. His publisher, Robert Havell, was an accomplished engraver who was permitted to change occasional details or even fill in backgrounds when Audubon was unavailable. The missing toe, together with the legend beneath, which erroneously represented the bird as a female, might well be evidence that the engraver felt the need to fill empty space in the original version and filled it himself by tracing and reversing a Wilson bird.

In Audubon's frenzy to meet publishing schedules, he occasionally surrendered to expediency, and whether he or his engraver did so in the case of the kite remains unknown. In *The Viviparous Quadrupeds of North America,* his second major work, he again borrowed from earlier work—fortunately, his own.

Having often observed the predator-prey relationship of owls and squirrels, he associated them in pictures and texts. Plate 46 of *The Birds of America* is devoted to a barred owl, rendered with a delicacy, balance, dynamism, and flow of line reminiscent of Oriental art. The bird is alighting on a branch only inches from a meticulously detailed eastern gray squirrel, and the painting is only flawed (or perhaps ironically enhanced) by the squirrel's impossible complacency. In the accompanying text of the *Ornithological Biography,* he recalled the haunting of his campsites by such owls: "How often when snugly settled under the boughs of my temporary encampment and preparing to roast a venison steak or the body of a squirrel, have I been saluted with the exulting bursts of this nightly disturber of the peace." In the text of his *Quadrupeds,* he returned to this leitmotif, noting that the gray squirrel's "search after food or its playful gambols until the light of day is succeeded by the moon's pale gleams, causes it frequently to fall a prey to the Virginia [great horned] owl, or the barred owl; which last especially is very abundant in the swamps of Carolina, where gliding on noiseless pinions between the leafy branches, it seizes the luckless Squirrel ere it is aware of its danger, or can make the slightest attempt to escape."

One such squirrel of Audubon's acquaintance must have escaped, however. Plate 7 of *Quadrupeds* shows two gray squirrels poised on a limb. One of them is the squirrel under attack in Plate 46 of *Birds,* precisely transposed in every detail.

Whether or not Audubon copied any of Wilson's work in 1810 or thereafter, he devoted much of his time to observing and drawing wildlife while business at the store deteriorated. Soon after the visit, he and Rozier loaded their merchandise on a flatboat and floated down the Ohio a hundred and twenty-five miles to Henderson, Kentucky, where they opened another store. This, too, was a bad choice, as the settlers were few and poor. For a while they employed a young clerk, but while Rozier labored, Audubon and the clerk "roamed the country," according to one biographer, "in eager pursuit of rare birds," and in comparably eager pursuit of game for the scantily provisioned table. While traveling near Frankfort, Audubon met a man he greatly admired, Daniel Boone, then in his seventies but still active. Boone was the "American woodsman" Audubon wished to be. Soon they were hunting squirrels together near the Kentucky River on land "thickly covered with black walnuts, oaks and hickories," Audubon afterward recalled, where "squirrels were seen gambolling on every tree." Audubon invited Boone to hunt with him again, on a longer wilderness ramble, in 1813. Failing vision and the infirmities of age caused the celebrated frontiersman to decline the invitation, but Audubon led parties of other hunters, using such opportunities to gather food as well as specimens. And the acquaintance with Boone and his fellow frontiersmen seemed to intensify his desire to explore the wilderness.

In December, 1810, Audubon readily accepted Rozier's

suggestion that they move on again, down the Ohio and up the Mississippi to Sainte Genevieve, in what is now Missouri. He left his wife and child at a friend's farm near Henderson. The partners rented a keelboat and, in addition to the usual supplies, they loaded three hundred barrels of Kentucky whiskey, a commodity calculated to bring a profit when all else failed. At the mouth of the Ohio, they were informed that stretches of the Mississippi were ice-choked, a condition to be expected at that time of year. They made camp for part of the winter, then pushed on but were delayed by ice again at the Big Bend of the Mississippi. Rozier was disgusted, Audubon delighted.

He visited Indian encampments, bartered chalk portraits of Shawnees and Osages for wildlife specimens, and roamed the woods, observing, collecting, drawing. Like the artist-naturalist William Bartram and the artist-ethnographer George Catlin, Audubon considered the Indians worthy of serious study. In his journals and in the *Ornithological Biography* he reported what he had learned of their manner of living and their customs.

By the time he and Rozier reached Sainte Genevieve, in early spring, their relationship was crumbling beneath the weight of their antithetic personalities and attitudes. They had paid for the whiskey at twenty-five cents a gallon and they soon disposed of it at eight times that price, but temporary solvency did not deter them from severing the partnership. Audubon walked back to Henderson, accompanied only by his dog and equipped only with a gun and a pack of sketching materials and scanty provisions. He spent the nights with Indians or at settlers' cabins or sometimes alone in the woods.

When he reached Henderson, he learned that his wife's brother, Thomas Bakewell, was to be financed by a group of Liverpool businessmen in establishing a commission house at New Orleans. Bakewell would be dealing in pork, lard, flour, and other commodities, and he would not object to a partnership with Audubon. But before Bakewell and Audubon could establish themselves in New Orleans, the War of 1812 ended any possibility of trading with Liverpool businessmen. The new partners then opened another store at Henderson. For a time it appeared that Audubon might devote himself to storekeeping after all, especially after the arrival of a second son, John Woodhouse Audubon, on November 30, 1812. Four weeks later, while

Audubon was exhibiting an unusual spate of commercial energy, he and Bakewell leased a tract of land on the river front and hired an engineer named David Prentice to design a steam-powered gristmill and sawmill. In 1817, Thomas W. Pears joined the partnership and the mill was erected. It was not profitable, though it was to become a landmark—"Audubon's mill"—until it burned down in 1913.

By the time of the milling venture, Audubon had made and saved over two hundred drawings of wild fauna, chiefly birds but also including a few mammals and reptiles. Many were rough chalk sketches, and they were far from the finished portraits, combining watercolors, chalk, and crayon, from which his famous plates were made. But they were the nucleus and inspiration for his later collections of masterworks, *The Birds of America* and *The Viviparous Quadrupeds of North America.* Moreover, he had already gained a minor reputation as an amateur naturalist, though he had no clear idea yet about publishing a work of natural history or earning his livelihood as a naturalist or an artist.

In the summer of 1818, he entertained a distinguished visitor, Constantine Samuel Rafinesque, a somewhat eccentric French-American naturalist born in Constantinople and by now widely traveled in America. Rafinesque had first visited the United States in 1802, visiting Bartram's garden and for several years making field trips near Philadelphia. In 1815 he had settled in America and begun teaching botany and modern languages at Transylvania University in Kentucky. He published works on banking, history, malacology, and ichthyology, as well as botany. He made a few worthwhile contributions to natural history, though one modern encyclopedia describes him, with some justice, as having written "not always with scientific accuracy." His chief eccentricity was a mania for discovering and naming new species. It was an obsession spreading swiftly among naturalists in that age of discovery and collecting, but in Rafinesque it reached an absurd extreme, and thirteen years after his visit Audubon was to write a humorous character sketch, entitled "The Eccentric Naturalist," for the *Ornithological Biography.* He called his protagonist "M. de T.," but well-informed readers recognized M. de T. as Constantine Rafinesque.

Rafinesque was lodged in a room that was occasionally visited by bats, darting through the open window and fluttering about on their nightly insect hunts. Audubon, hearing a loud noise one evening, rushed in and found that his cherished Cremona violin was being used to flail at the little flying mammals. A mere first glance at their blurred forms had convinced Rafinesque he had chanced upon a new species of bat, and he was in a frenzy to collect one. The violin suffered a battering in the process.

During this period of his life, Audubon was gaining a peculiar, unbridled energy and already beginning to exhibit the almost manic kind of ebullience that sometimes marks a genius with an *idée fixe*. Moreover, the rigors of life in a frontier town required comic relief, which sometimes took the form of exuberant pranks. One of Audubon's was to have serious consequences. Evidently a practical joke seemed to him a fitting revenge for the damage to his violin, and Herrick theorized that he may also have wanted to "vent his dislike of species-mongers." After assuring Rafinesque that he was not offended, he spent several days supplying his guest with descriptions, measurements, vernacular and scientific names, and drawings of unfamiliar fishes and mollusks. The following year, ten fictitious fishes appeared in a magazine article by Rafinesque, and in 1820 they appeared again in his little volume devoted to the Ohio River's natural history, *Ichthyologia Ohiensis,* each time with the acknowledgment that the data had been "communicated by Mr. Audubon." And in 1820 he also published an account of a new bird species, the *"Hirundo phenicephala,* scarlet-headed swallow." Field identification should have been easy from the description, except that it was another Audubon fiction: "Head scarlet, back gray, belly white, bill and feet black. A fine and rare swallow seen only once by Mr. Audubon near Henderson, Kentucky."

The prank tended somewhat to discredit both perpetrator and victim. Years afterward, when Audubon was seeking the favor of publishers and the support of the Academy of Natural Sciences, critics remarked that anyone who had foisted imaginary species on a fellow naturalist and on the public might be committing another hoax. Some of his plates illustrated birds not found in Wilson's works; perhaps a few of them were nonexistent.

In the years before and just after Rafinesque's visit, there were repeated changes of partners in Audubon's enterprises, but none succeeded in rescuing the investments. In 1819 the mill failed. By now his father and his wife's father were dead, the inheritances consumed, and Thomas Bakewell was impatient for the return of his money. In Henderson and Louisville, Audubon managed to borrow more. He then bought a steamboat and sold it at a good profit, only to find that he had accepted worthless notes in payment. With two black helpers rowing his skiff, he pursued the steamboat to New Orleans. There he lost a suit against the purchaser because the papers of sale had been improperly drawn. He returned, humiliated and defeated. Creditors seized his possessions and he was jailed as a debtor in Louisville. To gain his release he was forced to declare himself bankrupt. He had nothing left but his clothing, his gun, and his drawings, all deemed nearly worthless by the sheriff. Former friends at Henderson, both investors and others who had hoped the mill might bring new trade to the town, felt they had been betrayed by Audubon's indefatigable optimism and charm. He could find no employment, either there or in Louisville, until one day a friend paid him for a black chalk portrait. By default or necessity, Audubon the former businessman was now Audubon the professional artist, and he enjoyed an immediate if very modest success drawing portraits in chalk and crayon at Louisville and Shippingport, Kentucky. Sometimes he was able to charge as much as five dollars for a portrait.

A few friends remained, after all, and through them he soon found more remunerative employment in Cincinnati, mounting fish for Dr. Daniel Drake's recently opened museum. Drake admired his new taxidermist and paid him very generously—one hundred and twenty-five dollars a month—for the few months before expenses rose high above museum admissions. The Audubons were now settled in Cincinnati and Lucy Audubon was working as a governess for a local family while her husband resumed his drawing of portraits and opened a drawing school.

Again necessity or desperation may have influenced the direction of his efforts, as Cincinnati in 1820 held no bright prospects for him. He made a momentous decision, encouraged by Dr. Drake and Lucy Audubon, who agreed that his pictures were not only artistically superior to Wilson's but also more natural, often more accurate, and sometimes enhanced by more details of appropriate habitat. Thus, he was not merely the better artist but the better scientific explorer and reporter, and he had already portrayed some species unknown to Wilson or other naturalists.

Lucy Audubon, understandably fearful about supporting herself and her two sons, vacillated in her encouragement, but Audubon—unaware of the financial difficulties that had beset Wilson—regained his former optimism. He heard Wilson's name mentioned constantly, and once he saw a government expedition pass downriver, staffed by paid explorers and scientists. He became decisive: he would complete his collection of drawings and publish a truly comprehensive delineation of American birds. Perhaps he would succeed Wilson as the country's foremost naturalist.

Drake had been comparing Audubon's pictures with Wilson's and had correctly surmised that Wilson must have failed to find some species on his trip down the Ohio. A river expedition along the Ohio and Mississippi would therefore be an ideal way to begin. Lucy Audubon agreed to continue working as a governess to support the family, and she did so for more than seven years, first in Cincinnati and then in Louisiana.

On October 12, 1820, Audubon set off down the Ohio, accompanied by a young botanist, Joseph Mason, who was to receive art lessons in return for help in collecting specimens. On the day of departure, Audubon began one of his most detailed journals, the first one he regularly kept, and from that time forward he worked systematically toward his goal. "Without any money," he wrote, "my talents are to be my support and my enthusiasm, my guide in my difficulties, the whole of which I am ready to exert. . . ." At first, he followed the boat on foot, walking the banks to collect specimens and also to provide extra food for the crew and passengers since he could not pay the full fare. Journal entries show that his initial optimism and determination gave way temporarily to despondency when he passed Henderson and saw his old mill, when the captain of the boat joked about his poverty, and when he thought about his wife. He sat on the deck one day, gazing at a keepsake portrait he had drawn of her, and he thought he saw its expression grow sorrowful. Briefly, as some biographers have agreed, his depression may have approached insanity, but only until his mission took firm hold of his thoughts, giving his life a strong purpose. When he was not sketching birds en route down the Mississippi, he began to draw black chalk portraits of passengers and crewmen to help defray his expenses.

The immense valley and plain of the river was America's richest tract in avian numbers and variety, and at that time may have been richest, too, in other forms of wildlife. He drew and described in detail every bird he could find. Early in January, he reached New Orleans, without enough money even for a night's lodging but with his zeal again growing strong. Two weeks later he sent his wife twenty drawings, including his famous "Turkey Hen," "Great-footed Hawk," and "White-headed Eagle." On an accompanying list, he boasted of quite a few among them as "not in Wilson." Apparently working from memory, he was wrong about some; they had been in Wilson. But he was beginning to find unfamiliar species, and he was producing superior illustrations and descriptions of familiar ones. He wandered through the Louisiana bayous sketching live birds and shooting and drawing specimens. And having obtained a few drawing pupils, he was able to visit the New Orleans markets to buy or barter for dead birds kept in plumage.

His poverty might have been alleviated somewhat, had not the humiliations of poverty made him sensitive, sometimes irritable, often easily offended. During those years he supported himself as a portraitist, as a private art teacher until his irritability or arrogance led to dismissal, and even as a painter of street signs.

In June, 1821, he made a trip upriver to Shippingport. A fellow passenger, Mrs. James Pirrie, was sufficiently impressed by his work to hire him as a tutor for her daughter, and for nearly five months he and his assistant Joseph Mason lived at the Pirries' Louisiana plantation on Bayou Sara, West Feliciana Parish. In October, the two naturalists abruptly left for New Orleans, where Audubon again became an art teacher and resumed his ornithological studies with even greater ardor. He seemed to have resented tutoring as an interference with his real vocation. Finally, after some fourteen months and much pleading by letter, he persuaded his wife to join him with the two children. They arrived in December and endured a winter of privation.

In the spring, Audubon renewed his explorations, bartering for passage to Natchez with portraits of the captain and the captain's wife. Misfortunes continued as if, somehow, he attracted them. At this time a number of his sketches were stained by gunpowder, and in later years some of his plates were destroyed by water and fire. But Audubon had committed himself to perseverance. At Natchez and Washington, Mississippi, he taught French, drawing, and dancing to sustain himself. Joseph Mason was burdened by no such commitment; he was longing for the North. In July, 1822, he left for Ohio. To help him work his way home, Audubon gave him a gun, drawing paper, and chalks.

By then Lucy Audubon was employed as a governess in New Orleans. That fall she found a similar position at Natchez and joined her husband there, and in December he was able to take lessons in oil painting—his first such lessons—from an itinerant portraitist named John Stein. Undoubtedly the experience with oils improved his brushwork, but years afterward he confessed that he had never mastered the medium and would always produce most of his work—all his best work—with chalk, crayon, and watercolors.

The year 1823 began propitiously. Lucy Audubon was engaged by Mrs. Robert Percy, a neighbor of Mrs. Pirrie, to tutor her children and open a private school on her plantation, Beech Woods. She remained there for five years. Her younger son, John Woodhouse Audubon, went with her. Victor remained with his father at Natchez. In the spring Audubon left with his son and John Stein on a painting tour of the South, but lack of success terminated the project at New Orleans, and the Audubons, father and son, returned to Lucy Audubon at Beech Woods. There Audubon spent much of the summer, instructing his wife's pupils in music and dancing. And there was time enough to continue painting. During the brief period in and around West Feliciana Parish he painted eighty-two of his *Birds of America*. Among them were new discoveries such as the rough-winged swallow (*Stelgidopteryx ruficollis*), the Bewick's wren (*Thryomanes bewickii*), and the king rail (*Rallus elegans*).

In addition to these and other previously undescribed species, he painted some of his most famous portraits, including his ivory-billed woodpeckers (introduced to science by Mark Catesby); his mockingbirds (also introduced by Catesby) defending a nest from a rattlesnake amid a softly counterpointing spray of yellow jessamine vines and blossoms; and his Baltimore orioles—a female perched on the hanging basketwork of her nest and attended by two flamboyant males in the blooming foliage of a tulip tree.

The productive and idyllic period ended when Mrs. Percy had

the innocent audacity to ask that he brighten the cheeks in his portraits of her children. Audubon's sensitivity about criticism of his work often seemed arrogant though it was pathetically defensive; in this instance, he replied that he had painted sallow-cheeked children because the Percy children had sallow cheeks. Thereupon he left Beech Woods without even bidding his wife good-bye. Taking his son Victor, he returned to Natchez, but there both he and the boy contracted yellow fever. Lucy Audubon rushed to Natchez, nursed them until they could be moved, and then—with the approval of the forgiving Mrs. Percy—brought them back to Beech Woods to recuperate.

Audubon was impatient to leave again, this time because he believed his work was far enough advanced for him to seek publication. In September, 1823, he sent a package of drawings ahead to Philadelphia and then went to New Orleans to seek letters of reference from influential residents. In October, he went north, heading first for Shippingport and again taking Victor with him. He wanted the boy to experience one of his journeys; moreover, since he realized that publication might be a slow process and there was still cause for concern about supporting the family, he hoped to find at least a temporary home and employment for his fourteen-year-old son. They made considerable portions of the journey on foot, and Audubon noted proudly that Victor, though weakened by his recent illness, seemed to gather strength on the long hikes over rough backwoods trails, easily outdistancing a couple of adult companions gathered en route. At Shippingport, Victor became a clerk for an uncle, Nicholas Berthoud. Audubon stayed with him that winter, saving what money he could from the painting of portraits, street signs, and panels on river boats.

He made his way to Philadelphia in the spring of 1824, seeking patrons or an optimistic publisher. He found neither. He was advised to take his drawings to Europe, where he might find an engraver who could do superior work cheaply—a suggestion he remembered and eventually followed. While in Philadelphia he was befriended by the painter Thomas Sully, who gave him free instruction in oils; by the ornithologist Charles Lucien Bonaparte, who was probably known to most of the public only as the French emperor's nephew but whose work on the last, posthumously published volume of Wilson's *Ornithology,* as well as his own ornithological writings, contributed significantly to nine-teenth-century wildlife studies; and by an amateur naturalist named Edward Harris, who was to help finance a later western expedition on which he accompanied Audubon.

The Philadelphia trip was not, therefore, altogether futile. It seemed, in fact, auspicious when Audubon was invited to display his pictures before the Academy of Natural Sciences. The result was another calamity. No minutes of the meeting exist but the scene can be reconstructed from subsequent events and from later comments by Audubon and his adversaries. There, in the midst of the late Alexander Wilson's close friends and admirers, Audubon became so eager to extol his work that he did so at the expense of Wilson's. George Ord himself was present to admin-ister a tongue-lashing and Audubon replied in kind. The ex-change initiated one of the vitriolic feuds of nineteenth-century academia. When Audubon lost his temper, he also lost any im-mediate chance of publication, which probably was fortunate because neither his illustrations nor his written accounts of many species were really ready for publication in 1824.

At the beginning of August, he went to New York City, with letters of reference to Gilbert Stuart, Washington Allston, and Samuel Mitchill (the last of whom had already helped him almost two decades earlier). He was welcomed and made a member of the Lyceum of Natural History. Among prospective publishers, however, his Philadelphia reputation had preceded him. Even if he had not damaged his standing, they would have been reluc-tant to undertake the costly engraving and hand-coloring of prints and they had no reason to believe that a new book of orni-thology, however grand it might be in conception and execution, could compete with the sale of Wilson's eight volumes and the ninth that would be completed by Ord and Bonaparte.

Disgruntled and needing a change of scene, Audubon left in September on a journey that seems to have been more a pleasure trip than an exploration or a search for financial support. Tramping and taking deck passage on boats—for which he paid with the customary chalk and crayon portraits—he went to Al-bany, Rochester, Buffalo, Niagara Falls, and then southwest to Meadville and Pittsburgh. On this trip and especially while gaz-ing at Niagara Falls, apparently he composed himself, noting af-terward that he resolved there to take a more professional approach to his goal. In the fall he made a tour of exploration for birds along the shores of Lakes Ontario and Champlain, returned to Pittsburgh, and then traveled down the Ohio by skiff. In Cincinnati he was stranded, penniless, but in his usual way he managed to accumulate a few dollars and go on, first to Shippingport and then to the plantation at West Feliciana Parish.

After an absence of a year, he had returned in tatters, but he no longer felt the sense of defeat that had overcome him during the Henderson debacle or on his first birding trip down the Ohio. On the contrary, his missionary zeal was now so strong that he was prepared to forsake field studies and painting while somehow acquiring funds that would take him to Europe. There, he was now certain, he would find patrons and a publisher for his American paean to nature. Probably using his wife's money and certainly with her encouragement, he attired himself respectably, and at plantations in Louisiana and Mississippi he asked and received high fees as a dancing master, fencing instructor, and violin teacher. In the spring of 1826, with his own savings and his wife's, he took passage aboard a cotton schooner from New Orleans to Liverpool.

He arrived on July 21, began making inquiries and showing his pictures, and less than a week later was invited to exhibit his work at the Royal Institution of Edinburgh in the fall. Immediately he was proclaimed an "American genius." Soon he exhibited at Manchester; and although his success there was not as great as at Edinburgh, encouragement was sufficient for him to lay definite plans for the publication of what he now decided to call *The Birds of America*.

Through a printer and amateur naturalist named Patrick Neill, he met an engraver, William Home Lizars, who agreed to begin producing plates in Edinburgh while Audubon sought subscribers. The quest for financial aid had by now taught Audubon the chief technique of salesmanship—that is to say, showmanship. Wearing his hair in long curls and dressing in western American style, he regaled potential subscribers and fellow naturalists with stories of his frontier adventures, referring to himself as "an American woodsman" and building an image in the minds of listeners (and perhaps his own) of a new Daniel Boone. When necessary, he could also assume the manners of a French gentleman. He had regained the charm of his ebullient youth, and whether it was genuine or a stratagem, it succeeded.

Because money on which to live remained a problem, he continued to paint intensely not only for publication but for private sale, in the next few years producing from seven to ten copies of a number of favorite subjects—some that he could produce with facile speed, some that were particularly dramatic, such as his "Entrapped Otter." In view of his attention to mammals, it is possible that he was already planning, at least in a vague, hopeful way, for the production of his work on quadrupeds.

As to *The Birds of America*, the plan was to publish the work in parts of five plates each, engraved on copper in life size and hand-colored faithfully from his originals, at five guineas per part, and there were to be eighty parts completed in fourteen years. Eventually, there were eighty-seven parts, four hundred and thirty-five plates, over a thousand individual birds as well as thousands of background trees, shrubs, flowers, insects, and other animals. The cost for the entire set was one hundred and seventy-four pounds in England, and import duties raised the American price to a thousand dollars.

Everything about the undertaking was enormous: the preparation, the labor, the cost, and the size of the bound volumes. The first edition has always been popularly known as the "elephant folio" or "double elephant folio." The British term "elephant folio" has been used long and loosely, to designate either a book of the very largest size or a large size of drawing paper, usually twenty-three by twenty-eight inches. The sheets in this instance were even larger—twenty-six and a half by thirty-nine and a half inches—for Audubon had drawn most of the birds in life size and he wanted the portraits to be printed accordingly, in order to convey a uniquely accurate image of each species. Art critics have occasionally denigrated some of the pictures as being awkwardly posed, contrived, distorted, or clumsily stylized. Many are subtly stylized, to be sure, and a few may be awkward though Audubon is generally conceded to have been an artist of power and skill. He must have had difficulty fitting certain of his larger subjects into the chosen dimensions of the page, but he did so with considerable ingenuity. The poses of his great blue heron, his pair of Canada geese, his whooping crane, and several others are rather singular but certainly not unnatural to the species.

In accuracy and numbers, as well as size, the delineations were unique. Witmer Stone, writing for *The Auk* in 1906, compiled "A Bibliography and Nomenclator of the Ornithological Works of

John James Audubon," which, he explained, was a needed compilation in view of Audubon's "historic interest" and "preëminence in American ornithological literature. On the 435 plates of the original edition," Stone found, "there are represented 489 supposed distinct species of birds," and added in a footnote that "the name of the Golden-eyed Duck appears differently on the two plates where it is figured, but it was not [erroneously] intended to recognize two species." Audubon subsequently published his text, *Ornithological Biography*, an index which he called a *Synopsis*, and a smaller edition of the plates and text, adding new species as he progressed. The total was five hundred and eight birds thought to be distinct species—about twice the number Wilson had found.

"Of these," Stone explained, "474 are recognized to-day in the A. O. U. [American Ornithological Union] Check-list, 17 have proved to be identical with others, 10 are extralimital, 2 are hybrids, and 5 have never been found since." Audubon himself, striving for accuracy by conceding possible errors and trying to avoid the "species-mongering" of a Rafinesque, withdrew several birds from his final version, but two of those were subsequently validated as distinct species, after all, making a total of five hundred and ten properly identified and described. Of those, Stone added, "Audubon was personally acquainted with 385, while 74 were sent him by John K. Townsend from the Pacific coast and 51 he obtained from museums and other sources." The achievement was truly monumental.

In November, 1826, Lizars began engraving plates from the paintings then on hand, and by the end of the month was able to show Audubon the first proof, that of the "Turkey Cock." By March, 1827, the first two parts—ten plates—were ready. Audubon exhibited them at the Royal Institute of Edinburgh and in London before the Linnaean Society and before the Royal Society (which afterward elected him to membership). He now issued a prospectus and went from city to city selling subscriptions. He could not carry his wares to prospective buyers in the manner of Wilson because his portfolio of drawings and plates was huge and weighed about a hundred pounds. Therefore he engaged rooms in each city and issued invitations to viewings. Among the early subscribers were a number of celebrated personages, including the profligate, unpopular, yet perversely glamorous

King of England himself, George IV. Such famous men helped to set a small fashion, and at first sales mounted encouragingly. For that matter, during the next decade or so Audubon (and agents in Europe and America) found a thousand subscribers. However, many subscribers dropped from the list after paying for a few parts, as there were long waits before some of the parts were issued, and at two guineas per set of five plates the purchase was an expensive luxury. In addition to the subscribers who withdrew, there were others who failed to pay promptly. Audubon's publishing difficulties soon resembled Wilson's.

For a time, he supervised the engraving and coloring of plates, but had to abandon the practice in order to devote all of his time to seeking orders and earning an income by painting. By the time ten plates had been completed, he was growing more and more demanding, more and more impatient with the engraver Lizars, who informed him at that point that his colorists had gone on strike. Audubon then asked a London publisher, Robert Havell, Jr., to produce the third part. Havell underbid Lizars for the work of engraving and coloring, and he offered to extend generous credit. For the next eleven years, until *The Birds of America* was complete, he remained Audubon's publisher.

In the fall of 1828, having solved the immediate problems of production, Audubon spent eight weeks in Paris. He was accompanied by a new friend, William Swainson, an English naturalist and writer who had written a glowing review of his work in *Loudon's Magazine of Natural History.* Together they called on Georges Cuvier, who examined the paintings and reported to the Paris Academy of Sciences that they were "the most magnificent monument yet erected to ornithology." Baron Cuvier himself subscribed, of course. The Parisian sojourn garnered only a dozen other subscribers, but among them were King Charles X and the Duke of Orléans.

The following year Audubon returned to America. He spent much of the summer drawing birds at Great Egg Harbor on the New Jersey coast, where Wilson had done so much work in his last years, and in Pennsylvania at the forest cabin of a lumberman named Jedediah Irish. In the fall, he traveled down the Ohio to Louisville, where he was reunited with his two sons, and then on to Louisiana to join his wife, whom he had not seen for nearly three years. Lucy Audubon had been reluctant to leave her employment and come to England but when she saw how changed her husband was, how businesslike and practical, she agreed to return with him. They journeyed to Louisville, Cincinnati, Baltimore, and Washington—where the recently indigent artist was received by President Andrew Jackson—and then sailed for England, reaching Liverpool in the spring.

For some time, Audubon had been pondering the problem of writing a text to accompany his plates. He had intended to do so from the first, but realized that he needed the help of a more scholarly naturalist. Now he invited Swainson to collaborate, but Swainson had been stung by a disregard of his attempts to correct the ornithological nomenclature (a subject in which he fancied himself an expert) in the legends beneath the engravings. He would consider collaborating, but insisted that his well-established reputation entitled him to the publication of his name as coauthor, on an equal basis with Audubon. Audubon refused. Swainson, knowing Audubon's ferocious competitiveness with the scientific legacy of Wilson, replied caustically that he was glad his terms had not been met as he had decided to accept a better offer from Sir William Jardine to help prepare a new edition of Wilson's *Ornithology*.

Fortunately, Audubon moved from London back to Edinburgh at this time, and there he met William MacGillivray, an assistant professor of natural history at that city's famous university. MacGillivray was an extremely capable naturalist. He was about to be appointed curator of the museum of the Royal College of Surgeons, and a decade later, shortly after completion of the Audubon text, he was to become professor of natural history and botany at Marishal College in Aberdeen. By then he would be writing another valuable work of ornithology, *A History of British Birds*. But in 1830 he was young and unacclaimed. He was glad of the chance to collaborate in the writing of Audubon's text, to be called the *Ornithological Biography,* even if he was not to receive equal credit as coauthor.

MacGillivray accomplished for the *Ornithological Biography* what the Reverend John Bachman was later to do for *The Quadrupeds*. Both men exerted a strong steadying influence on the mercurial Audubon, and both were magnificent scientific collaborators. In a critical evaluation of the *Biography,* Elliott Coues perceptively concluded that Audubon's genius was vivid and ardent . . . but there was a strong and patient worker by his side,—William Macgillivray, the countryman of Wilson, destined to lend the sturdy Scotch fibre to an Audubonian epoch. The brilliant French-American naturalist was little of a "scientist". . . . The magical beauties of form and color and movement were all his . . . but Macgillivray's are the bone and sinew, the hidden anatomical parts beneath the lovely face, the nomenclature, the classification,—in a word, the technicalities of the science. . . . The anatomical structure of American birds was first disclosed in any systematic manner, and to any considerable extent, by him.

The text required five thick volumes, the first of which appeared in 1831, the last in 1839, shortly after the last plates were issued. The five volumes were published in Edinburgh, then partly reissued in Philadelphia and Boston. The first, dealing with the birds shown in the first hundred plates, was being printed in March, 1831, and Audubon left for London and then Paris with his wife. Then they returned once again to America. He wanted to visit Florida in order to find still more new birds, and he was able to secure a promise of government aid in the form of transportation from Charleston southward.

In October he arrived in South Carolina with two assistants, a landscape painter named George Lehman and a taxidermist named Henry Ward. They spent their first night in Charleston at a boardinghouse, and the next morning Audubon decided he must find cheaper lodgings. It was then, quite by accident, that he met John Bachman, Doctor of Divinity and pastor of the town's Lutheran church. Audubon was walking the streets under the guidance of a clergyman when Bachman happened by on horseback and was introduced. He had been a devoted amateur naturalist since boyhood, and he insisted that Audubon and both assistants stay at his home.

Audubon planned to remain in Charleston only a short time before boarding a government schooner to continue the journey. However, government vessels were not always available on schedule, and the visit so delighted both the host and his guests that the little expedition remained in town for a month. Audubon and Bachman spent much time together, observing wildlife, collecting specimens, making and comparing notes, and discussing natural history. Though Bachman's knowledge of ornithology was dwarfed by Audubon's, he had a more scholarly grasp of mammalogy. He had not yet made any significant contributions to the study of mammals, but Audubon inspired him to channel his interest into systematic research. By mid-April, when Audubon departed on the schooner *Agnes,* a friendship had been established firmly enough to survive future financial quandaries, scholarly and editorial disagreements, frustrations, and the herculian labors of an unprecedented scientific collaboration—the work on American quadrupeds—successfully completed in an age when scientific equipment and facilities were still crude. Audubon's sons married two of Bachman's daughters, and several members of both families eventually helped in the preparation of *The Quadrupeds.*

Bachman was well equipped for the role he was to assume. He was five years younger than Audubon, a strong worker, a thorough scholar, and a methodical compiler of natural data. In the years between the meeting and the collaboration, he continued to devote most of his time to the ministry, yet he gained recognition as a reputable scientist. He corresponded with eminent naturalists, a number of whom visited him. In 1838, a congress of physicians and naturalists in Germany invited him to address them on the topic of American natural science. He went to Freiburg, the site of the congress, via Great Britain, staying in London long enough to study the famous mammalian collection at the British Museum. And during those years he remained in correspondence with Audubon, who visited him several times, though neither man foresaw their future partnership.

Audubon reached St. Augustine aboard the *Agnes* and, in April, 1832, sailed from there on the revenue cutter *Marion* to explore Florida's east coast. He reached Key West, painting and recording birds, and soon afterward traveled north through Savannah and Charleston to Philadelphia, where he rejoined his family, and next to Boston to promote his publications. In August, he embarked on an ornithological exploration of the coasts of Maine and New Brunswick, ascended the St. John River, then returned to Boston and sent his son Victor to England to take charge of the publishing operation. In Boston that winter he became ill, apparently from overwork, but he recovered quickly and in June sailed for Labrador with his son John and four other assistants aboard the *Ripley,* a schooner chartered this time at his own expense.

He was observing mammals more and more diligently (though without detriment to his birds) and years later, writing in *The Quadrupeds* about the known range of polar bears, he would report that "during our visit to Labrador in 1833, we coasted along to the north as far as the Straits of Belleisle [Belle Isle], but it being midsummer, we saw no Polar Bears, although we heard from the settlers that these animals were sometimes seen there; (on one occasion, indeed, we thought we perceived three of them on an ice-berg, but the distance was too great for us to be certain)." He was not much more successful in collecting specimens of new birds on that expedition, although he did discover and describe a species which he named the Lincoln's finch (now called the Lincoln's sparrow, *Melospica Lincolnii*) after a young companion, Thomas Lincoln of Dennisville, Maine. And he brought back twenty-three bird drawings and seventy-three bird skins, as well as collections of plants and marine mammals.

Critics have charged him with writing excessively flowery and sometimes melodramatic prose in both the *Biography* and *The Quadrupeds*. There are self-indulgent passages, but most of the writing is a fine if flowery blend of personal narrative with natural history. His account of the Labrador exploration, in Volume IV of the *Biography*, was typical:

> On the morning of the 14th of June 1833, the white sails of the Ripley were spread before a propitious breeze . . . gaily wending her way towards the shores of Labrador. We had well explored the Magdalene Islands, and were anxious to visit the Great Gannet Rock, where, according to our pilot, the birds from which it derives its name bred. For several days I had observed numerous files proceeding northward, and marked their mode of flight while thus travelling. As our bark dashed through the heaving billows, my anxiety to reach the desired spot increased. At length, about ten o'clock, we discerned at a distance a white speck, which our pilot assured us was the celebrated rock of our wishes. After a while I could distinctly see its top from the deck, and thought that it was still covered with snow several feet deep. As we approached it, I imagined that the atmosphere around was filled with flakes, but on my turning to the pilot, who smiled at my simplicity, I was assured that nothing was in sight but the Gannets and their island home. I rubbed my eyes, took up my glass, and saw that the strange dimness of the air before us was caused by the innumerable birds, whose white bodies and black-tipped pinions produced

a blended tint of light-grey. When we had advanced within half a mile, this magnificent veil of floating Gannets was easily seen, now shooting upwards, as if intent on reaching the sky, then descending as if to join the feathered masses below, and again diverging toward either side and sweeping over the surface of the ocean.

Audubon returned from Labrador in the fall and visited Philadelphia, where an attempt was made to jail him on charges arising from old debts. It was an unpleasant echo of his Henderson years, but old grievances could no longer disrupt his work. With his wife and his son John, he spent that winter in Charleston, at Bachman's home, hunting, drawing, and writing, and in the spring sailed back to England with his family. By 1836, both sons were working as his assistants and they were developing into accomplished artists. Again he sailed for America, accompanied by his son John, and this time he had meetings with Washington Irving (who tried but failed to secure government patronage for him) and with the naturalists Thomas Mayo Brewer and Thomas Nuttall. After some initial difficulty, he gained access to the collection of birds brought from the West by Nuttall and John Kirk Townsend, a number of which (including new species) subsequently appeared in his plates and text. He planned an expedition to Texas, and in Washington he secured another promise of government transportation.

After wintering once more with Bachman—a visit on which he may have begun to plan *The Quadrupeds*—he traveled overland with his son and Edward Harris to New Orleans. From there, two government vessels took them to Galveston, where the now famous naturalist had a meeting with Sam Houston, president of the new republic. By June, 1837, they were back in Charleston, and John Woodhouse Audubon married Bachman's oldest daughter, Maria Rebecca. From Charleston they returned to Washington, met President Van Buren, and took passage back to England.

A year later, June 20, 1838, the last plates were issued. In bound form, the complete set filled four gigantic morocco volumes. And eleven months after that, the fifth and final volume of the *Ornithological Biography* was published, almost immediately followed by a full index of plates and text, entitled *A Synopsis of the Birds of North America*.

The family returned to America, and soon afterward Victor

Audubon wed Mary Eliza Bachman. Then arrangements were made to publish a "miniature"—octavo—edition of the plates and text. It appeared, in seven volumes, between 1840 and 1844, and was a great success. At last, Audubon was earning enough to begin paying substantial portions of the money he owed his publishers and other creditors, and to buy his wife a house of her own, something she had long wanted. He purchased about thirty acres of land overlooking the Hudson on the bluffs of upper Manhattan (at the present site of 157th Street) and built a house there. Lucy Audubon was sometimes called Minnie—a pet name, a term of endearment—by her husband and sons, and so he named the estate Minnie's Land. By the spring of 1842, the family was ensconced in the new house, as were a number of wild animals and birds in the years that followed, for Audubon liked to draw live models when possible and, despite charges to the contrary by various critics, he took great pains to observe animal behavior and to dissect fresh specimens. He was already engrossed in the planning of the second major opus, *The Viviparous Quadrupeds of North America.*

Probably he had been contemplating the work seriously since 1837. In 1839, with *The Birds of America* and *Ornithological Biography* just published, he had at last begun to live comfortably but still with apprehension about future funds to provide for his family. The problem might be solved by publication of another book and, characteristically, he was seeking new outlets for his restless energy even though the exertions of his most recent exploratory journeys had produced an alarming fatigue. (Of the Labrador expedition he had reported: "At times I felt as if my physical powers would abandon me . . . [and] my fingers were almost useless through actual fatigue at drawing. . . . As dark forced me to lay aside my brushes, I immediately went to rest as if I had walked sixty-five miles that day, as I have done *a few times* in my stronger days.")

In 1839, with the memory of exhaustion already dimming, he impulsively issued a prospectus for *The Viviparous Quadrupeds.* He had approached no publisher about it, nor had he prepared more than a few drawings and scanty notes, but he evidently assumed that, if necessary, he could do all the writing, reading of reference sources, collecting, identifying, and painting with little help from collaborators. John Bachman's reaction was instantaneous. "Are you not too fast in issuing your prospectus?" he asked in a letter to Audubon, and then cited reasons for his cautionary tone. "The animals have never been carefully described, and you will find difficulties at every step. Books cannot aid you much. Long journeys will have to be undertaken. . . . The Western Deer are no joke [to classify], and the ever varying Squirrels seem sent by Satan himself, to puzzle the Naturalists."

His wish was not to dissuade the great ornithologist from a Promethean endeavor in mammalogy, but to help him. The possibility of being allowed to participate made him bold enough to add: "I think that I have studied the subject more than you have. . . . Say in what manner I can assist you."

Audubon might have resented the implications, had they come from any other source, but his reply was to invite Bachman to assume equal status in the project. In January, 1840, Bachman accepted the invitation, thereby initiating one of the most important collaborations in the history of American field studies. The remarkable success of Bachman's contribution to the task can be seen in the data for every species in *The Quadrupeds*. There were, for example, those members of the Order *Rodentia,* the Family *Sciuridae,* "sent by Satan himself." The clergyman wrestled with Satan's emissaries and vanquished them, ultimately recognizing and including two dozen varieties of tree squirrels. That he and Audubon mistook several color phases and subspecies for separate species does not diminish the achievement when viewed in the context of classification in the mid-nineteenth century. The compilation of American mammals was an unprecedented advance.

Somewhat to Bachman's distress, they agreed that the task might never be concluded if they did not set practical limits to its scope by excluding winged mammals—the bats—as well as marine mammals not equipped with four terrestrially functional legs. Thus the sea otter was included, despite its webbed and somewhat flipperlike hind feet, but there would be no whales, manatees, walruses, seals, porpoises, and the like. The work would deal with America's terrestrial quadrupeds. On that basis, Bachman predicted there would be no more than a hundred or so species to illustrate and describe. He later doubled the estimate. The mammalogist Victor H. Cahalane has remarked that "even the realistic and hardheaded Bachman did not fully realize

*Loggerhead turtle, painted by John White on the
Carolina coast late in the 16th century.*

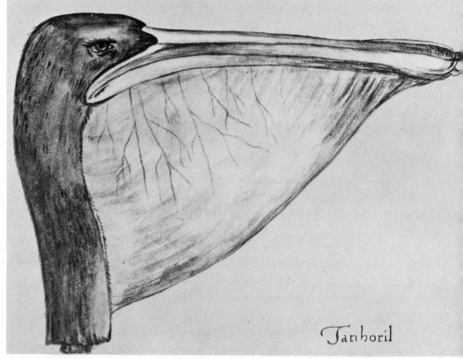

Alcatralsa . This fowle is of the greatnes of a Swanne . and of the same forme sauing the heade wᶜʰ is in length 16 ynches

Tanboril

John White's watercolor study of a pelican's head, a bird described by the painter-naturalist as "being of the greatness of a Swanne and of the same forme saving the heade."

FACING PAGE: *One of John Lawson's depicti* *of Carolina fauna, drawn between 1701 a* *1708. Some were drawn from specimens or p* *sonal observation; others (such as the fox-fa* *raccoon,* BOTTOM RIGHT, *using its tail to ca* *a crab) were based on sometimes fanciful* *counts by coloni.*

Mark Catesby's famous "Largest White Bill'd Woodpecker"—an ivory-billed woodpecker on a willow oak.

Plate 66 from Catesby's Natural History—*a catbird about to snatch an insect (probably meant to be a mayfly). Catesby was among the first naturalists to emphasize interactions of wildlife.*

William Bartram's portrayal of a Franklinia—discovered and saved from extinction by John and William Bartram, and named for their friend, Benjamin Franklin.

RIGHT: *Venus's flytrap (lower left) pictured by Bartram in a characteristically surrealistic mélange of Carolinian flora and fauna.*

BELOW: *Bartramian potpourri of "natural productions" discovered in America—disdainful of scale, incorrect in its association of elements from separate ecosystems, but adorable in its attention to small creatures such as reptiles, amphibians, and insects.*

Alexander Wilson's Mississippi kite. Audubon
was accused of plagiarizing this delineation.

Wilson's ivory-billed woodpecker, pictured with other woodpeckers. He portrayed them together to show comparative sizes of species.

(Courtesy of the New-York Historical Society, New York City)

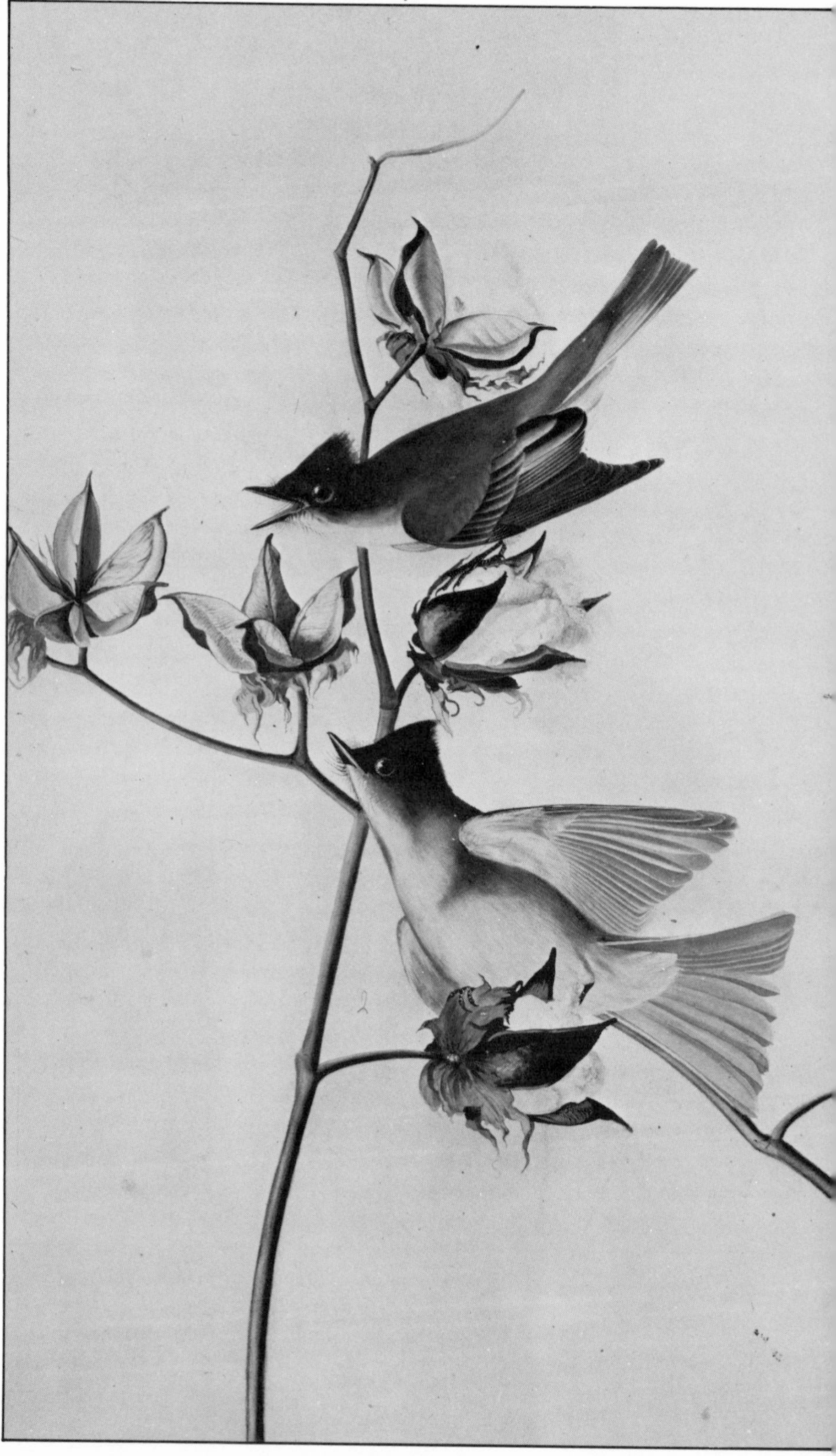

*One of Audubon's studies of the Mississippi kite,
showing the bird with its insect prey.*

ACING PAGE: *Plate 120 from John James Au-
ubon's* Birds of America—*eastern phoebes,
nown to Audubon as pewee flycatchers. This
as the species he used when he devised
merica's (and possibly the world's) first success-
ul bird-banding experiment.*

Audubon's mockingbirds, defending their nest from a rattlesnake. Critics declared the scene to be nonexistent in nature, but later biologists vindicated Audubon.

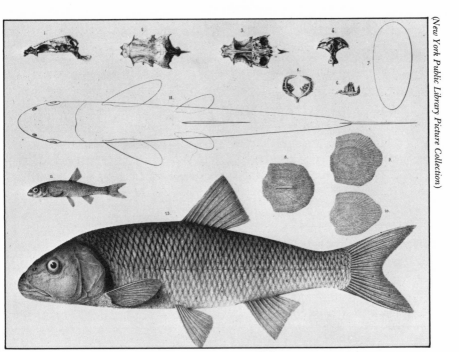

One of Auguste Sonrel's outstanding ichthyological illustrations for Six Species of North American Fresh-Water Fishes, *written by the naturalist David Starr Jordan under the joint direction of Louis Agassiz and Spencer F. Baird for the Smithsonian Institution.*

Island of St. Ignace, drawn by G. Elliot Cabot and lithographed by Auguste Sonrel for Louis Agassiz's account of Lake Superior's natural history.

(Author's collection)

ABOVE: *"The start from Green River Station"—an illustration from John Wesley Powell's Smithsonian report on the exploration of the Grand Canyon.*

RIGHT: *One of the Indians encountered on Powell's first Grand Canyon expedition and described in Powell's Smithsonian report.*

John Wesley Powell, conversing with a Paiute
Indian in southern Utah in 1873.

John Burroughs in typical pose on the porch of his rustic retreat. He disliked subjecting himself to publicity, but endured being adulated as a guru—the "Sage of Slabsides"—in order to propagandize the study and appreciation of nature.

the magnitude of the task on which they entered with such high hopes." Eventually Bachman described more than two hundred mammals, of which a hundred and forty-seven species plus eight regional "varieties" were depicted on a hundred and fifty plates.

It was still a pioneering age of natural history, a time when investigators, somewhat dazzled by their own continuing discoveries and influenced by the recognition accorded men like Rafinesque, tended to divide species into more species on the basis of sometimes insignificant physical differences. In more recent years, as taxonomy has built on itself and become more sophisticated, the trend has been to group minor variations of form as single species. The distinctions made by Bachman and Audubon among the tree squirrels and all the other groups have dwindled far below two hundred by modern reckoning, but they do represent one hundred and eighteen valid species. Their compilation of America's mammals was much more comprehensive and detailed than anything published before or for many years afterward.

Though Bachman's fame, like MacGillivray's, has been eclipsed by that of Audubon, his role was equally great. He determined the validity of the species that were collected, reported by correspondents, or found in previous writings. He compiled a synonymy of species names. He calculated their geographic distributions by collating the information in all available publications and documents, reports from correspondents, and his own observations as well as those of Audubon and many associates who became involved in the work. He wrote the basic scientific descriptions, including his own observations of behavior, habits, and habitat of animals with which he was familiar. He revised and edited comparable accounts, together with field observations and other information, provided by John James Audubon, John Woodhouse Audubon, and a number of other informants who volunteered or were asked for field observations and anatomical descriptions. And he combined all of this material into the final text.

He did all this without asking for personal remuneration; he was working for his own satisfaction, for a measure of recognition, for the enhancement of scientific knowledge, and in the well-founded hope that the endeavor would in future years help to provide for his daughters' families. In large measure for the sake of *The Quadrupeds* he declined the presidency of South Carolina College. During the dozen years consumed by research, correspondence, writing, and editing, he endured such personal calamities as the deaths of his wife and three of his eight children, including the daughters who had married John and Victor Audubon. And he continued to work when stricken by a number of ailments and an impairment of vision.

Mention has been made of the crudity of scientific tools and techniques—among other formidable obstacles. This crudity is poignantly evident in some of Audubon's early correspondence with distant informants and suppliers. Regarding the preservation of varying hares for shipment, he instructed Increase Smith, of Hingham, Massachusetts, that "the animals ought to be put in a Keg of Common Yankee Rum, and as soon as possible after death, cutting a slit in the abdomen of not exceeding *Two Inches* in length, and pouring Rum in the aperture until well filled." A man of Audubon's élan could not be deterred by the perishability of specimens or by such other obstacles as the obvious need for a far-western expedition that was as yet unfunded and might be terminated disastrously by storm, cold, hunger, thirst, flood, or Indian attack.

Fortunately, his many informants included some men of great ability in the natural sciences. In June of 1840, he began a correspondence with an adolescent admirer, a seventeen-year-old amateur naturalist named Spencer Fullerton Baird, who was observing birds and other wildlife in the vicinity of his Carlisle, Pennsylvania, home. Two years later, the brothers Spencer and William Baird were to discover two new species of flycatcher, and the following year would publish a list of bird species in their region. (Significantly, the last bird listed in Audubon's finally revised edition of the *Biography* was named *Emberiza bairdii*, Baird's bunting—now called *Ammodramus bairdii*, Baird's sparrow.) In 1841, Audubon wrote to young Spencer F. Baird—the future secretary of the Smithsonian Institution—about the scheme of *The Quadrupeds*, and in the ensuing years Baird not only supplied him with many specimens but also searched the literature for allusions to possible new species.

There were others, such as Audubon's ornithological colleague in Massachusetts, Thomas M. Brewer, and the English-American botanist Thomas Nuttall. John K. Townsend, who had been instrumental in adding new species to *The Birds of America,* lent the collaborators his excellent field notes and specimens, which included hitherto undescribed mammals from the Rockies and the Pacific Northwest. (The scientific designation of the whitetailed jackrabbit, *Lepus townsendii,* among others, honors Townsend, just as the classifications of several animals, such as the brush rabbit, *Sylvilagus bachmani,* honor Bachman. In the vernacular, too, the whitetailed jackrabbit was formerly known as Townsend's hare, and the brush rabbit—though it is a subspecies of cottontail and not a hare—was called Bachman's hare. Ironically, one of the animals named for Audubon is another subspecies called *S. auduboni,* Audubon's cottontail, which was not included in *The Quadrupeds.*)

There were still other associates who made essential contributions. Sir George Simpson, governor of the Hudson's Bay Company, supplied skins of arctic furbearers, and Audubon's old friend Edward Harris—in addition to supplying specimens, observations, and funds—arbitrated occasional disputes between Bachman and Audubon.

Bachman's sister-in-law, Maria Martin, was a skilled artist who worked closely with him. When Bachman required pictures of insects, plants, and mammals about which he was writing, she made fine drawings. She also worked as editorial assistant and copyist. Bachman's labor would have been far more difficult had it not been for his close relationship with Maria Martin. He was widowed in 1846, and two years later he married her.

Among all of these colleagues, the most important may have been Audubon's younger son. John Woodhouse Audubon had not assumed as large a role as his brother Victor in helping to supervise publication of the ornithological plates, but he had worked as a portraitist in England, Scotland, and America. He joined the new enterprise immediately as assistant artist, general aid, and secretary. Though he lacked John James Audubon's gifts as a naturalist, he also worked hard in the field, particularly in the winter of 1845–1846, when it became clear that his father could no longer endure the rigors of wilderness journeys and a proxy was therefore needed for an expedition into Texas to observe and collect animals. Though the trip was only moderately productive, he was able to contribute descriptions and paintings of such little-known animals as the kangaroo rat and the ocelot.

His painting of an ocelot foraging at the edge of a stream—crouched on an overhanging log and gazing down at a catfish—is one of the finest in *The Quadrupeds*. Following that expedition, he solved the problem of picturing a number of arctic and subarctic animals of which the collaborators could not obtain acceptable specimens. He did so by spending almost a year in England, painting northern Canadian species and other mammals in the collection of the British Museum.

He was accustomed to working in oils, but instead he emulated his father's methods and style in order to maintain uniformity in the folio, and he was so successful that many of the quadruped paintings have never been attributed with certainty to father or son. The artists' names beneath the plates are of little help. There is a plate depicting two "species" (actually subspecies) of lemmings. One of them, according to a passage of text by Bachman, was painted by John Woodhouse Audubon in London from a skin obtained on a tributary of the Peace River. However, the legend beneath the plate names John James Audubon as the artist.

Some of the other plates bear the father's name in *The Viviparous Quadrupeds of North America*—that is, the first edition, also known as the imperial folio—but are assigned to the son in an octavo edition: three smaller volumes, combining text and illustrations, published in 1849, 1851, and 1854, with the title appropriately condensed to *The Quadrupeds of North America*. This later edition credits John Woodhouse Audubon with seventy-two of the paintings, not including pictures on which both artists worked, and he probably contributed a few more. Critics have pointed out that his mastery of composition and the dynamism of animal movements never equaled his father's, yet some of the composition—chiefly background—was executed by other hands, and no one has been able to prove which Audubon painted some of the finest wildlife studies.

A number of backgrounds and plants were painted by Audubon's other son, Victor, an accomplished landscape artist who performed another valuable service by supervising the lithography, printing, and coloring to ensure fidelity to the originals. (The mammal portraits were lithographed, not engraved on copper as the birds had been.) To minimize growing costs and to expedite printing, he also condensed and further edited some of the text sent to him by Bachman, and a dispute arose when

Bachman objected. Nonetheless, he continued to prepare text for the typesetters, and his changes in no way marred the scientific, literary, or artistic value of the work. Both John and Victor Audubon sacrificed careers of their own to *The Quadrupeds*, and the extreme burden of the work probably shortened their lives. Victor Audubon died at fifty-one in 1860; his brother John died two years later at the age of forty-nine.

In 1839, at about the time Audubon had corresponded with Bachman about collaboration, he had also attempted to interest Robert Havell, publisher of *The Birds of America*. Havell had not yet been fully paid for the first publication, however, and he would not undertake another project of the kind. Audubon then discussed the scheme with J. T. Bowen, a skillful English-American lithographer in Philadelphia. By the time the Audubons took occupancy of Minnie's Land, an agreement had been reached whereby Bowen would lithograph and color the plates, while other Philadelphia publishers would set the type and do the printing.

Here, too, Bachman exerted his steadying influence. There was no question, of course, of picturing the larger mammals in anything approaching life size, but Bachman did not relish the notion of anything even as unwieldy as the elephant folio. He suggested that "the figures . . . may be given without any reference to any scale, those of a skunk full size, those above as taste or space will dictate."

With the approval of the lithographer and printers, Bachman and Audubon settled on a size of twenty-eight by twenty-two inches—the dimensions of the imperial folio—with most of the compositions horizontal but some (particularly those showing arboreal animals) appropriately vertical. The proportions easily accommodated roughly life-sized paintings of the smaller creatures: the skunks Bachman had mentioned, the hares and rabbits, the rodents and insectivores, the foxes, weasels, and so on. These were labeled "Natural Size," and the legends beneath pictures of larger animals supplied a key to their sizes. The bobcat was labeled "3/4 Natural Size," the collared peccary "4/7 Natural Size." Unfortunately, the printers omitted these notations in some instances, and there were also a few astonishing misprints. One of the two bison plates bore the roughly accurate scale of "1/7 Natural Size." The other bore a startling proclamation that it was "Natural Size." Fortunately, the text stated correctly that a large bull bison generally weighs almost a ton.

The plan was to issue the text in separate volumes, as had been done with Audubon's previous work, and to issue the portraits in thirty parts of five plates each, ultimately forming two volumes in the imperial folio at a total price of $300.

To attract subscribers, a few of the plates were rushed from the presses as early as 1842, but only about half were finished four years later, when Audubon's powers had begun to fail and his son John assumed responsibility for the remainder of the paintings. In the first year of preparation, working feverishly, Audubon had completed three dozen paintings as well as some descriptive writing, and he hoped to complete the pictures in 1842. He and Bachman originally thought that the necessary field studies and writing would take only an additional year, so that the text could be published in 1843. As they progressed, they began to realize the enormity of the scheduling error and of the opus itself. Audubon lived to see the last of the imperial folio plates, Volume III, issued in 1848, but he was to die in 1851, a year before the writing was finished, three years before the third and final volume of text came from the press.

By the time the first plates were published, in 1842, he had secured orders from a few subscribers, and he was also receiving a small income from his ornithological works, but with publication proceeding he was worried about funds and by midsummer he also felt an urgent need for western specimens and information. Having achieved fame as a naturalist, he hoped to persuade the government to support an expedition, and he went to Washington to present his case. His requests were denied, though in a manner of speaking the government's support was offered posthumously when, in 1857, Congress appropriated $16,000 for the purchase of a hundred sets each of *The Birds* and *The Quadrupeds*, for presentation "to foreign governments in return for valuable gifts made to the United States."

The trip to Washington was auspicious despite governmental rejection. At his hotel, he met a fur trader and financier, Colonel Pierre Chouteau, who became an immediate and enthusiastic patron. Chouteau would be happy to contribute specimens. Through the American Fur Company, he would also arrange a western expedition for Audubon, together with his friend Edward Harris and three modestly salaried assistants. Harris rented his farm in order to defray a fifth of the expedition's costs. On March 11, 1843, when Audubon was fifty-eight years old, the party set out for the upper Missouri and Yellowstone rivers. An American Fur Company steamboat carried them to their head-quarters, the Fort Union trading post, on the Missouri near its confluence with the Yellowstone. In that area, from June 12 to August 16, they observed and collected species ranging from prairie dogs weighing a couple of pounds to pocket gophers less than half as large and bison weighing a ton. Audubon narrowly escaped being trampled or gored; his excitement and curiosity overwhelmed his usually good judgment about approaching large, potentially dangerous animals, and a buffalo bull charged him.

On the day of his arrival, he saw his first bighorn sheep— twenty-two of them, a band of ewes, one lamb, and a few rams (young rams since, as Audubon astutely noted, mature males form bachelor flocks except at breeding time). He carefully noted their surefootedness and climbing prowess, and though he insisted that writing was tedious for him, his description of their habitat and behavior along the fringes of the Badlands was con-cise and evocative:

> In many places columns or piles of clay, or hardened earth, are to be seen, eight or ten feet above the adjacent surface, covered or coped with a slaty flat rock, thus resembling gigantic toad stools, and upon these singular places the big horns are frequently seen . . . looking like so many statues on their elevated pedestals. One cannot imagine how these animals reach these curious places, especially with their young . . . which are sometimes brought forth on these inaccessible points, beyond the reach of their great-est enemies, the wolves.

In his journal, which was to furnish new material for *The Quadrupeds,* he described landscapes and vegetation, animals, trappers, hunters, and Indians. Together with many drawings and specimens, he brought back a live badger, deer, and the diminutive buff-yellow fox of the Great Plains known as the swift fox (*Vulpes velox*). All the same, he knew when he reached home in autumn that the expedition had not been an unqualified suc-cess. He had not penetrated the Rockies, one of his goals, and he felt so old, so exhausted, that he knew he had made his last wilderness journey. Bachman had hoped for a great compendium of western information. Instead he received colorful generalities; and instead of precise scientific data, there were expendable anecdotes about some of the unfamiliar species. Audubon, in an uncharacteristically apologetic tone, wrote to Bachman that besides his many sketches he had, after all, returned with specimens which might represent some new bird species as well as a new variety of pronghorn antelope. His collaborator praised the birds but was forced to add that the pronghorn had probably been described in previous works. Bachman was correct. Audubon's contribution with regard to the pronghorn was only to prove that this unique American animal sheds the sheaths of its horns—unlike antlered species, which shed the entire structure, and unlike other horned species, which do not shed at all.

Bachman felt that Audubon had let himself be entranced by the Western game animals—the pronghorns and bison, wolves and grizzlies—at the expense of gathering precise data about the less glamorous skunks, rabbits, hares, ground squirrels, and the like. Additional specimens were requested from Fort Union, but their arrival did not redeem what Bachman considered to be the inadequacies of the written data. He went to Minnie's Land to consult with his collaborator and study some notes which Audubon had made but had not sent to him. Audubon refused to show him the notes until Bachman, employing the occasional intermediary Harris to deliver an ultimatum, threatened to withdraw from the project. The necessity of the ultimatum saddened Bachman. During his visit he had begun to understand both the paltriness of the notes and the errors that had begun to appear in manuscript pages sent by Audubon. His friend was slowly declining.

That year, fifty plates were issued—the first volume of the folio—followed in 1846 by the first volume of text. But in 1846 there was also more sorrow. Audubon's eyes began to fail, as did his faculties. It may be that he had suffered a stroke. Lucy Audubon wrote that he simply "drooped. Silent, patient sorrow filled his broken heart" now that he could paint no more. She walked him about and each night she serenaded him with a Spanish song he loved. But he had lost the power of concentration and he had lost interest in everything, even the book. He appeared to be suffering from premature senility.

In the first bleak month of 1851 he collapsed and declined rapidly. This time, without doubt, he had suffered a stroke. A few days later, on January 27, he died. He had been informed some time back that his old friend John Bachman was nearly finished, that the work would soon be completed and published. He may have understood, and perhaps the knowledge brought him some contentment.

His son had finished the paintings. John Bachman's vision, like Audubon's, had dimmed and still he remained at work. Unable to write, he dictated the last portions to Victor Audubon, and early in the spring of 1852 the last lines were put to paper. Bachman lived to be eighty-four. Before he died in 1874 he had seen the great treatise receive some of the praise it merited.

That praise has sporadically subsided and swelled. A few of the paintings were stiff and anatomically inaccurate, as some critics have said of both the birds and mammals. But they were the most copious, natural, and accurate portrayals of fauna yet published and the inspiration for later generations of nature artists and scientific illustrators. They influenced artists ranging from Ernest Thompson Seton to Louis Agassiz Fuertes to Roger Tory Peterson. And they advanced the concept of animals in a natural, ecologically sound environment rather than as stiff, isolated exhibits. Until recently, Audubon received less than full recognition for his attention not only to flora but to fauna other than his primary subjects. From 1821 to 1824 he had kept a sketchbook, filled with butterflies, moths, grasshoppers, sow bugs, snakes, wasps, lizards, caterpillars, toads, crickets, praying mantises, spiders, and dragonflies. The sketchbook survives, but was almost unknown until 1952 when Alice Ford published an excellent resurrection, *Audubon's Butterflies, Moths, and Other Studies.*

Some of the adverse artistic criticism arose from faulty reproduction. In two of the only three books of relatively recent vintage devoted to Audubon's mammals, the gray fox of his Plate 21 in *The Quadrupeds* walks in a crouch with its nose tilted skyward as if some invisible aerial phenomenon had startled it. The curious, unmotivated position appears excessively stylized, but only because a crucial detail has been lost in the printing. The same plate in the third book, benefiting from lithographic advances, reveals a subtle detail of the original plate; a small feather fluttering above the animal's head. In midstride, the fox has caught a tantalizing scent and lifted its head toward the delicate, gauzy breast feather floating above, perhaps wafted from a flushed goose or duck, perhaps from poultry at the farm in the scene's distant background. With the feather hovering above the raised snout, the picture—still unquestionably stylized—appears dramatically taut rather than unnatural, and it includes ecological implications not often found in the scientific illustrations of its time.

Another criticism (directed also at Wilson's work) concerned the haphazard arrangement of plates. The portraits were painted as opportunity (in the form of live models or mounted specimens) permitted, and the plates were then made as the pictures became available. Hence, the exigencies of nineteenth-century publishing dictated the arrangement, and in some modern reprintings the animals are presented in a toxonomic sequence that would have pleased both Audubon and Wilson.

A yet stranger criticism has been Audubon's alleged lack of charity toward rivals and his tendency to claim too much credit for discoveries. It is true that in *The Quadrupeds* he took Rafinesque to task for giving the aplodontia, or mountain beaver, then called the sewellel, a Latin designation on the basis of insufficient data. And the designation he used himself (supplied by the naturalist Sir John Richardson) has since been supplanted, as have many others proposed by Audubon and his contemporaries. But he did give due credit to Townsend, Baird, Brewer, and all the others who merited it, including his rival Wilson. "To Wilson," he wrote in his description of the Wilson's, or common, snipe, "is due the merit of having first shewn the difference between this bird and the Common Snipe of Europe; and it is honourable for the ornithologists of that region of the globe to have dedicated our species to so zealous and successful a student of nature."

Some critics have mourned Audubon's tendency to empurple the prose of his behavioral reports, while others have mourned Bachman's supposedly dull editing of Audubon's evocative accounts. Both of these contradictory charges are more faddish than well founded. Each entry of *The Quadrupeds* gives the animal's then accepted (or newly proposed) scientific name, its vernacular name, the plate number, a stipulation as to whether it is male or female, and whether adult or young. There is a key to size, followed by a brief generalized description and list of synonyms, then a detailed description covering coloration, dimensions, habits (including valuable notes on writings by previous naturalists), and geographical distribution, as well as general remarks. There is an account of muskrat habits that is poetic in its evocation of animals "disporting on a calm night in some mill-pond or deep sequestered pool, crossing and recrossing in every direction, leaving long ripples in the water behind them, whilst others stand for a few moments on little knolls or tufts of grass, or on stones or logs." But also included in the passage is data on foot structure and dentition, still used for distinguishing species, as well as precise measurements. Likewise, in the passage on the swamp rabbit there is a personal, perhaps quaint, tribute to the animal's prodigious swimming ability—as valid and biologically useful as it is vivid—and there is also information about the "visible depression in the anterior part of the frontal bone" and other differences in skull structure between this species and related forms. Such characteristics of skull structure remain in use today to distinguish related species.

In a brilliant and erudite "Historical Preface" to his *Key to North American Birds*, Elliott Coues called the period from 1800 to 1824 "The Wilsonian Epoch" and the period from 1824 to 1853 "The Audubonian Epoch." And in connection with what he called Audubon's "splendid genius . . . surmounting every difficulty and discouragement," he summarized the naturalist's contribution succinctly: "Audubon and his work were one; he lived in his work, and in his work will live forever."

Chapter 6
LOUIS AGASSIZ

Jean Louis Rodolphe Agassiz—or Louis Agassiz, as he preferred to be called—was descended from Huguenots whose family name meant "magpie" in Old French. In the nineteenth-century patois of the Swiss Canton de Vaud, the word *agassiz* probably retained its ancient connotation of one who talks a great deal, for the magpie was a vociferous bird and common in that region. Louis Agassiz was no master of ornithology; his specialties were paleontology, geology, ichthyology, and embryology. Yet the name was singularly appropriate for this Swiss-American naturalist who became one of the nineteenth century's most renowned scientific lecturers, a vociferous herald of new teaching methods as well as new theories and investigative procedures in the natural sciences.

At Harvard University he took scientific education out of the classroom into the field, established research projects and stations, and built a new kind of museum in which enormous collections were arranged to reveal the comparative zoological structure of specimens as well as their temporal and spacial distribution. His work in this connection—comparative paleontology and zoology—helped to provide a basis for modern knowledge of the structural development of life forms, despite his personal distaste for the implications of evolutionary theory. His unprecedented emphasis on advanced and original research within the auspices of academic institutions so drastically changed the character of those institutions that he has been called America's first university builder.

124

He has also, and justly, been called both progressive and reactionary in his views of natural history. As the son of a clergyman, he became an inevitable victim of the rift between theology and science. "In Europe," he remarked, "I have been accused of deriving my scientific ideas from the church. In America I have been called an infidel because I will not let my church-going friends pat me on the head."

He lived and died encased in a pious (he would have called it antimaterialistic) armor of implacable opposition to Darwin's theory of evolution and yet, in recorded conversations with students of his famous summer training school and marine biological station on Buzzards Bay, he conceded that some of his own discoveries seemed to lead toward Darwin's conclusions. Recalling his early work with fossil fishes, he declared: "At that time I was on the verge of anticipating Darwinism, but I found that the highest fishes were those that came first." As an example he cited the sharks, a very ancient group displaying larger, more complex brains and more specialized teeth and muscular systems than those of the later fishes.

How, then, could the later fishes have evolved from the earlier ones by any process of specialization through natural selection? He and many of his contemporaries failed to realize that the example and concomitant question reflected a misunderstanding of the evidence. Even today certain aspects of the mechanics of natural selection arouse debate. The process is generally thought to build changes out of random mutations among relatively small, isolated species populations in which such changes will not always be smothered by sheer numbers of the unchanged. This does not produce a unified, steadily progressing set of refinements or improvements in every aspect of a creature's structure. The pressure of natural selection operates to reproduce and perpetuate only the changes trending toward survival in a given environment. Evolutionary divergence cannot therefore be measured in terms of general "progress." It is true that sharks have developed relatively specialized brains and nervous systems, dentition, and a musculature that serves well with their cartilaginous skeletons, but sharks do represent an early, primitive group. The bony fishes that followed them are far more specialized in their adaptations to aquatic life.

Agassiz was a "special creationist" who interpreted his findings in paleontology and ontogeny as he interpreted the Old Testament, to fit either his convictions or the evidence as he saw it In 1850, nine years before the publication of Charles Darwin's great work, *On the Origin of Species by Means of Natural Selection, or the Preservation of Favoured Races in the Struggle for Life,* Agassiz felt compelled to clarify his views about human races. Some of those views conflicted with the Gospel, and in an article for the *Christian Examiner,* his heresy was almost as bold as Darwin's, for he asserted pointedly that the Bible could not be regarded as a textbook of natural history. Though pious, he was no biblical fundamentalist; had he believed that all mankind was the progeny of the Divine experiment in Eden, his unfortunate speculations regarding the creation, survival, and relative level of development of eight "species" of man would not have delighted slaveholders in the years before the Civil War.

Thus, in striving for objectivity, he came to some wrong conclusions even while preparing the way for successors to arrive at the right ones. He enlarged upon the findings of the brilliant German comparative embryologist Karl Ernst von Baer (who discovered the mammalian ovum and the embryonic notochord) demonstrating that primitive and Paleolithic life forms could be seen mirrored in the embryonic stages of "higher"—more complex—animals. But, like Baer, he was a teleologist who could not accept the metaphorically sentient if perhaps somewhat simplistic notion that ontogeny recapitulates phylogeny.

Elucidating the "Meaning of Orders" in his 1863 volume *Methods of Study in Natural History,* Agassiz dwelt on metamorphosis, a phenomenon that fascinated him. Using the butterfly to illustrate, he described "its three lives, as Caterpillar, Chrysalis, and Winged Insect," stressing that the three lives "make after all but one life," in which the earliest embryonic development resembles the adult development of a lower order such as that of the centipedes.

In a later chapter on "Embryology and Classification," he reminded readers of

> the general recognition that the caudate Batrachians, with permanent external gills, rank lower than the Salamanders, which lose their gills in the adult condition, while these again are inferior to the Frogs and Toads, in which the tail also is resorbed before the animal completes its growth . . . [and] among Fishes I have lately

discovered metamorphoses as extensive as those known to take place among Reptiles. Pisciculture being carried on upon so large a scale in some parts of Europe, it is surprising that the fact [a significant ichthyological discovery] should not have been ascertained long ago. . . . . The resemblance of an adult Skate, especially in the configuration of the face, the form of the mouth, the position of the nostrils, the arrangement of the gills, to some of the earlier conditions in the growth of the young Mammal, not excepting the human family, is equally striking.

Therefore, Agassiz explained, the astonishing discoveries in embryology revealed interrelationships among life forms, and further investigation would identify the membership of more and more life forms in their proper orders. In fact, he helped to establish embryology as a major tool of scientific classification. Yet he was equally positive that this was no evidence of evolution. Apparently he regarded it as evidence that the Creator, having completed a given experiment in producing one paleolithic order or another, incorporated features of that order in the early stages of construction of the next order. After all, he argues:

Whatever the changes may be through which an animal passes, and however different the aspect of these phases at successive periods may appear, they are always limited by the character of the type to which the animal belongs, and never pass that boundary. Thus, the Radiate begins life with characters peculiar to Radiates, and ends it without assuming any feature of a higher type. . . . The resemblance of the larvae of the Echinoderms to the Ctenophorae had not escaped my notice; but during the past year my son [Alexander Agassiz] has shown conclusively, in a series of microscopic investigations not yet published, that they are as truly related as the most circular or spheroidal of the type. . . . .

Indeed, modern Embryology leads at once to the consideration of the most occult problem, as to the origin of animals, suggested by these comparisons. What do these resemblances mean, from some of which we shrink as unnatural and even revolting? If we put a material interpretation upon them, and believe that even Man himself has been gradually developed out of a Fish, they are repugnant to our better nature. But looked at in their intellectual significance, they truly reveal the unity of the organic conception of which man himself is a part, and mark not only the incipient steps in its manifestation, but also, with equal distinctness, every phase in its gradual realization. They mean that when the first Fish was called into existence, the Vertebrate type existed as whole in the creative thought, and the first expression of it embraced potentially all the organic elements of that type, up to Man himself. . . . The philosopher's stone is no more to be found in the organic than the inorganic world; and we shall seek as vainly to transform the lower animal types into the higher ones by any of our theories, as did the alchemists of old to change the baser metals into gold.

Not for Agassiz the "transmutation," as he called evolution, of "lower" into "higher" creatures. Yet this same Agassiz was delighted, upon dissecting the gars he had caught in the Great Lakes, to discover that these Lepisosteidae represented a transitional form, a kind of missing link, between his beloved paleolithic fishes and the modern ones. If "reactionary" is taken to mean unreceptive to new ideas, the term is a gross injustice to him. He was equally delighted by what he called one of "the astounding discoveries of modern science—that of the immense periods which have passed in the gradual formation of our earth." His field studies of glaciation had been instrumental in establishing that astounding and fundamentally unbiblical discovery, which was still controversial when he died. He was similarly delighted when A. C. Jackson caught a pair of unfamiliar perch in Sausalito Bay, California, in 1852, and Agassiz was able not only to describe a new species, the black perch—which he named *Embiotoca jacksoni*—but to show that it bore living young rather than eggs. Until then, viviparous species were unknown to marine biology, and Agassiz did not mind in the slightest that some of his own discoveries, like this one, seemed to contradict some of his preconceptions about the development of species. If he vainly sought definitive answers to some of science's questions, he also sought and found new questions to be answered by his successors.

At Harvard University he established the concept of learning the natural sciences by field study and by the intense observation of specimens rather than by relying almost exclusively on texts and classroom lectures. At Harvard, too, he founded the great Museum of Comparative Zoology as well as a prototype marine research and instruction station for both undergraduate and postgraduate naturalists. Many biologists would agree that he was the greatest biologist and teacher of biology of his century. He was probably one of the century's greatest geologists as well. His field studies of glaciation, begun in his native Alps and concluded in America, explicated and proved the revolutionary theory that diverse geological features had been produced by at least one global Ice Age.

Louis Agassiz was born on May 28, 1807, at Motier-en-Vuly in French Switzerland. His father, Rodolphe Agassiz, minister of the parish, was the last of a long family line of Protestant clergymen. His mother, Rose Mayor Agassiz, was the daughter of a prominent rural physician. An intelligent woman who shared and encouraged the child's curiosity about nature, she was probably oversolicitous of his welfare and happiness, having borne four children before Louis and seen them all die in infancy.

The boy was tutored at home until he was ten years old. He was gifted with a peculiarly magnetic charm and leadership, first displayed when he involved his younger brother Auguste and his two little sisters, Cecile and Olympe, in all of his childhood interests just as he would later collect disciples and assistants like satellites around a moon. Louis and Auguste spent much of their time fishing and collecting animals and natural objects. The parsonage fountain, fashioned from an alpine boulder, became an aquarium. The house became a museum of stones and shells, the garden a menagerie of birds, mice, rabbits, snakes, and other small creatures.

At ten, Louis Agassiz happily left home for the Collège de Bienne, a preparatory school twenty miles from Motier. Four years later, with letters of recommendation from the headmaster and his teachers, he entered the Academy at Lausanne. He was poor at mathematics but displayed a startling aptitude for the natural sciences and languages. One of his teachers at Lausanne was Professor D. A. Chavannes, an entomologist who directed the canton's museum of natural history. The museum was an abode of ecstatic discoveries for the young student. He had already decided to become a naturalist, although the requisite studies would entail subterfuge because his family insisted he must become a physician in order to support himself.

Germany was succeeding England as the world capital of scientific education, and in 1824 Agassiz began two years of study at the medical school of the University of Zurich. His brother

Auguste went with him to study at the university before entering a career in commerce; they shared their rooms not only with each other but with a growing collection of birds, mammals, amphibians, reptiles, fish, shells, and rocks. Money was a constant problem. A wealthy gentleman, somewhat dazzled by Louis Agassiz's combination of scholarship, lightheartedness, and extroverted charm, offered to adopt him. The offer was graciously refused, though Agassiz was not entirely happy with his parents' plans for him and he may have been tempted by the prospect of being able to buy all the books he desired. A professor loaned him the magnificent 1815 treatise *Histoire naturelle des animaux sans vertèbres,* by the Chevalier de Lamarck (who, like the Comte de Buffon before him, was an early propagator of evolutionary theory). Agassiz persuaded his younger brother to help him make a manuscript copy of the entire two volumes. He had a prodigious memory for the texts he read, and he later commented that his inability to buy books "was, perhaps, not so great a misfortune . . . at least, it saved me from too great dependence on written authority." Lacking sufficient books, he spent all the more time dissecting animals, studying human anatomy, and examining specimens. In later years, he illustrated his lectures with actual specimens of the life forms he was describing—not pictures or written descriptions but the things themselves—and he encouraged students to study by handling and examining specimens for hours, even days, until they could perceive for themselves the unique characteristics of each life form as well as its similarities to others. Samuel Scudder, an entomologist, once wrote that the best entomological lesson he had ever received was an ichthyological session under Agassiz at Harvard. The Professor handed Scudder a fish and told him to look at it, and keep looking at it, without reference books, a magnifying glass, or any instruments whatever. "For three long days he placed that fish before my eyes," Scudder recalled, "forbidding me to look at anything else or to use any artificial aid." As a result of the simple three-day assignment—hardly a conventional teaching technique in the nineteenth century—Scudder saw and remembered more about anatomical adaptations than he had believed possible.

In 1826, after two years at Zurich, Auguste Agassiz went into business with an uncle and Louis Agassiz entered the University of Heidelberg, where he formed a close comradeship with two brilliant young botanists, Alexander Braun and Karl Schimper. One of their professors, H. G. Bronn, gave Agassiz a fossil collection which was to be used in lectures at Harvard some thirty years later. At Heidelberg he sought and received extracurricular lectures in zoology, botany, and paleontology. He expected to complete his formal studies there, but in the spring of 1827 a typhus epidemic struck the university, and Agassiz nearly died of the fever. He convalesced at Alexander Braun's home in Karlsruhe, where he was nursed by Braun's younger sister, Cecile, a talented artist. She drew the first known portrait of Agassiz, and later she was to provide some of the finest illustrations in his monumental works on fossil fishes and freshwater fishes. After regaining some of his strength he joined his family, now living at Orbe. During his brief stay at Karlsruhe he had become engaged to "Cily"—Cecile Braun—but his happiness was marred by the prospect of practicing medicine at Orbe after completing his academic training. Restless and in need of activity, he explored the region, cataloguing its plants—his first comprehensive treatise in natural history. Then he received word that Alexander Braun and Karl Schimper were transferring from Heidelberg to the larger university at Munich. Among its attractions were free lectures, cheap board and lodging, and a plentiful supply of excellent beer.

He joined them there as a medical student, and the triumvirate rented rooms from Professor Ignaz von Döllinger, a pioneer embryologist under whose guidance Agassiz studied embryology and became an adept microscopist. The rooms were transformed into a combination of museum, laboratory, lecture hall, living quarters, intellectual meeting place, and social club for young men who enjoyed fencing, swimming, climbing, arguing, singing, and beer drinking.

There at Sendlinger Thor No. 37, university professors frequently attended lectures and discussions conducted by a group of science students under the leadership of Agassiz. The group came to be known as the Little Academy. There Braun and Schimper made a valuable contribution to botanical understanding, the formulation of the principles of phyllotaxy, governing the arrangement of leaves on their stem or axis. There, too, Agassiz met a young artist named Joseph Dinkel, who for the next sixteen years would provide most of the splendid illustrations for Agassiz's works. And there another professor, C. P. J. von Martius, enabled Agassiz to produce and publish his first book.

In 1819 and 1820 Martius had toured Brazil with another naturalist, J. B. Spix, and had brought back a large collection of fishes, mostly from the Amazon River. Spix had begun work on the classification of the Brazilian species but had died in 1826. Martius now turned the specimen collection and notes over to his twenty-one-year-old student. Writing in Latin, then regarded as the universal language of science, Agassiz catalogued and described the fishes while Dinkel provided forty colored plates. English translations have been entitled *Brazilian Fishes* and *The Fishes of Brazil*; the original Latin text, published in 1829 while Agassiz was still a student at Munich, was called *Selecta genera et species Piscium, quos in itinere per Brasiliam.* Though flawed and incomplete, it was the most important account of a local fish-fauna published up to that time.

Agassiz possessed both the ego and ambition that often accompany genius, and he took clever pains to advance himself in academic circles. He dedicated his book to Georges Cuvier, the master of comparative anatomy, who was slowly untangling a jungle of arbitrary zoological classifications at the Museum of Natural History of the Jardin des Plantes in Paris. Cuvier read the book and was sufficiently impressed to write to Agassiz, stating that he intended to use some of the material in his own works. This easy success stimulated Agassiz next to write to that other towering presence among naturalists, Alexander von Humboldt, applying to accompany him on an expedition into the Ural Mountains. Humboldt rejected the offer, having already chosen his assistants, but he, too, was impressed. Both Cuvier and Humboldt were soon to advance the career of their young Swiss admirer.

While preparing the book on Brazilian fishes, Agassiz rushed with characteristic energy to earn a degree as Doctor of Philosophy—partly to assure himself of a teaching position and thus avoid becoming a physician, and partly because Martius believed the degree would add distinction to the book's title page. Both the book and the degree were a surprise to his parents, whose pride was somewhat mitigated by the conviction that only a career as a doctor would provide their son with future security. He mollified them with declarations that he had merely taken a brief detour from his medical studies. To prove it, he earned another degree within a year, this time as Doctor of Medicine, although he had no intention of practicing medicine. By now—1830—he had prepared a prospectus for another ichthyological work, *History of the Fresh-Water Fishes of Central Europe*. This had begun as a modest study of the species in the Lake of Neuchâtel, near his home, but quickly grew into a major opus which would be published in parts, from 1839 to 1842, with excellent lithographs, by his own press—a printing establishment to be founded at Neuchâtel in 1838. And while preparing the prospectus in 1830 he was also planning his epoch-making work in paleoichthyology, *Recherches sur les Poissons Fossiles*.

His family had moved to yet another parsonage, this time at Concise, on the Lake of Neuchâtel, and Agassiz settled there for a brief period, ostensibly to work as a physician though he occupied all of his time in research on living fish and their paleolithic ancestors. The enthusiastic academic reception of his first book, together with the respect accorded him by men like Döllinger, Martius, and Cuvier, had brought him a reputation as an accomplished naturalist, though he was now only twenty-three. He had access to central Europe's finest museum collections, a privilege not widely granted, but his research was languishing for lack of traveling money. He particularly yearned for Paris, where Cuvier was working with fossil fishes at the Jardin des Plantes. There now appeared on the Neuchâtel scene a *deus ex machina* in the person of Charles Louis Philippe Christinat, a pastor of the Canton de Vaud, an old friend of the family who was especially fond of Louis Agassiz. He supplied enough money for a journey to Paris, and additional funds for living expenses were provided by an uncle and by Johann Friedrich Cotta, the publisher who had produced *Selecta genera*.

Parental objections were quelled this time by references to cholera, which was raging through Europe and which could best be studied by young Dr. Agassiz under the medical savants of Paris. Taking Dinkel with him, Agassiz traveled by a circuitous route through Stuttgart (to examine fossil fishes), Karlsruhe (to see Cily and Alexander Braun), then Heidelberg and Strasbourg (to see more fossils). He learned little about cholera but amassed sufficient material concerning paleoichthyology and geology, as he said, "to join, without embarrassment at least, in conversation upon the more recent researches." The journey began in September, 1831, and December was half gone when Agassiz reached Paris.

He and Dinkel took a room at a cheap hotel near the medical school and even closer to the Jardin des Plantes. He sent word of his arrival to the Museum of Natural History, and the following day was summoned to the home of Cuvier. Jules Marcou, a later colleague and biographer of Agassiz, described the meeting as one might describe the goal of a pilgrimage: "He was absolutely astounded by the great erudition, the prodigious memory, and the extreme facility of Cuvier in passing from one arduous subject to another. . . . Agassiz had found his master, and his leader for life."

Cuvier must have been almost equally impressed by his visitor. A few days later he installed Agassiz and Dinkel in a corner of one of his laboratories, the one devoted to fishes, and there Agassiz immersed himself in the notes and specimens his master had been collecting for fifteen years. Cuvier was embarked on a difficult mission of immense value to future investigators of nature: to transform the Linnaean classification of animals from an arbitrary nomenclature of convenience (which was growing more inconvenient and bewildering with every newly discovered animal) into a system reflecting the zoological structure of species. No longer would each discovery be summarily labeled a species and crammed into the pigeonhole of a seemingly appropriate genus; accurate analysis and classification would replace confusion and provide new insights into nature. And in this undertaking he welcomed the collaboration of a man whose genius and tremendous vigor were apparent.

Agassiz had been studying the problems with regard to fossil fishes since 1829, while Cuvier had been gathering data on these and other fauna. It was Cuvier's custom to entertain colleagues at Saturday evening receptions. At one of these, in February, 1832, he presented to Agassiz a large portfolio of notes and drawings. He explained that he was delegating the work on fossil fishes to Agassiz, relinquishing to him all of his own materials and collections. With these as well as materials gathered from other museums and collections and in the field, Agassiz labored to extract the ancient life from the skeletal imprints left in the rocks. Until then, only eight generic types of fossil fishes had even been named in published treatises. Agassiz worked on his monograph for more than a decade, and the colossal *Recherches sur les Poissons Fossiles* ultimately yielded nearly a thousand varieties of fossils, rather than the previous eight, illustrated with one thousand two hundred and ninety plates. The work was published in five successive quarto volumes, from 1833 to 1844, with a folio "Atlas" of four hundred colored plates, most of them produced by Dinkel. In an article for the *Encyclopaedia Britannica,* David Starr Jordan (who studied with Agassiz at Harvard) noted that "the great importance of this foundation work rests on the impulse given to the study of extinct life itself." Though some of the groupings were necessarily tentative or crude, the monograph furnished the basis for all subsequent knowledge of the fish-fauna in primitive seas.

The work on ancient fishes also led Agassiz to collateral achievements. In 1837, he began publishing the results of investigations on fossil and living mollusks and echinoderms. Two volumes of his findings—*Description des Échinodermes fossiles de la Suisse*—appeared in 1839 and 1840, followed in 1840 to 1845 by several quartos of *Études Critiques sur les Mollusques Fossiles,* illustrated with nearly one hundred plates. By 1845 he had produced a half-dozen major monographs, including pioneer works on living freshwater fishes and on glaciation, as well as many relatively minor studies. His astounding productivity continued throughout most of his life. Marcou's bibliography, despite a few inaccuracies, furnishes an indication of this productivity; it lists four hundred and twenty-five articles and books.

Soon after beginning work with Cuvier, Agassiz called at the working room of Alexander von Humboldt in the Latin Quarter. Whereas Cuvier was known for his elegant, formal reserve, the great German naturalist and explorer was known among lesser scholars as "the terrible Humboldt"—famous for his savagely brilliant sarcasm. None of the savagery was inflicted on Agassiz, whose reputation and magnetic charm almost instantly prompted Humboldt to take him to breakfast at the Café Procop. Agassiz, whose scientific conversation normally erupted into monologues of epic length, sat silently for three hours, listening to Humboldt's account of experiences with electric fishes in Venezuela. When they parted, Humboldt's relation to Agassiz was almost that of a surrogate father.

Having won the aegis of the Barons Cuvier and Humboldt, Agassiz still faced the bleak probability that he would have to give up scientific research. He and Dinkel were living on two hundred francs a month, of which Dinkel consumed more than half. Describing his difficulties in a letter to his mother, Agassiz wrote, "I cannot even follow up my letters of introduction because I have no presentable coat." Negotiations had begun for the publication of the work on fossil fishes, but as yet the publisher had advanced no money (nor would the profits from his published works ever be sufficient to support Agassiz, whose expenditures continually exceeded his income as he purchased equipment, mounted expeditions, and hired artists, secretaries, and research assistants for each new project).

Agassiz requested no money from his mentors, but Humboldt became aware of the situation and in March, 1832, sent him a bank note for a thousand francs. Thus enabled to continue his research, Agassiz took Joseph Dinkel and Alexander Braun with him on a walking tour of the Normandy coast. It was Agassiz's first experience with living creatures of the sea and "the great phenomena presented by the ocean in its vast expanse." The journey stimulated his interest in marine biology, one of his several specialties in his later American years.

On Sunday, May 13, 1832, a few weeks after Agassiz returned, Cuvier, who had recently suffered a stroke, died of cholera—the disease Agassiz had ostensibly planned to study in Paris. The loss was shattering both emotionally and professionally. Through Cuvier's influence, Agassiz had hoped to secure a prestigious and remunerative academic position. Now Humboldt advised him to accept a professorship at the little University of Neuchâtel. Leaving much of his research material for Humboldt's use, he went home to Neuchâtel, established a museum—his first—in the Orphans' Home, and began giving his lectures in the only large available room, the chamber of the justice of the peace in the city hall.

He was determined not to stultify his university students by reading dull lectures from a book. On the first day, he launched his course in natural history by telling them about a hawk he had watched that day as it caught a mouse—how its beak and talons were adapted for catching and eating prey. It was a simple approach but a new and exciting one. Soon his classes were crowded. He had begun his secondary career as an inspired modern teacher of natural sciences.

He now had a modest but seemingly adequate salary, and through Humboldt's intervention the government paid him for the collections he had installed in the museum at the Orphans' Home. In October, 1833, he married Cecile Braun. Her brother Alexander, though he would always remain Agassiz's loyal friend, opposed the marriage. Subsequent events vindicated his judgment. Cily Braun joined Agassiz in his small, ugly, sparsely furnished lodgings. She spoke little French, and most of the people at Neuchâtel spoke only French. She was soon desperately homesick for Karlsruhe. Later, as her husband gathered assistants and became so engrossed in research that she was virtually ignored, and as financial difficulties once again mounted, she would feel herself to be surrounded by intolerable chaos. Evidently she was unhappy throughout most of her married life. The muscles of genius often seem to function best under the carapace of an egoist, and Louis Agassiz was a happy man who seldom noticed his wife's distress until she left him. Even then he did not seem to regard the separation as particularly serious, much less terminal.

The spring of 1834 was especially happy for him. The first volume of his *Poissons Fossiles* was being praised by zoologists and geologists, and the Geological Society of London awarded him the Wollaston Prize (with which went thirty guineas) and invited him to visit England. Soon, accompanied by Dinkel, he was touring the museums and private collections of England and Scotland, where the problems of traveling to and rummaging through unrelated arrays of specimens instilled in him a strong desire for a museum of comparative zoology—a desire that was to be realized at Harvard. Many collections of fossil fishes were placed at his disposal in England. He chose a multitude of specimens to be illustrated, and when he went home he left Dinkel in England to draw them. The artist remained at work there for several years. Agassiz had found a patron, the Earl of Enniskillen, to help pay Dinkel's expenses. He had also enlisted several enthusiastic scientific supporters, among them the outstanding geologist Sir Charles Lyell.

The following winter and spring were spent at Neuchâtel, working chiefly on fossil echinoderms, their classification, and their relation to the periods of formation of the strata in which they were found. Cily was pregnant, and even her self-absorbed husband was permitted to have no doubt about her unhappiness, her yearning for home. And so he left her in Karlsruhe that summer while he went back to England. He hired a second artist for a projected work on the English fossil fishes and obtained many subscriptions for it, but then, experiencing the usual financial difficulties with a prospective publisher, he decided he would establish his own printing and lithography enterprise at Neuchâtel. There, on December 1, 1835, Cily Agassiz bore her first child, a boy who was named for her brother Alexander. Two months later the English geologists added the Wollaston medal to the prize they had bestowed on Agassiz. Never before had so young a naturalist won the medal; there could be no further doubt about Agassiz's future career.

Years before, at Lausanne, he had become acquainted with a naturalist name Jean de Charpentier, who was now director of the salt works at Bex. In 1834, Charpentier had read a short paper before the Helvetic Society of Natural Sciences at Lucerne. The premise of the paper was that the boulders sprinkled over the region where Charpentier lived had been deposited there by ancient glaciers. The theory struck Agassiz and most of his colleagues as preposterous but now, in 1836, Charpentier invited Agassiz to visit him at Bex for the purpose of studying the glaciation of the Chamonix, Diablerets, and Rhône valleys. Agassiz, still scornful of the glaciation theory, accepted the invitation as an opportunity for a pleasant summer holiday with his wife and child. But after a summer of walking the valleys with his host, Agassiz embraced the new theory; in fact, he was convinced that Charpentier's hypothesis was too small in scope—that glaciers had once covered large portions of Switzerland, perhaps of Europe, perhaps of still greater portions of the world; that glaciers might even have influenced the topography and geological features of many large areas of the planet.

Agassiz summoned Karl Schimper first to Bex and then to

Neuchâtel to study the question further. He wrote about it to Humboldt, who admonished him: "No more ice, not much of echinoderms, plenty of fishes, recall of ambassadors *in partibus* [a not very oblique reference to Dinkel in England], and great severity toward the book-sellers, an infernal race, two or three of whom have been killed under me."

In July, 1837, the Helvetic Society of Natural Sciences met at Neuchâtel, expecting to hear the society's recently elected president, Louis Agassiz, discourse on fossil fishes. Instead, he delivered an address, startling in its imaginative scope and incredible premises, on an entirely new concept: the Ice Age.

Fellow naturalists were astonished to hear Agassiz, the thorough, admirably skeptical scientist, announce that a sheet of ice, perhaps miles thick, had once covered much of the earth:

> Siberian winter established itself for a time over a world previously covered with a rich vegetation and populated with a large mammalia, similar to those now inhabitating the warm regions of India and Africa. Death enveloped all nature in a shroud, and the cold [at the period of its greatest severity] gave to this mass of ice, at the maximum of tension, the greatest possible hardness.

Agassiz duly acknowledged the investigations of Charpentier, and also stated that the ideas he now promulgated were a combination of his own "and those of M. Schimper." Monsieur Schimper must have been worried at the time about the reception of those ideas, but eventually he tried to claim exclusive title to the concept of *Die Eiszeit*. The claim was so absurd that it probably accelerated Schimper's plunge into obscurity.

During this same period Agassiz also acquired another assistant who was eventually to become troublesome. He was Edouard Desor, originally enlisted as a secretary but later acknowledged as a capable scientific assistant. Unfortunately, Desor was equally competent at spending Agassiz's money and at alienating Agassiz's wife and colleagues. Yet he remained at Neuchâtel until 1846, rejoined Agassiz in America, and continued in his employ until 1848. He might have remained still longer, had he not misappropriated funds and plagiarized some of Agassiz's findings, or had not Agassiz's mother refused to send his children to him in America while Desor remained in his house. Upon being dismissed, Desor sought revenge by spreading malicious gossip about Agassiz, but managed only to ruin his own reputation. He eventually returned to Europe in disgrace.

The year of Agassiz's Revelation of the Ice Age, 1837, was also the year when his second child, Ida, was born; when his father died; when his mother began staying with him for extended visits; and when his wife began to take frequent refuge at Karlsruhe with her children. The following year Agassiz's lithography and printing plant began operation with twenty employees. He also hired several additional scientific assistants, lodging them in his home. The house was now both laboratory and dormitory, and debts mounted with the chaos. In the same year he was nominated for membership in the Royal Society of London, and attractive offers arrived from large universities, but he was held to Neuchâtel both by his publishing activities and by his new glacial studies. He led expeditions into the mountains to gather evidence, and as he published additional findings the former skeptics began to acknowledge the probable validity of his theory.

In 1840 in the Bernese Oberland, he used a monk's hut as a base camp for explorations. The hut, situated on a glacier, was slowly moving with the ice; he measured its progress until finally it disappeared beneath the lip of the glacier. Then he found a natural shelter under a great overhanging block of slate on the moraine of the lower Aar Glacier and, with a number of assistants, stored his provisions there, set up a kitchen, hung a blanket over the entrance to hold in warmth and keep out the wind, and christened his new camp the Hôtel des Neuchâtelois. Month after month, year after year, Agassiz and his assistants observed and computed the glacier's rate of movement. They also noted the changing relative positions of a series of stakes driven into the ice in a line across the glacier, and of eighteen prominent boulders that were being carried along by the glacier. Other scientists had asserted that glaciers were pushed forward by freezing water underneath—that is, by the pressure of expansion. Agassiz disproved this and showed that gravity controlled glacial movement, as it controls the flow of a river. The enormous mass of ice must be flowing like a viscid fluid, though very slowly, for the stakes at the center moved fastest and slanted forward. The base of the glacier was not being pressed forward; on the contrary, the surface moved faster, particularly at the center.

In 1840 he published his two-volume *Études sur les Glaciers*, a work whose importance vied with that of the *Poissons Fossiles*, for in it he showed that in a geologically recent period ice covered Switzerland, and he concluded astutely that "great sheets of ice, resembling those now existing in Greenland, once covered all the countries in which unstratified gravel (boulder drift) is found."

But he had not proved his case to his own satisfaction or quenched his own curiosity. In the summer of 1841—several months after the birth of his third child, Pauline—he had his assistants lower him by rope more than eighty feet down into a natural glacier well so that he could measure its depth and study the laminated structure of the ice, revealed by blue bands. Shortly afterward, he led a small party on an ascent of the Jungfrau to make further observations and measurements. And he continued to publish accounts of his glacial findings, one in 1846 and another in 1847.

By then his printing enterprise at Neuchâtel had become hopelessly insolvent. It had closed down in 1845, having produced a score of volumes that only the rich could afford to buy. Again Humboldt rescued him. The canton was under the protectorship of Prussia, and Humboldt helped to persuade the King of Prussia to grant Agassiz fifteen thousand francs for a visit to America. Leaving his son at school in Neuchâtel and sending his wife and daughters to his mother's family at Cudrefin and then back to Karlsruhe, he departed in the spring of 1846, traveling via Paris and England. His family astutely discounted his assurances that he would return. In England, he visited Charles Lyell, who arranged for him to give a series of well-paid lectures at the Lowell Institute in Boston. The crossing, begun on September 19, 1846, was long and stormy—newspapers erroneously reported that the ship was lost—but with relative imperturbability Agassiz used his time at sea to improve his English.

He arrived in October, was warmly welcomed by John Lowell, and visited New York, Princeton, and Philadelphia before beginning the series of lectures in Boston in December. Among the distinguished scholars he met in Philadelphia was Spencer F. Baird, who was to become Assistant Secretary of the Smithsonian Institution in 1850 and its secretary in 1878. They became lifelong friends, despite occasional scientific differences as well as friction regarding the disposition of various specimen collections. It was at Agassiz's urging that Baird, in the late 1850s, inaugurated a system of specimen exchanges with the great museums of Europe. A few months after their first meeting, a long, fairly voluminous correspondence began, and in the ensuing two and a half decades it resulted in valuable exchanges of information and specimens.

Though Agassiz and Baird did not collaborate in any major scientific enterprises, in 1849 the Smithsonian Institution published an illustrated description of *Six Species of North American Fresh-Water Fishes,* prepared under their joint direction, with descriptions written by David Starr Jordan and drawings by Auguste Sonrel (who had done the lithographic work at Neuchâtel and was brought to this country to continue producing illustrations for Agassiz at Cambridge).

Agassiz arrived in the United States at a time when there was both governmental and popular interest in geology because of the well-founded general assumption that the land held vast mineral deposits of tremendous value. It was also a time of intense interest in education, when the people of a young country, lacking the traditions of Europe, were striving self-consciously to overtake or assimilate the culture of the Old World. Lyell himself had lectured at the Lowell Institute, which had recently been established through a bequest of the Lowell family of Boston to present free or low-cost educational lectures. Such endeavors were very popular, for only a small minority could afford to attend the nation's colleges. Agassiz began his series of Lowell Institute lectures in December, 1846, with a discourse on "The Plan of the Creation, Especially in the Animal Kingdom." Though he received an ovation, he was distressed by his awkwardness in English. He resorted to French for some of his subsequent lectures, such as "Les glaciers et l'époque glaciaire." Attendance was high even at the lectures given in French.

After a couple of months he was joined by Count François de Pourtalès, who had been a favorite pupil at Neuchâtel and had accompanied him on alpine expeditions. Soon, using some of the dwindling grant from the King of Prussia, Agassiz sent for two more Neuchâtel associates, Edouard Desor and Charles Girard.

He was not yet certain how long he would be able to stay in America, but he planned to establish at Cambridge the same kind of laboratory he had operated in Switzerland. His financially unsupported scheme was not so impulsive as it seemed. The Harvard administration had been considering the addition of a scientific school, and early in 1847 Abbott Lawrence, a textile manufacturer, agreed to donate sufficient money for the establishment of the Lawrence School of Instruction in Theoretical and Practical Science.

Agassiz repeated his series of Lowell lectures in Albany and then, accompanied by Pourtalès, in Charleston, South Carolina. Agassiz thoroughly enjoyed being feted by the fashionable society of Charleston, and was even more gratified when he and Pourtalès were able to retire briefly to nearby Sutton's Island, where they studied and collected jellyfish, turtles, mollusks, fishes, and insects. Next, in the summer of 1847, John Lowell took Agassiz and Desor on a tour to Niagara Falls and up the St. Lawrence, where Agassiz was deeply impressed by the richness of the fauna and by the abundance of glacial markings in the rocks. His theory of the Ice Age was already widely accepted, but Agassiz himself felt a need to discover further proofs and at the same time to amass a more detailed knowledge of glaciation. At the great rapids of the St. Lawrence, according to Jules Marcou, Agassiz made the final decision "to consecrate the remainder of his life to the study of the natural history of the New World."

Upon returning to Boston, he received an invitation from Professor Alexander D. Bache, Superintendent of the Coast Survey, to join a cruise on the steamer *Bibb* along the shores of Cape Cod to Martha's Vineyard and Nantucket. The purpose of the cruise was to survey Boston Harbor, but for Agassiz it was a chance to observe and collect marine life, and he said that he learned more in a single day aboard the *Bibb* than he could learn in months "from books and dried specimens." It was probably at this time that he began to think about the advantages of teaching science outdoors, in the natural world, by conducting courses at a marine biological laboratory. Dr. Bache was thinking about a different, if related, possibility—the benefit to the country and to science of having a trained scientist accompany future coastal surveys, just as naturalists had been taken on earlier voyages of exploration. Thereafter the resources of his agency were always open to Agassiz, who eventually cruised almost the entire Atlantic and Pacific seaboards on Coast Survey vessels.

The summer's activities had been beneficial in yet another way. Agassiz, who had always been robust and indefatigable, was recuperating from an attack diagnosed as nervous prostration. It was a malady that would recur throughout his life. The first seizure had come while he was arranging living quarters for his newly arrived staff. He had rented a house on the East Boston waterfront and there he fitted out a laboratory and kept a dory for use in aquatic studies. From the beginning there was friction among the staff, evidently instigated in large part by Desor. The management of the house, even including such elementary matters as providing food, was a constant problem. But, once again in 1847, the *deus ex machina,* Pastor Christinat, appeared on the scene.

During the political convulsions of that period in Europe, Prussia lost control of its Swiss properties and Agassiz could foresee the end of his royal Prussian patronage—surely another factor in his decision to remain in America. The European upheavals included small as well as large revolutions, and one of the smaller eruptions had occurred in Charles Louis Philippe Christinat's canton. As a result, Christinat had been living in exile in Italy and France. Now he had come to America and he was soon managing the tangled affairs of Agassiz's home. The men of the establishment deferred to the strong-willed "Papa" Christinat, who was even able—to a small extent—to curb the mischief of Desor. He remained as *maitre d'hôtel* and self-appointed guardian until Agassiz was widowed and about to take a second wife. Christinat, knowing Agassiz's tendency to let his money be squandered by subordinates or devoured by quixotic projects, forecast doom unless a rich wife could be found. He was so infuriated by Agassiz's choice that he left the house and never returned. After serving as pastor to a Swiss congregation in New Orleans, he eventually returned to Switzerland, where he died in 1855. Fortunately, Agassiz's second wife was to prove a far better choice than Christinat had predicted.

In October of 1847, a month after Christinat's arrival, Agassiz delivered a series of twelve lectures at the College of Physicians and Surgeons in New York. The *New York Tribune* printed them in full, then reissued them in pamphlets. Agassiz's English was becoming more fluent, and he was receiving recognition as one of the world's most illustrious naturalists. Returning to Boston, he gave another course of lectures at the Lowell Institute and at last, in January, he received the offer of a permanent professorship at Harvard. He still seemed to feel a little unsure of himself as an American and, despite his earlier decision to remain in this country, he wavered briefly. But the turmoil in Europe was increasing. In February, the French Revolution of 1848 erupted; there was revolution in Neuchâtel as well, and rioting in Berlin. Gratefully Agassiz accepted Harvard's chair of zoology and geology, established especially for him. And in June he enjoyed a further satisfaction: the publication of his first American work, a textbook entitled *Principles of Zoology*, written in collaboration with an eminent Bostonian conchologist, Dr. A. A. Gould.

Edouard Desor, recently dismissed by Agassiz, had also helped in the preparation of the book. Now he charged that Agassiz had failed to pay him for the work. He made other accusations, some directly, some in the form of rumors: Agassiz had allegedly plagiarized Desor's writings and had borrowed money from him and failed to repay it; Agassiz mistreated his assistants; Agassiz had always mistreated his long-suffering wife, abandoned in Europe; Agassiz was sleeping with a servant girl.

Dignity demanded that most of the charges be ignored, but those involving plagiarism and financial cheating had to be refuted if Agassiz was to retain his standing among academics. In rather characteristic Bostonian fashion, friends suggested arbitration by a private tribunal of three respected citizens. Agassiz chose John A. Lowell as a member of the panel; Desor chose Dr. D. Humphreys Storer; and Lowell and Storer chose Thomas B. Curtis to serve as umpire of the proceedings. Three tribunals were held rather than one, because Desor was twice dissatisfied with the verdict. It was decided that Agassiz must pay Desor a hundred dollars for extra assistance in preparing the textbook, although Desor had already received his full salary. The third tribunal, with Agassiz's approval, conducted a four-month investigation of all accusations and rumors—even the one involving the servant girl. Agassiz was completely exonerated and his place in American university life thus assured.

He began his tenure at Harvard somewhat unconventionally,

by organizing a kind of traveling summer school—an expedition of ten students, three doctors, and two businessmen, led by Agassiz himself and Jules Marcou. Agassiz carried a box of chalk and a roll of black canvas to serve as a portable blackboard. The days were devoted to observing, collecting, and taking notes; and each evening he lectured. The expedition journeyed west to Niagara Falls and then, by foot and canoe, along the shores of the Great Lakes. In his *Life, Letters, and Works of Louis Agassiz,* Marcou enumerated the "main results of the exploration":

> first, an extension of the glacial theory of Agassiz to include all the shores of Lake Superior, almost an inland sea; second, a thorough knowledge of the fishes of Lake Superior and their comparison with those of the other great Canadian lakes; third, a comparison of the vegetation of the northern shores of Lake Superior with that of the Alps and the Jura Mountains; and fourth, large collections of fishes, reptiles, birds, shells, and insects, rocks, minerals, and fossils.

It was at Lake Superior that Agassiz caught a gar which he recognized as the same fish he had described in fossil form as a transitional type between ancient and modern groups. (There, too, he visited copper mines which his son Alexander would later investigate. Alexander Agassiz was to buy an interest in those mines and thereby accumulate a considerable fortune at last for the family.) Two years after the expedition, there appeared a volume entitled *Lake Superior: its Physical Character, Vegetation and Animals, compared with those of Other and Similar Regions,* by Louis Agassiz, with contributions by other scientists, elegant illustrations by Auguste Sonrel, and a narrative of the tour by J. Elliot Cabot.

When Agassiz returned to Cambridge, late in August of 1848, sad but not unexpected news from Europe awaited him. His wife had been afflicted with tuberculosis for some time; on July 27, two days before her thirty-ninth birthday, she had died. Her daughters were living with their grandmother, her son with Alexander Braun. Agassiz resolved to send for his children as soon as possible.

He moved from the house in East Boston to one in Cambridge, closer to the university, and located an old bathhouse on the Charles River where he could store apparatus and specimens. The bathhouse collections were the nucleus of his future museum. In his garden he kept live specimens, as he had done in Switzerland and as Audubon did at Minnie's Land in New York. In addition to the usual rabbits, turtles, and so on, his animals included two opossums and an alligator. Residents also included an array of assistants whose upkeep cost more than Agassiz was earning, though his extracurricular lectures added significantly to his income.

He made a prolonged visit to Philadelphia in the late winter and early spring of 1849, delivering a course of lectures there and studying at the library and museum of the Academy of Natural Sciences. Returning to Cambridge, he renewed a recently acquired habit of visiting often at the home of Professor C. C. Felton. He was extremely fond of Dr. and Mrs. Felton, and still fonder of another frequent visitor, Mrs. Felton's sister, Elizabeth Cabot Cary. That spring, Agassiz and Miss Cary announced their engagement. In June, his son Alexander arrived from Europe and, fortunately, he and Elizabeth Cary immediately liked each other.

The marriage took place the following spring. That summer the Agassiz daughters, Ida and Pauline, arrived. The second Mrs. Agassiz was an understanding mother to them, but in other respects she was totally unlike her predecessor. The house was put in order, the assistants dismissed or ordered to do their work at the university. Money remained a problem but she knew how to keep track of it, use it frugally, and coax her husband to press for extra grants. Most important, perhaps, she sympathized with his goals, understood his needs, shared some of his enthusiasms, and possessed a keen enough intellect to be a comrade and literary assistant to him.

In the winter of 1850–1851, Dr. Bache arranged for Agassiz to join another Coast Survey cruise, this time exploring the reefs and keys of Florida. For governmental use, he calculated the effects of the Gulf Stream and its currents on the reefs, the probabilities of reef-shifting, the relations of reefs to one another, and so on. His findings were incorporated into new charts and used in the placement of markers, signals, and lighthouses. While performing these duties he also examined minute corals and massive coral formations. He returned with a large store of data, some of which he developed into new lectures, and he brought back specimens and drawings from which plates were to be made at the government's expense. He became so engrossed in the study of corals that he never completed the report in a form suitable for publication with the plates, and his son finished the work after his death. He did, however, publish his findings with regard to corals, significantly increasing the scientific understanding of them. There was, for example, a chapter on coral formation in his 1863 volume, *Methods of Study of Natural History*. In it he explained, among other details, that

> Coral Reefs are found only in tropical regions: although Polyps, animals of the same class as those chiefly instrumental in their formation, are found in all parts of the globe, yet the Reef-Building Polyps are limited to the Tropics. . . . The geographical distribution of animals according to laws regulated by altitude, by latitude and longitude, by pressure of atmosphere or pressure of water, by temperature, light, &c. . . . presents a most important field of investigation. . . .
>
> As soon as the little Coral is fairly established and solidly attached to the ground, it begins to bud . . . dividing at the top or budding from the base or from the sides, till the primitive animal is surrounded by a number of individuals like itself, of which it forms the nucleus, and which now begin to bud in their turn, each one surrounding itself with a numerous progeny, all remaining, however, attached to the parent. . . . I have myself counted no less than fourteen millions of individuals in a Coral mass of Porites measuring not more than twelve feet in diameter. The so-called Coral heads, which make the foundation of a Coral wall . . . are known in our classifications as the Astraeans, so named on account of the star-shaped form of the little pits crowded upon their surface, each one of which marks the place of a single more or less isolated individual in such a community.
>
> Thus firmly and strongly is the foundation of the reef laid by the Astraeans; but . . . for their prosperous growth they require a certain depth and pressure of water, and when they have brought the wall so high that they have not more than six fathoms of water above them, this kind of Coral ceases to grow. They have, however, prepared a fitting surface for different kinds of Corals that could not live in the depths from which the Astraeans have come. . . .

Agassiz would have liked to extend his coral explorations, but he was forced to return in March, 1851, to defend himself in a libel suit. Two years before, an Albany schoolteacher had published an inaccurate and misleading chart of American geological formations for use in public schools. A capable geologist named James Hall showed it to Agassiz. Hall and Agassiz then wrote denunciations of the chart, feeling that by doing so they were fighting quackery and serving the cause of public education. The publisher of the chart filed a libel suit against them, seeking damages of twenty thousand dollars. Eminent geologists volunteered to testify for Agassiz, but he returned from the Florida Keys to do so for himself, scientifically and brilliantly. The embarrassed counsel for the plaintiffs moved for dismissal. Agassiz's willingness to denounce charlatanism and defend scientific accuracy—at the risk of his career and income—immediately made him a hero to American scientists.

Next, to augment his earnings and because he liked Charleston, he accepted a teaching position at the medical college of that city's university. He was to lecture there for the three months between Harvard's fall and spring courses. At the same time he would be able to establish a laboratory on Sullivan's Island for the study of marine life. He was additionally pleased because his son was becoming increasingly devoted to the study of marine biology and was developing into an able naturalist.

While in Charleston in 1852, he was notified that the Prix Cuvier had been awarded for the first time, and that he was the recipient. He was probably Charleston's most celebrated resident, and he was happy there although the climate had always seemed to disagree with him and he had felt ill during previous visits. Then, in the Christmas season, he was stricken by malaria. When he had convalesced, doctors advised him to leave the region and not return. He resigned his professorship at the medical college.

In terms of the status accorded him by posterity, his final departure may have been a blessing. His inflammatory "racial" lectures had been delivered during visits to Charleston, possibly in deference to the topical interests of his audiences. In 1847, he had told the Literary Club of Charleston that Negroes were a distinct species, an example of the pluralistic thesis of "special creation" in which he staunchly believed; they had been produced at a time and in a geographical locale quite different from the time and place of white origin. Later he made similar assertions, and in 1854 and 1857 he was to contribute essays to patently biased books of racial theory in which he divided humanity into eight "types"—Caucasian, Arctic, Mongol, American Indian, Negro, Hottentot, Malayan, and Australian. That there were distinct races with distinct physical characteristics no one disputed, of course, but on occasion Agassiz added evaluations of their relative merits. He stated that the black man could never be the physical equal of the white man. He said so at the time of the Civil War in answer to questions put by Samuel Gridly Howe, of the government-sponsored American Freedmen's Inquiry Commission. On other occasions, he even offered the speculation (which he could have refuted easily by personal observation in the South) that mulattoes, being hybrids, would tend to be infertile. He favored emancipation and the gradual, cautious education and elevation of blacks, but his statements must have grieved, perplexed, and shocked his Abolitionist friends in Cambridge and Boston. And they must have been pleased when he made his final departure from Charleston.

He went home by the kind of circuitous route to which he was addicted, with stops at Mobile, New Orleans, and St. Louis, an exploration of the Mississippi River, and a visit to Washington to lecture at the Smithsonian Institution.

When he reached Cambridge at last, Harvard built a house for him. On the top floor his wife and son—with his encouragement and help—opened a school of natural history for young ladies. It was a typical Agassiz educational innovation. The school remained in operation for several years, and its tuitions somewhat alleviated the family's financial distress. One of the students, Anna Russell, eventually became Alexander Agassiz's wife.

Harvard must, indeed, have treasured its professor of zoology and geology; in addition to the gift of the house, the university turned over to him first one floor and then the whole of Engineer Hall to hold his growing specimen collections. Next, the treasurer raised money to purchase the collections, for which Agassiz eventually received more than twelve thousand dollars. Moreover, Abbott Lawrence, who died in 1855, made a fifty-thousand dollar provision in his will to guarantee Agassiz's continued employment.

By the following year, perhaps earlier, he decided he must publish the results of all his American studies. He planned to do so in ten volumes under the general title of *Contributions to the*

Natural History of the United States. No publisher dared to inaugurate such a venture without first safeguarding the investment in early volumes by accumulating a minimum of five hundred subscriptions. Agassiz, though still regarded by many as a distinguished foreign visitor, was so popular in America that when he announced his intention the subscription list swiftly grew to twenty-five hundred names. The author himself was astonished: "What do you say to that for a work which is to cost six hundred francs [twelve dollars] a copy, and of which nothing has as yet appeared? Nor is the list closed yet, for every day I receive new subscriptions—this very morning one from California! Where will not the love of science find its niche!"

His enthusiasm was not enduring, however. Poor health and the demands of other projects ended the endeavor after the publication (from 1857 to 1862) of four volumes. There were two volumes devoted to radiate species and one that was an exhaustive study of the embryology of American turtles—three arcane books whose value might elude even a very scholarly layman. The other—his first—was the *Essay on Classification.* Marcou and other commentators have ranked it as the most important contribution Agassiz made to natural history during his American years. It emphasized the philosophical aspects of its subject; one might call it a reconciliation of theology and science. This emphasis must now seem quaintly dated to many scientists, although in the nineteenth century it probably contributed strongly to the acceptance of scientific theories. But its most valuable point was the recognition that "the changes which animals undergo during their embryonic growth coincide with the order of succession of the fossils of the same type in past geological ages." Surely, it effectively presented the case that ontogeny did, after all, recapitulate phylogeny, though it concluded that the evidence proved the hypothesis of special creation rather than evolution.

Its conclusions aside, the essay was of enormous value to naturalists then and afterward. And despite Agassiz's conviction that he never really mastered English, it was so lucidly articulated that passages have been included in literary anthologies. It strikes a modern reader as poignantly ironic that such well-marshaled evidence could be so well articulated in defense of such dubious conclusions:

There are entire continents, North America, for instance, in which the paleozoic rocks have undergone little, if any, alteration, and where the remains of the earliest representatives of the animal and vegetable kingdoms are as well preserved as in later formations. In such deposits the evidence is satisfactory that a variety of animals belonging to different classes . . . have existed simultaneously from the beginning. . . . In Russia, in Sweden, in Bohemia, and in various other parts of the world, where these oldest formations have been altered upon a more or less extensive scale, as well as in North America, where they have undergone little or no change, they present the same general character, that close correspondence in their structure and in the combination of their families, which shows them to have belonged to contemporaneous faunae.

He completed the volume on his fiftieth birthday, May 28, 1857. The following evening a special dinner was given for him by the Saturday Club, whose members included Oliver Wendell Holmes, Ralph Waldo Emerson, Nathaniel Hawthorne, Edward Everett Hale, and James Russell Lowell. There is no record showing which members attended that dinner, but it is known that Holmes and Lowell recited poems written for the occasion, as did Henry Wadsworth Longfellow, who stood and began, "It was fifty years ago. . . ." In Longfellow's poem—not one of his best but a touching tribute—Nature was an "old nurse" who showed Agassiz a book of marvelous stories "Thy Father has written for thee," and then invited Agassiz to venture

> Into regions yet untrod;
> And read what is still unread
> In the Manuscripts of God.

Soon afterward, Henry David Thoreau sent Agassiz four casks of Concord fish, among which Agassiz is said to have found a new species. Subsequently, he visited Thoreau for a restful day of turtle hunting. And that summer there was an Adirondack camping trip on which Agassiz was accompanied by Lowell, Holmes, and other scholars. (Agassiz was one of the very few naturalists who did not become hunters in order to gather their own specimens, and it is possible that he did not even carry a gun on this expedition. Emerson did, however, and Longfellow decided to forgo the trip because, with a man like Emerson carrying a gun, he said, "somebody will be shot.")

In that same year, James Russell Lowell, as editor of the newly founded *Atlantic Monthly*, persuaded Agassiz to contribute scientific essays, and Agassiz's father-in-law provided a house at Nahant where a new marine laboratory could be opened. There was no question that the Swiss expatriate had become America's foremost naturalist. During this period he was directing his greatest efforts toward the raising of funds for his cherished goal, a museum of comparative zoology at Harvard. Once again his charm became more important than his scientific genius as he accumulated bank notes and pledges through subscriptions, bequests, donations—he even succeeded in extracting money from the notoriously frugal Massachusetts legislature by emphasizing his project's potential benefits to agriculture. And in June, 1859, he was able to lay the cornerstone of the museum's first wing. Then he embarked on a summer journey with his family to London, Paris, and finally to Montagny for a visit with his mother and other surviving relatives. He returned in September, and although the trip was supposed to have been for pleasure, he brought with him new collections for the museum. The north wing was nearly finished. A dedication ceremony was held in November, 1860, and Agassiz began conducting his zoology classes there.

For the next few years, he spent most of his time at Harvard. His few lecture tours were necessarily restricted to the North. Nationality had evidently never meant very much to him, but he felt strongly that the Union must be preserved and, with the outbreak of the Civil War, he decided he must affirm his loyalty to the country that had adopted him even though he had never taken the trouble to adopt it. Therefore he applied for his first naturalization papers. The attainment of citizenship was no longer as simple as it had been for Alexander Wilson or John James Audubon. Spiritually, Agassiz had become an American; he became one legally as well in January, 1865, when the war was almost over.

The coming of peace brought new opportunities for exploration. He had wanted to see Brazil ever since he had written about that country's fishes, over thirty-five years ago. And the yearning had been whetted by thoughts of the Amazon when he toured the Mississippi. Now, one of his friends, Nathaniel Thayer, offered to turn a private Brazilian excursion into a col-

lecting expedition for the museum by taking Professor and Mrs.
Agassiz and hiring six assistants. Agassiz accepted the offer with
alacrity, of course, and arranged to bring along several students
who could afford to pay their own expenses. Free passage was
secured on the Pacific Mail steamer *Colorado,* and Agassiz was enabled to explore and collect in the tropics for sixteen months,
along the Amazon and elsewhere.

Afterward, as usual, he incorporated his findings into lectures.
And in 1868 another book appeared. This time, however, he was
not the primary author. He contributed many passages, particularly those dealing with natural history, but *A Journey in Brazil*
was written mostly by Elizabeth Cary Agassiz, his talented wife.

The following year there was a short voyage with Pourtalès,
again on the Coast Survey steamer *Bibb,* to the Bahamas and
around Florida; it was an opportunity to perform deep-sea
dredging experiments and thereby collect new fauna. Soon after
the trip, Agassiz delivered a brilliant address to commemorate
the centennial of Humboldt's birth, and then he suddenly became ill, this time very seriously. For a while he could not speak;
he had probably suffered a stroke. All the same, he was prepared to undertake further explorations.

Another invitation came from the Coast Survey, which was
preparing to "send a new iron surveying steamer round to California. She will probably start at the end of June."

After repeated delays, the ship finally left Boston early in December, 1871, making her way through a snowstorm and heavy
seas. The new ship was the *Hassler*—new but shoddily built, with
a defective engine and dredging lines not long enough for deep
work. Elizabeth Agassiz and the captain's wife were the only
women aboard; Mrs. Agassiz kept a journal, for use in *Atlantic
Monthly* articles as well as in a subsequent book. It was an arduous trip, and disappointing in some ways. When the vessel
reached Santiago, Agassiz received word by telegraph from Dom
Pedro II, Emperor of Brazil, informing him of his election to the
French Academy of Sciences. His response was that "the distinction unhappily is usually a brevet of infirmity, or at least of old
age, and in my case it is to a falling house that the diploma is
addressed. I regret it the more because I have never felt more
disposed to work, and yet never so fatigued by it."

All the same, he was heartened by the glacial evidence he

found on South American islands, by the breeding colonies of sea birds around the Strait of Magellan, and by the sight of the strange fauna Darwin had described on the Galapagos Islands.

The trip was terminated at San Francisco, where Agassiz rested for a month before returning overland to Cambridge. He arrived home in October, 1872, still tired but enthusiastic about yet another idea for the education of naturalists. He wanted to establish an outdoor summer school and perhaps a marine biological observatory for teachers of natural history. The legislature was considering his request for funds, and as usual he had publicized the idea in the hope of securing donations. Now he received a startlingly generous offer from John Anderson, a New Yorker who owned an island called Penikese, off New Bedford in Buzzards Bay. The offer consisted of the island itself, with its furnished house and barn, and fifty-thousand dollars to open and begin operating a school there.

At Cambridge on June 26, 1873, after beginning preparations and seeing for himself that months might be required for the opening of the school, Agassiz printed an invitation to prospective students for that very summer, stressing that the instruction would be free. "I have at last decided," he wrote, "to open the Anderson School of Natural History, on Penikese Island, at 12 o'clock, on the 8th of July next." By personally urging on the carpenters, masons, and everyone else involved, and by taking a physical hand himself, he opened the school on schedule. It served as a prototype for many subsequent marine research and training stations.

In October, he dedicated an *Atlantic Monthly* article to his wife, and he opened his classes in the lecture rooms of his Harvard Museum. And on a Monday morning in December, he arrived on time for his class but suddenly felt a tremendous fatigue that prompted him to return home. He went to bed, fell asleep, and died on December 14, 1873. James Russell Lowell wrote a lugubrious elegy to him, in which he mourned:

> At last, arrived at where our paths divide,
> "Good night!" and, ere the distance grew too wide,
> "Good night!" again . . . .

The sincerity of sentiment surpassed Lowell's poetic talent. More to the point is a prosaic but accurate evaluation by one of

Agassiz's academic heirs at Harvard, Stephen Jay Gould, who teaches biology, geology, and the history of science. Gould has written of Agassiz that regardless of the comfort southern slave-holders may have taken from his less scientific speculations, he was "the greatest biologist of mid-nineteenth-century America."

Chapter 7
JOHN WESLEY POWELL

The single indomitable force in the establishment of the United States Geological Survey, John Wesley Powell was also founder of the Smithsonian Institution's Bureau of Ethnology, and he was a climatologist, hydrologist, paleontologist, conchologist, botanist—a paradoxical man who was irresistibly drawn to specialized investigations but whose mind was too restless for the citadel of laboratory, library, or specialization. A correlative paradox was his drive to attain the insights and knowledge of a quiet intellectual by the means of a man of action, a scientific adventurer. It is a conflict endemic to naturalists, for many of whom it may well be the primary urge toward field studies.

Perhaps Powell's greatest achievement was the introduction of organized, well-funded research in the natural sciences as a legitimate function of the federal government. Geologists might argue, however, that his major scientific contribution was his explanation of crustal uplift, erosion, and sedimentation, the forces that determine the shape and features of great portions of the earth's surface. His pioneering classification of Indian languages might also be nominated as his major contribution to natural sciences, particularly by ethnologists who hold the study of human societies to be as much a part of natural history as the study of plants or animals.

He has been called "the father of land preservation in the West," for it was Powell who first effectively lobbied for the withholding of vast expanses of the public domain in order to conserve water, minerals, timber, pasturage, and other natural resources and to prevent their monopolization by individual speculators or private corporations. He has also been called "the father of irrigation and land reclamation"—a title that now carries almost equal degrees of honor and reproach because of the unforeseen damage done to the environment by ill-conceived dam building, marsh drainage, and the like where short-term benefits have sometimes turned into ultimate deterioration. In one of the Powell biographies, *The Man Who Rediscovered America,* John Upton Terrell has said that Powell's monument is not the stone marking his grave in Arlington National Cemetery but "the largest man-made lake on earth, Lake Powell, which reaches out behind Glen Canyon Dam for hundreds of miles into the vast Plateau Province he opened to the world."

Glen Canyon Dam, completed in 1964, and Hoover Dam, completed in 1936, are but two of the many huge storage, flood-control, and power-generating dams erected on or near sites originally suggested by Powell on the basis of his geological explorations.

There are also those who consider his greatest monument to be the Geological Survey's topographical and geological mapping of the entire United States, a project whose enormity Powell himself underestimated. The task has required nearly a century to bring to a stage that might loosely be called completion. In this connection he explored and mapped the last large unknown region in the contiguous states and territories—the plateau and canyons of the Colorado River. He was a one-armed Civil War veteran, wiry but of less than robust physique, who led the first successful expedition down the dreaded and treacherous rapids of the Colorado. And out of that heroic expedition came his once-controversial theory of canyon formation, a theory which, in amplified form, is now an accepted tenet of geology.

Some of his flaws seem petty, others appropriately heroic. His expeditions and later his bureaus were pervaded by nepotism. He was often inconsiderate of subordinates, occasionally imperious, somewhat disdainful of rivals. He could be intentionally forgetful—devious, in fact—in sending collections of plants, fossils, minerals, archaeological artifacts, and so on, not always to the institutions to which they had been promised but to those most likely to support future projects. He made impulsive decisions.

He indulged in bureaucratic and Congressional politicking, at one time even bartering influence with a railroad promoter.

He was a utilitarian naturalist to whom "abstract science" seemed a contradiction of terms, for he regarded science as a tool for the material benefit of man; thus his geological findings were directed toward the transformation of American deserts into green farmland, his anthropological findings toward assimilating the American Indian into the "superior" white society (without, however, the continuation of traditional cruelty toward Indians, without the genocide officially sanctioned at that time, and without sacrificing any salvageable record of Indian culture). Later naturalists have challenged the desirability of altering the environment to the degree he advocated, and later ethnologists and sociologists (and many Indians) have mourned the burial of Indian ways beneath white culture. Powell was so self-assured that now and then he stated a scientific speculation as if it were an observed proof rather than an unproved theory. Yet his goal was always an unusually altruistic urge to broaden man's knowledge, thereby improving his condition, and he won the almost reverent loyalty of most of his subordinates, while attaining difficult goals of enormous value to the scientific study of nature.

In 1951, a biography entitled *Powell of the Colorado* was published by William Culp Darrah, a professor of biology who had also written works on geology, paleobotany, and the history of science in America. Darrah pointed out that in the second annual report of the U.S. Geological Survey, Powell proposed a system of geological nomenclature and cartographic standards which, in modified form, remain in use. He also pointed out that "the conservation movement, the development of a federal land policy, the elevation of science in government bureaus to a position of dignity, were in large part inspired and directed by Major Powell."

In 1830, a thirty-year-old Welsh-English Methodist minister named Joseph Powell emigrated to the United States with his wife Mary and two infant daughters. Earning a subsistence as a tailor and farmer but unswervingly committed to the ministry, he settled temporarily at Mount Morris, on the stage road southeast of Palmyra, New York. There, on March 24, 1834, a son was born. In the hope that the child would some day enter the ministry, his parents named him after John Wesley. Another son, William Bramwell Powell, was born two years later. Eventually there were eight children, five sisters and three brothers. For many years there was barely enough money to provide for the large family, and Joseph Powell kept moving them west, hoping eventually to establish a large enough, prosperous enough farm to support them while he supplemented the income with tailoring but devoting himself more enthusiastically to the duties of a circuit-riding preacher. At first the education of the children was limited to home tutoring and reading, but it was not desultory. At five, "Wes" Powell recited the Gospels from memory.

The Powells moved across New York and then to the Welsh settlement of Jackson, Ohio, a day's journey from Chillicothe. They bought a small parcel of land, and neighbors helped them raise a temporary log cabin and then a frame house. It was a period of heated debate between the older settlers, from the South, and many newcomers from the North. Abolition meetings in Jackson were attended by such celebrities as Whig Congressman Joshua Giddings and Liberty Party leader Salmon P. Chase, future Secretary of the Treasury and Chief Justice of the Supreme Court. These and other Abolitionists were guests in the Powell home. At Jackson's new log schoolhouse, the sons of proslavers stoned Wes, and so he was sent at the age of about nine to take tutoring in the home of George Crookham, a remarkably active three-hundred-and-fifty-pound self-taught scholar who was to become one of the county's first commissioners of education. Under Crookham's guidance, the child read such works as Gibbon's *The Decline and Fall of the Roman Empire* and Hume's *History of England.* In addition to this unconventionally heavy reading, there were hikes and field trips to study at first hand the rudiments of geology, botany, various other facets of natural history, and archaeology. Not far away were the mysterious ancient works left by the Mound Builder Indians, and there were also mineral deposits to investigate. (Reverend Powell himself, while digging a well in 1842, discovered a coal vein that made possible a local colliery.)

Crookham, who had helped a number of runaway slaves to reach Canada, showed Wes Powell the nearby caves where they were hidden when they reached this waystop on the underground railroad. The boy also accompanied Crookham and

Dr. William Mather—Ohio's first state geologist—on survey trips. For a future explorer and naturalist, it was an unconventionally effective primary education.

After eight years at Jackson, the Powells bought a homestead at South Grove, Wisconsin. Mary Powell tutored the younger children, but Wes was already better educated than his mother and he now received no schooling except by means of the books he read. The elder Powell tailored and rode his circuit while the family raised wheat, corn, and flax, and kept hogs, sheep, chickens, and two cows. At the age of twelve, Wes became the farm manager. It was about then that he first had a chance to observe Indians at close hand. A band of Winnebagos camped there en route to Chicago and again when they returned; they had gone to the city to collect payment—much of it in cheap calicoes, blankets, and shoes—for lands that had been taken from them. The lands included the homestead Joseph Powell had purchased from the Government.

There were Indian mounds in Wisconsin as well as in Ohio, and there were the remains of much more recent aboriginal settlements and encampments. When the boy was about fourteen, he began to assemble a little museum of artifacts, as well as collections of flowers and insects. His father, noting his developing interests, advanced all the arguments he could muster to discourage the boy's preoccupation with natural history and persuade him to prepare for the ministry; he succeeded only in persuading him that it was time to leave home to acquire more schooling. In 1850, Bram Powell was fourteen, old enough to take over the farm management and grain-hauling chores. Wes, encouraged by his sister Mary's new husband, William Wheeler, decided to remedy his deficiencies in mathematics, grammar, and classical languages in order to prepare for college. He attended school at Janesville, twenty miles away, while working for his room and board at a Janesville farm. The following year the Powells moved to another farm, across the state line in Illinois, and Wes returned to help them. For a while he studied at home, but the old arguments resumed when his father insisted that he would send him to Oberlin only to study for the ministry.

In 1851, Wes Powell walked the thirty miles to Jefferson County, Wisconsin, obtained a teaching certificate, and began instructing farm children in a one-room stone building. The next year the Powells moved again, this time to Wheaton, Illinois, the site of a new Wesleyan college, Illinois Institute, of which Reverend Powell had been elected a trustee. Curiously, the West was far more progressive in educational matters than the East was, and the Institute was coeducational; it was not, however, well endowed or well staffed, and at first could offer no science courses. Wes Powell came to Wheaton and could have pleased his father by remaining at the Institute, but the lack of scientific studies prompted him to leave again and take a teaching job near Decatur. With encouragement from another brother-in-law, John Davis, both Wes and Bram Powell took private courses at a local academy, and in 1855 Wes entered the scientific department of Illinois College at Jacksonville.

That year he also set off on a summer field trip to study the mollusks of the Mississippi drainage. He bought a small skiff, rowed up the Mississippi to St. Paul, sold the boat, and walked across Wisconsin. He spent four months collecting and sending home specimens, and his discoveries so elated him that he spent several summers thereafter rowing along the tributaries of the Mississippi.

He must have been an outstanding elementary teacher, for he earned a higher than average salary in the "common schools" despite his youth and lack of formal training. In 1856, he had sufficient funds to trek across Michigan to collect shells and reptiles. Upon reaching Detroit, he visited his mother's brother, Joseph Dean, and almost immediately fell in love with Dean's daughter Emma. Both families initially opposed a marriage between first cousins, but during the long courtship the Deans and Powells became reconciled to the inevitable.

In 1856, Powell also descended the Mississippi all the way to New Orleans. His observations and collections were extensive, and it is unfortunate that his only surviving notes (perhaps he made no others) are mere lists of those collections and the places visited.

Illinois Institute—still undercapitalized and soon to be reorganized as Wheaton College under the auspices of the Congregational Church—had now begun to offer scientific courses. All of the Powell children attended, but Wes remained only a short time because in 1858 he was able to realize his ambition of matriculating at Oberlin. His education was sufficiently advanced so that he was accepted in the class of '61. He now studied Greek, Latin, and botany—not theology—but his father's disappointment was mitigated by the fact that Oberlin was a militantly Christian and militantly abolitionist institution. Young Powell fared well scholastically. While there he accumulated an extensive wild-plant collection and, with the help of some fellow students, completed a survey of the local flora. Yet he soon lost interest in Oberlin and departed.

At Jacksonville, he had studied independently for a while with Jonathan B. Turner, a great teacher, liberalizer of education, and lover of experimentation. Turner had successfully introduced the Osage orange (*Maclura pomifera*) as a hedgerow shrub to provide natural fencing for prairie farms, and he had his own experimental farm. In 1858, he helped to organize the justly celebrated Illinois State Natural History Society, whose first objective was to explore the state and enumerate every plant, animal, and mineral. Powell immediately joined, and was elected to the curatorship in conchology. This provided him with free passes on railroads and steamers, as the transportation lines were cooperating in the deposit of collections by the Society at Illinois State Normal University in Normal, near Bloomington. Powell, who later became secretary of the society, had already amassed a herbarium of nearly six thousand plants, as well as a large collection of land and river mollusks, and collections of minerals, fossils, and snakes.

Once, at Wheaton, he carried a fruit jar into the woods and there he simply picked up a large rattlesnake and deposited it in the jar. Such incidents earned him an exaggerated reputation as a young wizard of natural history who possessed a consummate knowledge of the state's wildlife and its habitat and habits. No single primary interest yet held him; he kept shifting his concentration from one specialty to another—plants, reptiles, mollusks—and a lack of scientific literature at that time in America, together with his own lack of funds for books, prevented his identifying some of his specimens. Each winter he taught school, planning to save tuition money with which to further his education, and each spring he sacrificed the plan to a wanderlust as zealous as that which had drawn his father westward from one town to another.

In the spring of 1857, he had boarded a train to Pittsburgh

and explored stretches of the Allegheny, Monongahela, and Ohio. That fall he collected minerals in Missouri's Iron Mountain region below St. Louis, lingering until his money was gone, then vainly looking for work in St. Louis, and finally pawning a watch for his fare back to Decatur.

By 1858, when he celebrated his twenty-fourth birthday, he was a teacher at Hennepin, Illinois, at a very good salary. He was a slightly built young man, not quite five feet seven inches tall, weighing perhaps a hundred and twenty pounds, fairly good looking but with a bulbous nose and a full rusty beard—he called it auburn—already tobacco-stained. Coal was mined near Hennepin, and Powell searched the piles of waste for fossils. He also found extensive sand and gravel deposits, providing evidence of glacial drift. He was becoming progressively more interested in geology. That spring he explored the Illinois and Des Moines Rivers, observing how soils and vegetation followed the drift and rock formations, pondering how such knowledge might be applied to agriculture. While continuing to teach, he also embarked on lecture tours, visited Emma Dean several times, wrote to her regularly, and busied himself with the promotion of science in the curriculum of Illinois schools. In 1860, he was appointed superintendent of Hennepin public schools, and that year his mollusk collection won a prize at the fair of the Illinois State Agricultural Society. By March of 1861, he was also commissioner of conchology for the newly chartered and reorganized State Natural History Society, but he was spending less time studying shells than military engineering and tactics, for his travels in the South had convinced him that war was imminent.

When news reached Hennepin of the firing on Fort Sumter, his brother Walter had already joined the home guard in Decatur. Wes summoned Bram to Hennepin to replace him as superintendent of schools, then enlisted on May 8, 1861, and left the same day for Joliet, where the 20th Illinois Volunteer Infantry was being organized. He was elected sergeant major of Company H, and on June 13 was promoted to second lieutenant to fill a vacancy. Soon the 20th Illinois was steaming down the Mississippi to St. Louis and then to Cape Girardeau. Powell helped to plan and erect the town's fortifications. He came under fire during the siege of Lexington, but spent most of that year at Cape Girardeau, where boredom prompted him to organize and train an unofficial, unauthorized company of light artillery and engineers. General Ulysses S. Grant, soon after replacing John C. Frémont as department commander, ordered this group to take charge of one of the town's four main fortifications, and Powell became an acting captain of artillery.

After accompanying Grant on a tour of inspection, he requested and received a week's leave to go to Detroit and get married. On November 28, 1861, he wed Emma Dean, and he brought her back with him to Cape Girardeau. He was then commissioned captain of artillery and raised a siege company which quickly became Battery F, 2nd Illinois Light Artillery. Among the men serving under Powell was his brother Walter, who had reenlisted.

In March, 1862, the battery was shipped upriver, almost to Savannah, Tennessee, and emplaced the guns on the bluffs above Pittsburg Landing. About two miles west of the landing, at Shiloh Church, General William Tecumseh Sherman was holding an extremely exposed position with recently recruited troops, while other divisions were scattered nearby but out of sight of one another. On Sunday, April 6, the Union forces were attacked by the Confederates, who had deployed large numbers of troops around the Federal concentrations. The Battle of Shiloh had commenced.

Battery F received no orders, nor could Powell locate anyone in authority. Finally, at about 8:30 A.M., he moved his battery forward, but the Union troops were retreating, there was no place for the gunners to make an effective stand, and Powell had to wheel about and retire, abandoning one gun to pursuing Rebel forces. Drawing his artillery half a mile in six minutes, Powell led his men to the lines on Sherman's left, commanded by Generals W. H. L. Wallace (who was mortally wounded in the battle) and B. M. Prentiss (who was captured). Prentiss, fighting gallantly, was forced back to yet another position, and Powell helped him to hold it. The battery performed brilliantly. By early afternoon it had become a primary Confederate target. The area of the sunken road and peach orchard where Prentiss held his position was christened the Hornet's Nest.

Shortly after four o'clock Powell raised his right arm, as he had been doing continually, to signal his men to fire. A half-spent minié-ball from a Southern rifle smashed into his wrist and was deflected into the flesh near his elbow. There was throbbing pain, then numbness as blood spurted from the jagged wound. Walter Powell eased his brother down beneath a large tree and applied a tourniquet. Then General Wallace rode up and announced that since the position was nearly surrounded and he could not leave his men, he expected to be captured. He did not want the wounded artillery captain left behind or taken to a Southern prison camp. He therefore put Captain Powell on his own horse and told him to race for the landing. Later, Powell dimly remembered being helped from the horse and put aboard a boat. His battery escaped capture but before the battle ended it lost four men killed, six wounded, and a score of horses.

Emma, waiting anxiously at Savannah, stayed by his side at the hospital until laudanum had helped him to sleep, and afterward she nursed him. Dr. William H. Medcalfe, a druggist in civilian life but now the Surgeon of the 49th Illinois Volunteer Infantry, tried unsuccessfully to remove the bullet. On April 8, after administering a little chloroform, he amputated the arm below the elbow.

When Captain Powell had recuperated somewhat, though the arm continued to throb and pain, he decided to remain in active service if Emma could accompany him to each new post. General Grant issued a "perpetual pass" for her, and on June 30, 1862, Powell rejoined his Battery at Corinth. Assigned to recruiting duty and sent north, he spent that summer and much of the next winter in Illinois, then rejoined his unit for the campaign against Vicksburg. After the Battle of Champion's Hill, men under his direction built two bridges overnight to replace one burned by fleeing Confederates. He was present during the Vicksburg siege—which he recalled as "the forty hardest days of my life"—and in late June and early July his men dug trenches and connecting "saps" up a steep slope toward the enemy parapets, then dragged the heavy guns to within seventy yards of the Rebel works, thus contributing to the Confederate decision to surrender. By then, Powell weighed no more than a hundred and ten pounds, and his arm was a constant torture, for the nerves were regenerating.

He obtained sick leave to have it resectioned, but was on duty again that fall. After helping to organize and train a black regiment at Vicksburg, he was with his own battery again during the bloody Atlanta campaign and on part of Sherman's "march to the sea." His brother Walter had been captured, reported missing, escaped from Camp Sorghum in South Carolina, and recaptured raving mad after wandering about for two days. Later, when Walter Powell was paroled in a prisoner exchange, he appeared moody and unpredictable, for he had not recovered from his ordeal. He never did; eventually he succumbed to insanity, though not before proving himself hardy and skillful on geological expeditions led by Wes Powell.

The Captain rose to the rank of Major, Chief of Artillery of the 17th Army Corps, and at the end of 1864 was ordered to Springfield for the reenlistment and reorganization of his regiment, which had served its full three years. Still in pain, he felt that he had served well and that the war would very soon end in victory. Therefore, on January 4, 1865, after discussing the decision with his wife, he requested and immediately received an honorable discharge. Shortly afterward, his application for a disability pension was disallowed on the astonishing ground that he had allegedly deserted his post during the Battle of Shiloh. He was quickly exonerated, however, and the pension was granted.

On the first of May, all of the Powells went to Chicago to await the funeral train of President Lincoln, which stopped en route to Springfield so that thousands, like the Powells, could pay their last grief-stricken respects to the Emancipator. Having done so, Major Powell felt he could now concentrate on the course his life was to take with the coming of peace.

Without much hesitation, he declined a lucrative county clerkship—reward for a local hero—to accept a professorship in geology at Illinois Wesleyan University at Bloomington. The salary was hardly a temptation, but the opportunity for innovation was. William Culp Darrah mentions the striking parallel in the concerns and teaching approaches of Powell and the ebullient Swiss-American, Louis Agassiz: "Instruction in the natural sciences . . . was generally uninspired and insipid, depending upon the traditional textbook and recitation method. Louis Agassiz was instigating a one-man revolution in the teaching of zoology at Harvard; independent of his efforts [and evidently without any knowledge of them], it fell to Wes Powell to do the same for geology." Geology, however, was too limited a domain for Powell. Within a year he enlarged his status to professor of natural science, teaching botany, comparative anatomy and physiology, systematic zoology, geology, mineralogy, natural philosophy, and logic of natural science, and in addition offering lectures on such subjects as cellular histology, prehistoric man, and insects harmful to vegetation.

Like Agassiz, he inspired numbers of future naturalists by encouraging them to see for themselves the processes of nature. In laboratory classes, his students performed mineralogical experiments such as extracting ores from the natural materials in which they were deposited. His botany students ambled about the streams, woods, and prairies, examining plants, amassing a herbarium. They used Powell's own microscope to observe the structure of flora. To gain insights into germination, they dissected fruits and planted seeds. The zoology students went on comparable field trips and performed comparable experiments. Powell moved through the laboratory, watching them sort the stomach contents of such creatures as birds and snakes, jovially encouraging the squeamish among them to conquer inhibition with curiosity, to mess up their dissections if necessary so that they might take joy in discovery.

Soon Powell transferred to Illinois State Normal University because that institution was more liberal in the interpretation of professorial duties and, being state-supported, could be persuaded to help finance the projects he was beginning to plan. He talked to Emma about making an expedition into the Rocky Mountains, and in 1867 he appeared before the state legislature three times to solicit funds for an adequate museum and a paid museum curatorship at Normal. In this matter, too, he closely resembled Agassiz. The museum was established, and of course Powell became curator. He immediately utilized the new position to further his plans, proposing in his acceptance speech that he be sent on an exploring and collecting trip into the Colorado Rockies; $500, half the year's museum allocation, was granted to help defray costs, and each teacher or student on the expedition was to pay his own way.

Powell had a charming temerity in raising funds. In April he went to Washington, saw General Grant, and arranged for rations to be provided at government rates for a party of twelve. He also arranged for the army to provide an escort from Fort Laramie through the Badlands (a precaution he never repeated, because the expedition convinced him that military protection was unneeded and that, in fact, it was regarded by the Indians as a menacing gesture). Next he visited railroad and express-company executives and secured free passes as well as free shipment of supplies and specimens. In exchange for a promise of duplicate specimens, he obtained additional financing from Illinois Industrial University (the progenitor of the University of Illinois), and in exchange for topographic measurements he obtained a loan of scientific equipment from Joseph Henry, Secretary of the Smithsonian Institution. This was the beginning of a long and mutually beneficial association with the Smithsonian.

Powell was to be the expedition leader and official geologist. His wife, who had taken an interest in natural science, was to be one of three ornithologists in the party. There were also two entomologists, a botanist, two zoologists, a herpetologist, a mineralogist, and an artist (George D. Platte) who would record some of the scenes and natural phenomena encountered. Two professors wanted to accompany the group but were unable to make the trip. Except for Powell, the party included no established professionals; three were college seniors, the others amateur naturalists.

On June 1, 1867, the expedition left Council Bluffs, Iowa, where General Sherman had supervised the provisioning and persuaded Powell to follow a southerly route, avoiding the Badlands because of current Indian uprisings. The explorers rode horses and used mule teams to draw two heavy wagons. Along the way they joined a pioneer train of fifty-two wagons and traveled for some time with the settlers. On the first of July they reached Denver. They wished to explore Pikes Peak and its environs. A road led to their destination but they chose a shorter though more difficult route. With guides recruited at Denver, they made their way into the mountains, driving wagons that each carried twelve hundred pounds of freight. Along one stretch they climbed fifteen hundred feet to cover three winding miles; at another point they had to dismantle the wagons and manhandle them over gigantic boulders. But in less than three days they reached Bergen's Park, a narrow twenty-mile valley of pastures and twinkling streams where a few settlers raised cattle. They remained there nearly a month, exploring and collecting while Major Powell sketched and studied mountain formations.

Late in July they made the difficult ascent of Pikes Peak. The 14,110-foot peak had been discovered in 1806 by Lieutenant Zebulon Pike; it had been climbed by three members of Major Stephen M. Long's 1820 expedition, and had been the focal point of a gold rush in 1859, but Emma Dean Powell was the first woman ever to reach the summit. The group remained on the crest for only an hour, but that was too long. Night—an exceedingly cold, windy night—overtook them before they had descended below the timberline. Having no shelter, they built a big fire and kept close enough to the flames to be in danger of scorching themselves as they waited out the hours of darkness. Their reconnaissance of approaches had not been extensive enough, and the route they chose necessitated a difficult climb; it was a route probably never taken before or since.

Next they explored the South Platte to its source and penetrated the surrounding mountains, making observations and collecting specimens. The group disbanded at the end of summer, but the Powells stayed to explore part of the Colorado, above its junction with the Green River. For two months they studied the topography and formulated plans to survey the Colorado the following summer. Before leaving, they persuaded four local men who had guided and assisted them to join the next expedition.

Upon returning to Illinois, Powell began to inventory the Colorado collections—thousands of insects, nine hundred birds, and several hundred plants, as well as reptiles, mammal skeletons, fossils, and minerals. He also lectured, taught, and embarked on a second fund-raising campaign, working sixteen hours a day before rushing to Washington to secure additional governmental support.

Once again free transportation was arranged, and instruments were obtained from the Smithsonian in exchange for data concerning the area to be explored. It was agreed that this time the party would attempt an ascent of Longs Peak, which had never been climbed. Of the twenty-one people who joined the expedition, Mrs. Powell was the only woman. Two were newspaper correspondents, several were professional biologists, and the others were students and amateurs. The Major's brother Walter, having temporarily recovered from the mental instability caused by his Civil War experience, went along in the capacity of zoologist.

On July 1, 1868, they arrived by train in Cheyenne, and from there used horses, mules, and wagons to reach Denver. From Denver they rode to Hot Sulphur Springs, on the Grand, and there they established a headquarters. During three months of exploration and specimen-collecting, they recorded the altitude, longitude, and latitude of much hitherto unknown country. They traversed the Colorado range from Lincoln's Peak to the South Platte and they studied the Gore Mountains, the highest peak of which was later named Mount Powell.

On August 20, the Major, his brother, and five other men left a spur camp at the headwaters of the Grand for the trip to and up Longs Peak. Several attempted ascents were aborted because their way was blocked by slides, perpendicular cliffs, hidden canyons, and the like. Finally, one of the men, L. W. Keplinger, left their timberline camp in a last attempt to find a negotiable route. Darkness brought a thunderstorm, and Keplinger failed to return. Jack Sumner, a guide who was to accompany Powell on his next and most important expedition, went out to look for Keplinger, and at about ten P.M. both men returned. They had found a route. On August 23, 1868, they made the first climb to the 14,255-foot summit of Longs Peak. From the mountain top they could see all the way to Denver. Before descending, they made temperature and barometric measurements and erected a marker.

One of the men on the 1868 expedition, W. H. Bishop, had the task of replenishing supplies at the headquarters camp, hauling provisions from Empire City through Berthoud Pass. He made eleven trips, thereby crossing the Continental Divide twenty-two times before the end of summer. Following an advance group led by Walter Powell, the expedition traveled two hundred miles west of the Divide, and a winter camp was eventually established on the White River. From there they advanced to the Green, camping en route at the foot of Aspen Mountain to wait out a three-day blizzard. There was a railroad crossing at Green River Station, and from there many members of the expedition left for home. The Major, his wife, Walter Powell, S. M. Garman, W. H. Bishop, and several mountaineers—including Jack Sumner—returned to the White River camp. Before reaching it they encountered two grizzlies, which subsequently provided extra winter meat, robes, and lamp oil.

Powell spent many of the winter evenings at a nearby encampment of Ute Indians, learning their language, recording their customs and myths. With several students, he had begun compiling a Ute vocabulary. Powell made a point of going unarmed among the Indians, and it became his custom always to do so. He was never molested, even when he roamed through areas inhabited by hostile bands. His Ute vocabulary was the first ever recorded. These Indians had seen few white men, and they provided an opportunity to study Ute culture in its pure form, unmodified by contact with white civilization. By spring, the Major was a devoted ethnologist, and his collection of Ute crafts was welcomed by the Smithsonian as revelatory.

This was Mrs. Powell's last expedition with her husband. The men deeply respected her stamina and skill, but they resented her steadily increasing officiousness, and they intensely disliked her assumption that she was as much in command as the Major and empowered to give orders. One member left the expedition as a result. It would not happen again, for the next expedition was to be too arduous for any woman.

Powell had explored the area sufficiently to confirm that a vast network of canyons along the White River and then along the Green into the Grand—the upper Colorado—though nearly inaccessible by land, could be thoroughly surveyed by a boat strong enough to withstand the pounding in the many rapids. On government maps, the upper Colorado region was marked by blank spaces representing areas a hundred to two hundred miles wide, three hundred miles long. It was largely an unknown region, the last such area of significant size between the Atlantic and Pacific below Canada and above Mexico.

The Major planned not only to examine a three-hundred-mile labyrinth of mystery but to extend the exploration along almost a thousand miles of river, much of it uninhabited, much of it not even charted except on a few rough Mormon sketch maps.

The canyons of the Colorado system meandered through about fifteen hundred miles of land without a white settlement or military post. Beginning where the Green flowed into the Grand, the Colorado's gorges averaged three thousand feet in depth, and there were places where the canyons were twice as deep, though no one yet knew how many such places existed or where some of them were. And although it was common knowledge that the river had a steeper drop along its flowage than most rivers, no one knew how steep. It was for Major Powell to discover that in the nine-hundred-mile course from Green River Station in Wyoming to the Rio Virgen in Arizona, the altitude of the river dropped a mile—three times the drop of the Mississippi.

Government parties had explored several sections of the canyon in 1853, 1857, and 1859. A group led by Lieutenant J.C. Ives in 1857 had ascended a portion of the Colorado, and an eminent member of that expedition, geologist John Strong Newberry, had written the first accurate account of it. He had also theorized about the formation of the canyon maze, and when Powell later formulated his theory of canyon development he acknowledged having been strongly influenced by Newberry's insights.

None of those previous expeditions had navigated the upper Colorado, though a few bullboats of buffalo hide stretched over round willow frames had swirled through relatively short stretches of the Green. Powell studied all available maps, sketches, and reports, and he talked to the region's Indians, settlers, Mormon missionaries, and the nomadic mountain men who were continually looking for new trapping regions. He even contacted James White, who had made a dubious claim (Powell later realized it was a preposterous claim) to have rafted all the way from the San Juan River junction in Utah down through Arizona to Callville in eleven days. No raft of any construction then known could have been drifted, rowed, poled, pulled, and portaged down that treacherous chain of white-water rapids.

The starting point in Wyoming was easily chosen: Green River Station, east of Fort Bridger. Union Pacific flatcars could bring the boats to the railroad bridge there. Again Powell went to Washington, secured President Grant's approval of army rations for twelve men, and renewed his various arrangements with supporting universities and with Joseph Henry and Spencer F. Baird of the Smithsonian. Then, at the Bagley Boat Yard in Chicago, he had four boats built to his specifications. Three were twenty-one-foot double-ribbed white-oak craft with double stem and stern posts and four-foot reinforcing bulkheads at the ends. The buoyancy of the bulkheads would help keep the vessels afloat if they capsized. Each boat was equipped with eighteen-foot oars and a hundred and thirty feet of stout hemp rope. The fourth boat was rather similar in design but was a white-pine sixteen-footer. Its lighter construction and somewhat sharper lines made it faster and more maneuverable than the others. It was to be the lead boat. It would carry Major Powell, and at dangerous points in the stream he would lift a flag to signal back to the other vessels. When he and Walter Powell arrived at Green River Station with the boats in early May, 1869, the other men were already encamped outside the little town. The greatest of the Powell expeditions was about to begin.

He had not recruited experienced scientists. He knew that he could quickly train his assistants to make the observations, take the measurements, and record the data he wanted. What he needed was a crew of tough outdoorsmen, attracted to perilous adventure. All of them felt Major Powell's enthusiasm for discovery, and they served without pay. Once again accompanying the Major was Jack Sumner, hunter, trapper, Colorado guide. Another member was Oramel G. Howland, a printer and editor from Vermont who had worked in Denver for the *Rocky Mountain News*. He had summoned his younger brother, Seneca Howland, from the East to join him on this expedition. William Dunn was another who had previously served with Powell; he was a rugged and usually ragged mountaineer. One more who had been with Powell before was William Rhodes Hawkins, who sometimes called himself Billy Rhodes or just "Missouri." His service in the Union Army had terminated abruptly after some minor violation of the law, and he was, at least technically, a fugitive. He was a wild young man, known to consort with thieves; like Sumner, the elder Howland, and Dunn, he had accompanied the previous expedition. He had been unjustly suspected of complicity when a teamster named Gus Lanken stole two of that expedition's mules and then fired on his pursuers. But he had been exonerated, and was now happy to come along as cook and general assistant.

George Bradley was a former sergeant major stationed at Fort Bridger; he had been recommended to Powell because he was intelligent, strong, interested in the region's geology, and a skilled boatman. Andrew Hall was a twenty-year-old adventurer (often erroneously reported as being only sixteen) who had

fought Indians and been a plainsland drifter before this opportunity came.

Then there were the Major and his brother Walter, and, finally, an English adventurer named Frank Goodman who had
not been recruited but had haunted the camp at Green River
Station until Powell accepted him. Goodman proved to be less
adept than the others as a crewman, and less eager to work hard;
he was probably the only poor choice, although Walter Powell—
always ill-tempered and unpredictable—was even less popular
among the men.

Just before Major Powell arrived, one Samuel Adams—who
called himself Captain Adams—appeared at the camp and attempted to take command. Powell had little difficulty sending
him away, but later this rather eccentric impostor claimed to
have explored the canyon country thoroughly prior to 1869, and
before he was exposed he managed to have newspaper stories
printed in an effort to brand Powell as the impostor.

Before breaking camp, the men practiced their boating and
scientific duties. The Major would pilot the expedition, make the
important decisions (though he was fairly democratic in his practice of consulting the others), and take latitude and longitude
measurements. He and George Bradley would note geological
measurements, descriptions of strata, and related information.
Oramel Howland was in charge of mapping the river. Compass
readings were to be taken at every bend, and observers in each
boat would estimate the distances from point to point. Three
times a day the altitude at the water's edge would be recorded,
and the height of the canyon walls computed. Each man famil-
iarized himself with the workings of the barometers, but Walter
Powell and William Dunn would take most of the barometric
readings. Astronomic readings would also be made every fifty
miles.

The boats started down the Green River on May 24, 1869. In
the lead was the *Emma Dean,* named for the Major's wife, followed by the *Maid-of-the-Canyon*, the *Kitty Clyde's Sister*, and the
No-Name. Apart from several groundings, the first few days were
easy and relatively uneventful. Powell and his men had reason to
think that they had loaded enough provisions for twice the time
this trip would take. They camped from May 27 to May 30 below

Henry's Fork, among cottonwoods set against a backdrop of twelve-hundred-foot bluffs that were nearly perpendicular on one side—the first canyon to be climbed and surveyed. Already Powell was beginning to construct geological sections, examining, analyzing, describing, and diagraming segments of surface and successive strata. The vivid red bluffs caused the first canyon to be called Flaming Gorge; the next was named Canyon of the Rapid for the roaring white waters that tumbled through it, dropping several feet in a very short distance. Others were eventually given equally descriptive names. Some names were majestic or serenely picturesque—Grand Canyon, Split Mountain Canyon, Glen Canyon. Many were indicative of the river's terrors—Hell's Half Mile, Whirlpool Canyon, Desolation Canyon, Cataract Canyon.

Little cargo or equipment could be carried in the small pilot boat. The others each carried two thousand pounds of cargo. Despite this tonnage and the added weight of the crewmen, the vessels were proving to be reasonably maneuverable, buoyant, and very sturdy. But there was no way to run some of the wilder or shallower rapids. On the last day of May and again on the first of June, the boats had to be eased down rapids by roping and dragging. The night of June 1 the men camped at Ashley Falls, named for a mysterious inscription—"ASHLEY 1825"— painted high on a rock. It was not until later that Powell learned of an 1825 bullboat expedition through this segment of the river. It had been led by General William H. Ashley.

At first Powell and his crew made their way in a leisurely manner, again stopping several days to make observations. On the fifth, they came to a place where the canyon was three miles wide. Then it began to close in again, and the men's journals show that the going suddenly became difficult and dangerous.

June 8: The canyon narrows. The walls are two thousand feet high. A rumbling can be heard as boulders are carried along by the surging water. In the early afternoon a terrible roar warns of a chute. Powell debarks to find the best path for a portage while Dunn signals the others to land. The *No-Name* ships too much water to be maneuvered out of the current. It breaks up on the rocks. Goodman nearly drowns before his mates, the Howland brothers, can pull him out onto a midstream sandbar. The water is rising and the three men are stranded. Sumner takes the *Dean* out and makes a hazardous rescue. The spot is named Disaster Falls. The *No-Name*'s cargo of provisions is a total loss, but the men believe that they have more than enough left. The real calamity is the loss of three barometers. But the boat's after-compartment snags on rocks downstream. Sumner and Hall are able to retrieve the instruments, together with a two-gallon jug of whiskey that had been stowed against the Major's orders. Regarding the whiskey, the Major relents.

June 17: In Utah's Badlands now. Camp is made on a narrow island covered with pines. A gust of wind carries a lick of flame from the cooking fire into the brush. The trees ignite, the island is ablaze. To escape, the men run a hazardous rapid in the dusk. The fire has taken part of Walter Powell's mustache, and several of the men are scorched. The mess kit is lost. Hereafter the bailing cups—one cup per two men—will have to be used for coffee.

June 18: The Yampa River is reached. Again the expedition halts for several days to make thorough observations. A sack of spoiled rice must be discarded, but some trout and a big whitefish are caught, and a large buck is shot. There is still no real fear about the provisions. Progress is delayed for another few days when both Sumner and the Major become ill.

June 27: The going becomes so easy that the boats travel sixty-three miles in one day. But now there are swarms of mosquitoes, so thick and voracious as to become a torture.

June 28: The expedition reaches the Uinta River, just above the confluence of the White and Green. The first stage of the voyage has been completed safely. Major Powell and several of the men travel overland to the Uinta Indian Agency to observe the Utes and replenish the expedition's supplies. Powell sends letters home. In the East, John A. Risdon, a swindler, escaped convict, and horse thief, has announced to the world that the expedition has ended in calamity and he is the sole survivor. He is raising funds for himself very effectively, as is still another impostor who calls himself Jack Sumner. Fortunately, Mrs. Powell knows the real Jack Sumner, and she knows too many details of the expedition to be fooled by Risdon. Both men are publicly exposed when Powell's letters arrive. At the Uinta Agency, Goodman leaves the expedition; no one regrets his going. But the crew is somewhat shaken to learn that the Indian Agent is in Salt

Lake City, purchasing stores, and the Indians have very little to sell or barter. Powell must discard two hams that have turned rancid, three sacks of moldy flour, and a large quantity of wormy beans. Government maps show no more outposts of civilization for nearly eight hundred miles, and supplies are dwindling. The men find an Indian garden planted on an island. Hall, Dunn, and the normally scrupulous Major steal half-grown beets, turnips, carrots, and potatoes. Bradley dislikes the potatoes and eats none of them. Every other man becomes briefly but violently ill.

July 8: While climbing a sheer rock wall to take measurements, Major Powell finds himself on a minuscule ledge, unable with his one hand to pull himself higher, unable to back down, clinging to a fingerhold and in danger of falling to his death. Bradley, who is above, looks down and sees the danger. He pulls off his drawers—all he is wearing on this blistering day—and lowers them to the Major to be used as a rope. Powell lets go of the fingerhold, grabs for the rope, and is hauled up. Bradley has saved his life.

July 9: Bradley finds fossil shark's teeth. A stop is made to repair the boats, which are showing the wear of pounding over boulders.

July 11: The *Dean* swamps in a swirl of white water, with a loss of oars, watches, bedding, a barometer, and two rifles.

July 16: The previously uncharted junction of the Green and Grand is reached. A four-day stop is made for observations and repairs. Much flour can be saved by sifting it through mosquito netting to get rid of damp lumps and mold, but two hundred pounds must be discarded, leaving only six hundred pounds more. Powell notes that this is a good spot from which to observe a solar eclipse, predicted for August 7, but he is persuaded to move on because the provisions may not last until civilization is reached.

July 22: Powell closely examines strata which dip away from the river in opposite directions. He has been pondering the origins of this canyon country, and here he has found the axis of a fold formed during crustal uplift. The process of formation is becoming clearer to him. He writes in his *Geological Notes* that today he has "unraveled the mystery of the rocks."

July 26: Major Powell and five others climb a side canyon, looking for pitch to calk the leaking boats. Intense heat drives all of them back except the Major. He stuffs two pounds of pitch into his empty right sleeve and clambers down in a sudden rain squall.

July 27: Little meat remains. Two mountain sheep are sighted and killed. They are regarded as a godsend.

July 28: A muddy little river is discovered and named Dirty Devil Creek. (Later it will be renamed the Frémont River.)

July 29: The ruins of ancient Pueblo cliff dwellings are found and explored. Artifacts are gathered.

July 31: The San Juan River is reached. The expedition has come one hundred and sixteen miles from the junction of the Green and the Grand; in that leg of the voyage eighteen portages have been made, forty-five rapids run. The Major calls another halt to make observations. The men are worried now about such delays. Bradley writes in his diary that Powell "ought to get the latitude and longitude of every mouth of a river not known before and we are willing to face starvation if necessary to do it but further than that he should not ask us to wait, and he must go on soon or the consequences will be different from what he anticipates."

August 3: The expedition moves on, and the men are able to kill another sheep.

August 7: They climb a bluff to watch the predicted eclipse, but clouds obscure it. They are suffering now from exposure and hunger. The second week of August brings abnormally cold, torrential rains. Some of the bedding having been lost, there are only four blankets among them. After one of the rainstorms, the blazing sun appears and in half an hour the temperature rises to one hundred and twenty-five degrees.

August 13: They encounter fierce rapids again, and tremendously high canyon walls. Powell knows approximately where they are and what is in store for them. They are at the upper end of the magnificent and terrifying abyss to be named the Grand Canyon of the Colorado. It has been seen before but not often, and never explored. Powell records his reactions in his journal:

> We are now ready to start on our way down the Great Unknown. Our boats, tied to a common stake, are chafing each other, as they are tossed by the fretful river. They ride high and buoyant, for their loads are lighter than we could desire. We have

but a month's rations remaining. The flour has been resifted . . . the spoiled bacon has been dried, and the worst of it boiled; the few pounds of dried apples have been spread in the sun, and reshrunken to their normal bulk; the sugar has all melted. . . . The lighting of the boats has this advantage: they will ride the waves better, and we shall have but little to carry when we make a portage.

We are three quarters of a mile in the depths of the earth, and the river shrinks into insignificance, as it dashes its angry waves against the walls and cliffs, that rise to the world above; they are but puny ripples, and we but pigmies, running up and down the sands, or lost among the boulders.

We have an unknown distance yet to run; an unknown river to explore. What falls there are, we know not; what rocks beset the channel, we know not. . . . The men talk as cheerfully as ever; jests are bandied about freely this morning; but to me the cheer is somber and the jests are ghastly.

. . . We run six miles in a little more than half an hour. . . . There is a fall below, and a bad rapid, filled with boulders . . . so we stop to make a portage. . . .

. . . With great care, and constant watchfulness, we proceed, making about four miles this afternoon, and camp in a cave.

The lines regarding jests are poignantly revealing, for the men were defying fear with their gallows humor, and some of them felt that the Major was not only a man without fear but callous regarding their worry. His own record shows that he was far from callous, but hid his concern to avoid lowering morale still further.

August 27: Having passed the mouth of the Little Colorado more than two weeks ago, the men have already come much farther downriver than the Mormon estimate of the distance from the Little Colorado to civilization. The Howlands and William Dunn are convinced they must starve if they continue to follow the serpentine course of the river. They can move faster overland, and they are determined to try. It is a clear night. After talking to Oramel Howland and failing to dissuade him, the Major uses the sextant to determine their position by dead reckoning. He calculates that they are now only forty-five miles from the Rio Virgen—forty-five miles from safety and food. Even if the winding of the river doubles that distance, they should be able to reach a Mormon settlement in two or three days, four at most. The baking-soda can has been lost in the river and they are living on little more than unleavened bread, but there is flour enough to last that long. Nonetheless, Dunn and the Howlands remain determined to go their own way overland.

August 28: The barometers and collections are cached, the *Dean* abandoned here at Separation Rapids, because now there will be only six men to handle the boats. The remaining flour is made into biscuits and divided equally. Each of the three who are to go overland is armed with a gun and ammunition. The other six men take the *Maid* and the *Sister* out into the current, run the rapid, and wave a last farewell to the three they have left behind, three silhouettes on a cliff.

August 29: The rapids subside, the country flattens, rolling desert appears. The men know that within a day they will reach the Rio Virgen—the point of deliverance. In his journal, Powell describes their emotions and conversation as they camp that night:

> Now the danger is over; now the toil has ceased; now the gloom has disappeared; now the firmament is bounded only by the horizon; and what a vast expanse of constellations can be seen!
>
> The river rolls by us in silent majesty; the quiet of the camp is sweet; our joy is almost ecstasy. We sit till long after midnight, talking of the Grand Cañon, talking of home, but chiefly talking of the three men who left us. Are they wandering in those depths, unable to find a way out? are they searching over the desert lands above for water? or are they nearing the settlements?

August 30: In the morning one of the crewmen sights a band of Paiutes in a valley. "They see us," Powell notes in his journal, "and scamper away in most eager haste, to hide among the rocks. . . . Two or three miles farther down, in turning a short bend in the river, we come upon another camp." Powell, "being able to speak a little of their language," shouts that they are friends. The Indians flee, except for a man, a woman, and two children. After a little reassuring talk, the Indians beg for tobacco, but the white men have almost none left. Instead, Sumner gives them a little piece of colored soap which the Indians accept enthusiastically, "rather as a thing of beauty than as a useful commodity, however." Powell and his men push on. Early in the afternoon they come to the mouth of the wide, muddy Rio Virgen. Three Mormon men and a boy are standing in the river,

netting fish. The six explorers have come safely through an adventure that had turned into an ordeal. They are taken to a
cabin and banqueted. They have completed the exploration of
the last great unknown region in the United States.

The three men who chose to go overland never reached the
settlements. Powell learned later that they were murdered by
normally peaceful Shivwit Indians who thought they were prospectors. The arrival of prospectors was too often followed by
white settlement and the eviction of Indians. Moreover, these Indians had heard a rumor that several white prospectors had
abused some Indian women, and they assumed that Dunn and
the Howlands were the guilty men.

Major John Wesley Powell was suddenly famous—a national
hero. While planning the next expedition, he made a tour of
public appearances. He talked about hydrology and erosion in
the vast basin of the Colorado (later adopting Frémont's name
for it—the Great Basin); and he speculated on the age of the
canyons, basing his deductions on calculations of the alluvial deposits carried to the Gulf by the Mississippi. Those calculations
could be stated as one inch of soil per two hundred and sixty-five
years, and the assumption of a similar rate for the Colorado
River would place the age of the canyons at 60,000,000 years.

However, Powell noted that much more time might be needed
for the evolution of the canyons because much less rain falls in
the Colorado basin than in the valley of the Mississippi; therefore he astutely surmised that the canyons might be even older
than he had estimated. He then described a complicating factor,
the formation of alpine lakes and streams whose descending
waters must also have influenced the evolution of the plateau
and canyon surfaces as they washed down for countless centuries.

He was invited to contribute a brief account of the canyons to
a revised edition of Dr. William A. Bell's *New Tracks in North
America*. Here, too, he stressed the formation of topography by
water, and he offered a fully formulated and expanded theory
in 1874, in a report to the Smithsonian which was subsequently
printed as a book, *Exploration of the Colorado River of the West and
Its Tributaries, Explored in 1869, 1870, 1871, and 1872*. In it he
explained that there had been an uplift—a "wrinkling" and

"folding" of the earth's crust along the plateau of the Colorado, "down-turned as well as up-turned wrinkles, or, as the geologist would say, there were synclinal as well as anticlinal folds."

He added that "the upheavel was not marked by a great convulsion, for the lifting of the rocks was so slow that the rains removed the sandstones almost as fast as they came up. The mountains were not thrust up as peaks, but a great block was slowly lifted, and from this the mountains were carved by the clouds. . . . We speak of mountains forming clouds about their tops; the clouds have formed the mountains. Lift a district of granite, or marble, into their region, and they gather about it, and hurl their storms against it, beating the rocks into sands, and then they carry them out into the sea, carving out cañons, gulches, and valleys, and leaving plateaus and mountains embossed on the surface."

The river, then, had been flowing when the plateau rose, and as the fold was lifted the river cut its channel, deeper and deeper until the present canyon was formed. The causes of crustal shifting and faulting were not yet known when Powell delineated the three great processes of formation—uplift, erosion, and sedimentation—the cycle of topographic development which was to be expanded into the new science of physiography.

He worked out and diagramed the theory in detail over a period of half a dozen years, but he comprehended the basic elements immediately, in 1869. Today perhaps this and related theories seem rudimentary, but when Powell arrived at his conclusions no one fully comprehended the enormous energy of falling water, the concept, as he explained it, that a mighty river was like a moving saw and the crustal uplift was like a log being raised against the teeth of the saw, which cut farther and farther in as the log—the plateau—slowly rose.

Powell's recognition of erosion on so tremendous a scale was revolutionary, as was the word "slowly" in this context. It was a time of heated scientific controversy between the "Catastrophists," who held that great topographic formations were the result of sudden, cataclysmic upheavals, and the "Uniformitarians," who believed that the formations (except for volcanoes and sudden faulting by earthquakes) were built up at an imperceptible rate by natural processes which are still going on and can be measured. Many geologists perceived the logic and evidence of Powell's theory, but more than a generation passed before it gained universal acceptance by scientists, for it upset the tenets of the catastrophic school.

Early in 1870, Powell began raising funds anew. His goal was a second expedition down the Colorado. He was satisfied with the geological findings of the first expedition, but not with the specimen and artifact collections, most of which had been cached at Separation Rapids. He also wanted an opportunity for further study of the Indians of the region. And apparently even more important to him was his realization that the cartographic work of the first expedition was far from complete. The second journey was to be essentially a longer, more thorough mapping venture, entailing exploration and careful survey of lateral canyons and the bordering plateaus. Largely owing to the influence of such men as Salmon P. Chase and Senator James A. Garfield, Congress appropriated $10,000 for Powell's use in the fiscal year ending June 30, 1871, for a "Geographical and Topographical Survey of the Colorado River of the West." An allocation of $12,000 was later added for a continuation of the project in the following year.

Powell's selection of a chief topographer for this ambitious undertaking was characteristic. He hired his sister Nell's husband, Almon Harris Thompson (often referred to as Harry Thompson in subsequent writings by Powell and colleagues). Thompson was superintendent of Bloomington schools. As better-qualified topographers were readily available, it was a clear and typical instance of Powell's nepotism, but it was also typical in that it worked out well. Thompson developed into an exceptionally fine topographer and deputy expedition leader; and Nell Thompson, who often accompanied him, was an able assistant.

Certainly there was need of a reliable deputy leader, because Powell planned to take long absences from the group in the field—partly to arrange for supply wagons to haul provisions to designated points along the route in order to avoid a repetition of the food shortage that nearly doomed the first expedition; and partly to visit and study the Utes, Paiutes, and Shoshones of the region. (When the time came, he also absented himself several times to visit his wife, who was waiting in Salt Lake City and was undergoing a difficult pregnancy; their only child, Mary Dean Powell, was born there on September 8, 1871.)

Powell never regarded these subsequent Colorado River expeditions as important enough to require his continual presence; to him they were merely a mapping survey made possible by his great exploratory adventure of 1869. The preface of his *Exploration of the Colorado River* contains a generous acknowledgment of Thompson's work: "Professor A.H. Thompson has been my companion and collaborator during the greater part of the time, and has had entire charge of the geographic work; the final maps will exhibit the results of his learning and executive ability." But there is no recognition of any other members of the second field party; the text does not even contain a single specific mention of the 1871–1872 explorations, despite the inclusion of those years in the full title of the report. The nearest Powell comes to such recognition is to cite the conclusions of "Mr. G.K. Gilbert, a geologist of Lieutenant Wheeler's corps," with regard to the effects of "the Glacial Epoch" in "the region of the Great Basin"—conclusions helping to substantiate aspects of his own theory. He refers to Gilbert's findings as presented in a paper to the Philosophical Society of Washington in 1873. Gilbert was a member not of Powell's expedition but of a War Department survey west of the hundredth meridian under Lieutenant George Wheeler. Gilbert wrote to Powell in 1873, requesting technical advice about the geology of the region being surveyed, and—to the vast annoyance of Lieutenant Wheeler—was soon afterward added to the Powell staff.

The ten men who served under Powell during the 1871–1872 expedition included his brother-in-law, Thompson; a talented seventeen-year-old self-taught artist named Frederick S. Dellenbaugh, who was a distant relative of Thompson and was hired primarily as a boatman but who became a capable assistant topographer; a twenty-year-old cousin, W. Clement Powell, who had no particular training but was hired as another boatman; a guide named Jack Hillers, hired as a last-minute replacement because Jack Sumner was snowed in at the time of departure; E.O. Beaman, a professional photographer from New York; and five friends of Powell or the Powell family—F.M. Bishop, J.F. Steward, S.V. Jones, Andrew Hattan, and Frank Richardson. Bishop was a surveyor, Steward a capable amateur geologist, and Jones a surveying and mathematics student. Richardson and Hattan had no suitable training, but Hattan served reasonably well as a cook. Richardson, who apparently had neither the presence of mind nor the physical coordination of a wilderness explorer, soon burned out the seat of his pants by sitting on a hot coal. He had a peculiar facility for hurting himself, and before long, at the Major's suggestion, he resigned and went home. The others performed well. In 1908, Dellenbaugh published a fine book, *A Canyon Voyage,* recounting the experiences of the expedition.

In the summer of 1870, Powell brought F.M. Bishop and an assistant named Walter Graves to Utah for a preparatory exploration of the plateau, including a selection of supply routes and a search for waterholes. Powell asked Brigham Young to recommend a guide, and thus he acquired the services of Jacob Hamblin, an idealistic and outstandingly successful Mormon missionary who had been instrumental in securing Mormon treaties with the Utes and Shoshones.

With Hamblin, Powell visited and studied Utes, Paiutes, Shoshones, Kaibabits, Shewits, Moquis (Hopis), and other Indian groups. During a long visit among the Tusayan pueblos, he deduced from their utensils that these Hopis were related to the ancient cliff dwellers whose ruins he had discovered. He also deduced from their language and mythology that the relatively sedentary Hopi people were linguistically related to the nomadic Utes, Paiutes, and Shoshones. Powell swiftly won the trust and admiration of Indians, who gave him the Paiute name Ka-pu-rats, meaning "One-Arm-Gone." Hamblin was of great value to him, and he in turn helped Hamblin by speaking before a council of belligerent Navahos at Fort Defiance. As a result, on November 5, 1870, Hamblin was able to sign a peace treaty between the Mormons and the Navahos.

The second river expedition pushed into the stream at Green River Station on May 22, 1871. The men were provided with three boats, the *Emma Dean,* the *Nellie Powell,* and the *Cañonita,* improved versions of the big oaken boats used in 1869 and built at the same Chicago yard. Each was a twenty-two-foot craft with a twenty-inch keel, drawing twenty-two inches of water, with a square stern topped by a heavy oarlock to hold an eighteen-foot steering oar. Other equipment was also improved. Each man had a life preserver and a rubber bag for blankets. There were more or less watertight rubber sacks for most of the provisions too.

During the periods when Powell stayed on the river with the party, he piloted, signaled, and commanded from an armchair lashed atop the middle bulkhead of the *Dean*. It was an excellent lookout perch, though by making the craft top-heavy it may have contributed to a swamping that almost took Powell's life on September 3, 1872, in a chute some distance below the Sockdologer Rapid. With Powell in the boat were Hillers, Dellenbaugh, and Jones. As the Major stood up to get a better view, thus making the boat still more top-heavy, a large wave struck. The *Dean* capsized. Dellenbaugh and Jones managed to catch hold of the boat. A moment later, as Dellenbaugh related in *A Canyon Voyage*,

> the Major and Jack shot up alongside as if from a gun. The whole party had been kept together in a kind of whirlpool, and the Major and Jack had been pulled down head first till, as is the nature of these suctions on the Colorado, it suddenly changed to an upward force and threw them out into the air. . . . We joked him [Powell] a good deal about his zeal in going to examine the geology at the bottom of the river, but as a matter of fact he came near departing by that road to another world.

Lacking a right hand, the Major was less adept than some of the others in the water. Hillers and Dellenbaugh righted the craft, then helped Powell and Jones climb aboard. They probably saved the Major's life. (Hillers became Powell's very able staff photographer after Beaman left to establish himself as an independent Western photographer; Clem Powell was asked to assume Beaman's duties, but he proved to be inept with wet-plate equipment.)

The expedition charted the river in detail, then established a winter camp in the Mormon settlement at Kanab and continued to map the region. Powell left the group and again went to Washington, where he began politicking for continued government support. He and Mrs. Powell now made their permanent residence in the capital so that he could be close to the institutional directors and legislators with whom he dealt. He agreed to do some quiet lobbying for a bill favoring construction of the Great Southern Railroad because railroad promotor A.C. Osborne was able to influence several congressmen to advocate continuing survey work. Powell wished to conduct a new and extensive survey of the Western arid lands in order to establish sites for reservoirs, dams, canals, and other means of storing and distributing water for irrigation. He also wished to continue his studies of the Indians.

In 1872, a new agent, George W. Ingalls, was appointed for the Paiutes and related tribes of southeastern Nevada and the adjacent portions of Arizona and Utah. He was a replacement for one of the typically inept and corrupt Indian agents who had misappropriated funds. Powell had by now begun an attempt to persuade congressmen to end military supervision of the Indians, reform the Bureau of Indian Affairs, and in general treat the aboriginal peoples humanely. Ingalls and Powell admired each other, and the Major was happy to ride with the new agent through his district, aiding him as adviser and interpreter. He informed Ingalls that the Indians he knew in several similar regions wanted to establish farms but could not because the whites had taken almost all the good valleys in the southern part of Utah Territory and adjacent areas. However, he suggested Uinta Valley and Grass Valley as reservation sites, and his suggestions were heeded.

In 1873, he was appointed special commissioner to accompany Ingalls on visits to Indians in Utah and eastern Nevada. He took advantage of this opportunity to continue his work on Indian languages, mythology, social organizations, customs, arts, and general way of life. Afterward he submitted a four-part report containing an estimate of the number of people in each tribe, the condition of each tribe, recommendations for reservation placements, and a plea to halt all military actions against the Indians. White fears regarding Indian uprisings in the region were unfounded, since the census of the entire area of Powell's tour showed a total Indian population of only 5,500. This included Utah, parts of Arizona and Nevada, eastern Idaho, and southeastern California. Powell emphasized the need to educate and "elevate" the Indians, referring to their "savage" culture as a social phase of development comparable to childhood, but he believed that most of them were eager and able to gradually absorb themselves into the white way of life.

The tone of his report was undeniably condescending, and not because he felt the need for diplomacy in negotiating with the Great White Chiefs in Washington but because he was sincerely convinced that the Indian, though *potentially* the equal of the white man, represented a childishly savage culture that had not yet been environmentally influenced to evolve as European civilization had. The report and his other ethnological writings must be interpreted within the context of his time. In 1873, the report was actually very progressive in its tone, conclusions, and recommendations. His suggestions concerning reservation sites were carried out. His suggestion that military operations and expenditures be replaced with constructive expenditures and an emphasis on agriculture was ignored. He regarded his reform attempt as a failure, and so it was, but undoubtedly it influenced later government policy.

Scientifically far more important than the report were his completed vocabularies of all the Ute and Shoshone tribes; the recording of their myths, social institutions, dress, religious ceremonies, customs, and arts; and the collections of Indian products sent to the Smithsonian. (Smaller collections of duplicate artifacts were sent to Illinois Wesleyan, Illinois Normal, and several museums.)

Under the aegis of the Smithsonian, Powell now had continuing governmental funding and an official title as director of the "Geological and Geographical Survey of the Colorado River of the West and its Tributaries." He launched another of his quiet campaigns, this time for the consolidation of the several Western surveys being conducted by the War Department and the Land Office of the Department of the Interior.

A dispute between a survey under Lieutenant George Wheeler and that of Ferdinand V. Hayden (who had explored the Yellowstone region and had been instrumental in the establishment there of the first National Park) brought a congressional inquiry. At the hearings, Wheeler and Hayden were sufficiently vituperative toward each other to damage their standing. Moreover, the inquiry revealed that their appropriations were much higher than Powell's, and were rendered even more costly by their military escorts. Powell remarked that he neither needed nor wanted any military escort. The result of the inquiry was, for the time being, inconclusive. Hayden would continue his survey of the Rocky Mountain region, while Powell's survey would be designated as the "Second Division of the Survey of the Western Territories," technically under Hayden's jurisdiction, though directed by Powell.

The Major now had an adequately financed survey and drew a

personal salary of $3,000, most of which he spent for supplies and the services of assistants. He did not need the salary for himself and his family, as he had a sufficient income from lectures, magazine articles, and the sale of photographs. (He shared rights and royalties with his staff photographers, and the stereoscopic views were particularly profitable.)

In addition to lecturing and writing articles, Powell found time for an 1874 exploratory trip to the junction of the Snake and Yampa rivers and into the Dry Mountains and Cameo Mountains, while Thompson's party, operating independently, mapped southern Utah and the neighboring portion of Arizona. In 1874, he also completed his *Exploration of the Colorado River* and submitted the report to Smithsonian Secretary Joseph Henry. The following year it was published as a book by the Government Printing Office. The first of the book's three parts contained Powell's journal of the 1869 exploration of the Green and Colorado rivers, the land exploration of 1870, and a report by Harry Thompson of a trip to the mouth of the Dirty Devil. The second section contained Powell's geological descriptions, discussion, theories, and diagrams—his great contribution to geology. Appended to all this was a third brief zoological section completely irrelevant to the Colorado. It contained a comparative discussion by Elliott Coues of two genera of pocket gophers, or "pouched rats," a second paper by Coues on the cranial and dental characters of one of these genera, and scientific notes by G. Brown Goode concerning a gopher known in Florida and Georgia as a "salamander." Evidently a printing of these zoological reports had been ordered, and the Government Printing Office appended them to Powell's work as a publishing convenience.

Powell had contributed papers to the *American Journal of Science* and other scholarly publications, but it was the book that established his scientific reputation. It was followed within a year by his *Report on the Geology of the Eastern Portion of the Uinta Mountains*, published by the Government Printing Office in 1876. This book gave full credit for the mapping to Thompson, Bishop, and a newer member of the staff named H.C. DeMotte. Again, in this text, he advanced his geological theories, offered additional evidence, and now made a point of comparing natural and manmade erosion. Clarence King, a fine geologist who had led a War

Department survey of the region of the fortieth parallel beginning in 1867, had been offering speculations on the sudden upthrust of mountains. Here was well-substantiated evidence in two books that he was wrong in assuming catastrophic origins, as were most naturalists specializing in geology or various paleological studies. Only a few European geologists at that time promulgated tentative theories akin to Powell's.

Next, as part of his crusade to reserve lands in the public domain and begin irrigation of potential agricultural regions, he completed a *Report on the Lands of the Arid Region of the United States.* He submitted it to J.A. Williamson, chief of the General Land Office, who forwarded it to the new reform-minded Secretary of the Interior, Carl Schurz, and in 1878 the Government Printing Office published it.

Among other points, Powell contended that two-fifths of the United States was too arid for agricultural use but that significant portions could be reclaimed by irrigation. For many years the report's recommendations were ignored or refuted, but eventually—particularly during Theodore Roosevelt's administration—they strongly influenced government policy. Shortly before Powell's death, the first bill authorizing large-scale reclamation was enacted.

Costly irrigation surveys were not popular among congressmen during the economic doldrums of 1877 and 1878. But the desire to reduce expenditures made this a propitious time for another effort at consolidating the Western surveys. Curiously, Powell lobbied for consolidation under the direction of Clarence King. He had, at least for the present, become more interested in anthropology than in geology and therefore did not want the post for himself. Powell succeeded not only in the campaign for a single geological bureau but in his nomination of its chief. The United States Geological Survey was established, and Clarence King reluctantly accepted from President Hayes an appointment as director. (King privately stated that he planned to remain in office only long enough to organize the bureau and begin its operations.)

Appended to the survey bill was an authorization and appropriation for the establishment of an ethnological survey under Smithsonian direction. It was another success for the protean one-armed Major, who spent almost the last half of 1879 touring the West—much of the way by stagecoach—as a member of a newly authorized Public Lands Commission. Among the tour's significant investigations were the observation of an experimental irrigation system in California and the study of the destruction of agricultural bottomlands by sand and gravel washings from California placer mines. Once again Powell's recommendations were temporarily unheeded, but he returned to assume the directorship of the Bureau of Ethnology.

Shortly after the Civil War, he had lectured on prehistoric man at Illinois Wesleyan, and others were offering rudimentary courses on paleolithic man, but in 1879 no American university yet offered a course in modern ethnology or its parent discipline, anthropology. The bureau helped to legitimize these studies and pioneered in amassing sufficient information so that they could be taught at universities.

Three years previously, Powell had asked Joseph Henry's permission to study and publish the many Indian vocabularies that had been deposited in the Smithsonian collections. In 1877, disregarding the rather substantial differences between geology and ethnology, he had the temerity to publish as one of his Rocky Mountain Survey reports a work entitled *Introduction to the Study of Indian Languages.* In preparing it, he had, of course, made good use of the Smithsonian's Indian vocabularies. After Joseph Henry's death in 1878, Spencer F. Baird became Secretary of the Smithsonian Institution; Baird was quite familiar with Powell's earlier works but it was because of the language study that he unhesitatingly chose the Major as his ethnological director.

Powell's ethnological views had not changed. He was strongly influenced by Lewis H. Morgan, a student of ancient civilizations, who interpreted social development as a cultural analogue of Darwinian evolution. He supplied Morgan with information on Hopi kinship and inheritance customs for use in an 1877 book, *Ancient Society.* Powell's version of the Morgan thesis was that all societies (assuming that their environment exerts pressure for cultural evolution) pass through three main stages, from savagery to barbarism to civilization, much as a human passes from childhood to adolescence to adulthood. It was a simplistic theory, a reflection of its time, but it did not diminish the Powell contributions to genuine ethnological knowledge.

Albert Gallatin had published a North American linguistic map in 1836 but it was, of necessity, inaccurate and far from complete. The Bureau of Ethnology soon began work on a new map, while also compiling a useful bibliography of North American philology. The map and accompanying text required thirteen years to complete and publish. Meanwhile, in the bureau's seventh annual report, Powell published his classifications of linguistic groups, a work still regarded as one of the great achievements in the study of American Indians.

Another outstanding achievement of the bureau was the *Handbook of American Indians*, which was conceived primarily as a dictionary of names designating tribes and languages, but was expanded to include additional information and became a standard reference.

Powell hired specialists to investigate and report on such diverse matters as mortuary customs, home-building, and sign language. (He became a good friend of Alexander Graham Bell, whose work with the deaf had led not only to telephonic experiments but to research into sign language that would enable the deaf to communicate more easily and effectively.) In addition, Powell's bureau consulted with the government regarding Indian treaties and boundaries (the incompetent Bureau of Indian Affairs having lost many of its records) and compiled an index of all treaties made from 1606 to 1885.

When Clarence King had been in office two years, he resigned from the Geological Survey, as expected, and President Garfield nominated Powell for the vacancy. The Senate promptly confirmed the nomination. Powell was now director of two important, federally funded scientific bureaus. He had undoubtedly become the nation's most powerful and influential scientist. He continued King's policy of establishing regional survey offices and pursuing studies of mineralogy, stratigraphy, and paleontology, as well as the infant disciplines of geochemistry and geophysics. Despite his advocacy of applied rather than abstract science, he reduced the Survey's role as a mining bureau—initiated by King—to put more emphasis on scientific investigation and on agriculture.

In 1882, he asked Congress for authority to "complete a geological map of the United States." Previously the survey had mapped only portions of the West. This maneuver would give his operations nationwide scope and at the same time, since the mapping project would obviously take a number of years to complete, would assure continued financing. The authorization was granted, and the project proved to be even more ambitious than its originator realized.

It has taken until recent years to complete (more or less) the Geological Survey's quadrangle maps, most of them extending thirty minutes in each direction, bounded by meridians and parallels and employing a scale of two miles to the inch. Additional maps are scaled four miles to one inch, and others are scaled one mile to one inch. There are still larger maps depicting special-purpose or special-detail areas. From the first, these were much better maps than others prepared in the same period. The improvements included accurate contour lines, plus hachures and colors to show topographical features. And the large-scale maps have always been exquisitely detailed.

University degrees, awards, memberships in the most prestigious scientific and philosophical societies now came to Powell, and he enjoyed them. More travail and disappointment also came to him. A series of congressional hearings was conducted from 1884 to 1886 in order to review the expenditures of all governmental scientific agencies. The goal was to coordinate scientific activities and ultimately to economize without reducing scientific endeavor. The National Academy of Sciences recommended a single all-encompassing "Department of Science," an idea that had also occurred to Powell and that he advocated at the hearings. Opposition came from the War Department, which foresaw a loss of control over its remaining surveys, together with a reduction of appropriations. Opposition also came from those who disliked Powell's plan for an irrigation survey because they wanted public-domain lands opened to speculation. And it came, too, from magnates who resented the survey's interest in mining as an invasion of the private sector. Thus, ironically, Powell and the concept of a scientific department were severely criticized by Alexander Agassiz, whose copper mines had made his family wealthy. Afterwards, in 1886, Powell received an honorary degree from Harvard, "the Agassiz school," as a peace offering. Nothing at all came of the proposal to coordinate scientific research until the mid-twentieth century when the National Science Foundation was established.

Powell was summoned repeatedly to testify at the hearings. He did so in 1884 while suffering from a severe eye infection that left his sight impaired. More distressing to him was an anonymous report, circulated among the legislators, to the effect that his administration of the Geological Survey was marked by incompetence, political machinations, favoritism, autocracy, and gross extravagance. Evidently the report was compiled by a small coalition of rivals who had failed to secure federal appointments or had lost scientific positions, together with people representing vested interests in mining, land speculation, water-rights speculation, and similar exploitation.

An audit by the Treasury Department proved he had been both honest and skillful in his disbursements. His appropriation was increased rather than reduced, and in 1888 he was at last authorized to inaugurate an irrigation survey, beginning in New Mexico, Colorado, Nevada, and Montana. He certified reservoir and dam sites, to be reserved by the government in order to prevent speculation by private irrigation contractors and land investors. Inevitably, however, land grabs were made, suits and countersuits initiated, jurisdictional disputes arose, and there were delicate problems concerning the damming of such rivers as the Rio Grande, since any diverted and stored waters had to be shared equitably with Mexican farmers. Moreover, there was strong opposition by economy-minded people who believed in the astonishing dictum that somehow, miraculously, "rain follows the plow." It was a period of increased rainfall, tending to support such a belief. In the summer of 1889, Powell accompanied the Senate's select committee on irrigation, making an inspection tour of arid lands. The party stopped at Bismark to attend North Dakota's constitutional convention, and Powell was asked to speak. In his somewhat weak but deliberate and self-assured voice, he delivered the speech that was probably his most famous. He told the delegates:

> There's almost enough rainfall for your purposes, but one year with another you need a little more than you get. . . . There are waters rolling by you which are quite ample . . . and you must save these waters. . . .
>
> You are to depend hereafter in a great measure on the running streams—in a small part on your artesian wells, and in part on the storage of storm waters.

Don't let these streams get out of the possession of the people.
. . . Fix it in your constitution that no corporation—no body of
men—no capital can get possession of the right of your waters.
Hold the waters in the hands of the people.

Yet opposition mounted, and emotion often overwhelmed reason on both sides. Some critics accused Powell of proposing to
dam the Grand Canyon—and indeed, he had done so! Congress,
becoming impatient for the completion of the survey and an immediate panacea for the 1890 drought—the worst in history—
became strongly critical of Powell, although the drought was
merely one of his predictions come true. Interim measures were
tried, a few dams were built, and Powell attempted to explain his
views in papers that coined such words as *runoff*. Then it was discovered that, in his ambitious desire to map three million square
miles of America, he had diverted some irrigation-survey funds
for cartography. Although he was in charge of his own disbursements, his right to do this was questionable. In 1892, Congress
curtailed the budgets of all research agencies, and his appropriation was reduced. Moreover, it was allocated for specific pur-
poses so that he could no longer control disbursements.

In 1893, the appropriation was raised slightly, but Powell had
already decided to retire and had chosen as his successor Charles
D. Walcott, an old friend and employee who had done excellent
work in the canyon country.

Powell was beginning to feel old, and his arm had once again
become hypersensitive and throbbingly painful. In the spring of
1894, after submitting his letter of resignation, he entered Johns
Hopkins Hospital for corrective surgery. Instead of amputating
still more of the arm, the surgeons removed the regenerating
nerves, and at last Powell was relieved of his recurring torture.
While recuperating, he revised the report on the canyon exploration, replaced many of the old woodcut illustrations with photographs, and had it published by Chautauqua Press as *Canyons
of the Colorado*.

Then, in 1895, he wrote three geological essays for the first
volume of monographs published by the National Geographic
Society, which he and his brother Bram had helped to organize
in 1888. Unfortunately, his writing style had deteriorated with
age, and the three essays—intended as guides for teachers and
students—were excessively florid but not excessively informative.

In 1898, he made his last real geological contribution, a very short article for the *Journal of Geology* enumerating possible causes for movements of the earth's crust. This paper advanced the theory of isostasy, the main facet of which holds essentially that a general equilibrium in the earth's crust is maintained by a yielding or flow of rock material beneath the surface under gravitational stress. Though somewhat simplistic in its original form, it led to later, more complex and sophisticated principles and is still regarded as a major geological theory. Powell was not the first to formulate it, but evidently he had worked on some aspects of the hypothesis with G.K. Gilbert, who did formulate it. Unfortunately, when Powell mentioned the theory again in his last work, *Truth and Error*, he claimed credit for having first proposed it. He probably did so innocently, as his memory of past activities had become faulty.

For the last few years of his life, Powell summered on the coast of Maine, and there he pondered and worked on the plan of a trilogy that he apparently regarded as the summation of his life's learning. The first book, *Truth and Error*, was to be a survey of nature and man's knowledge of nature; the second, *Good and Evil*, was to be a review of man and his philosophy as the manifestation of nature's greatest achievement; the third, *Pleasure and Pain*, was to be a review of human activities, reasoning, and the ultimate power of a union between man and nature. He completed only the first book and a few random essays scheduled for revision and inclusion in the second and third.

Truth and Error, or The Science of Intellection is a peculiar blend of narrative, science, speculation, theorizing, and not very profound metaphysical philosophy. Powell denounced the metaphysical philosophers, yet he was obviously influenced by such thinkers as Kant, Spencer, Hegel, Comte, Hume, Adam Smith, Mill, and Milton! He consciously adopted some of their terms and unconsciously adopted some of their attitudes.

In the first chapter, "Chuar's Illusion," he begins with a personal narrative: "In the fall of 1880 I was encamped on the Kaibab plateau. . . ." And then he launches into an exposition demonstrating that his Indian friend Chuar, being a product of a savage culture and therefore childlike, misunderstands the operation of such natural forces as gravity. Later he postulates a strange blend of biological evolution and teleology, the teleological aspects of which are in strong opposition to Darwinian theory. He mixes scientific doctrines with philosophy until the reader becomes aware that this is a valiant but confused, somewhat puerile and mechanistic attempt to compose a philosophy of science.

Friends tried to dissuade him from publishing the book. He published it, nevertheless, in 1898, and dedicated it to a colleague, Lester Ward, a paleobotanist, ethnologist, and sociologist. Almost every review of the book, including Ward's, was scathing. Powell published rejoinders, but seemed less distressed than might have been expected. Probably he felt that posterity would vindicate his efforts.

Although he was growing infirm, he spent part of the winter of 1900–1901 with a member of his Bureau of Ethnology staff, William H. Holmes, on a short expedition to Cuba and Jamaica to study the Carib and Arawak Indians. The exertions of the trip left him ill and exhausted. A rest at his summer cottage in Maine failed to revive him. In November, he suffered a stroke. In January, he seemed to have recovered, though he needed assistance to walk. In May, the Powells left Washington again for Maine; he did not expect to return from the summer cottage.

After suffering severe chest pains on June 24, he deteriorated progressively. He knew he was dying, a prospect he faced with utter calm though he had long ago rebelled against his father's Methodism and had come to believe only in a doctrine of humanism and scientific rationalism much like that of his contemporary, Robert Ingersoll. There were lines in *Truth and Error* that could be construed as atheism, and Powell retained the courage of his convictions while awaiting the end. On September 17, 1902, he fell into a coma, and on September 23, he died without having regained consciousness.

Several years previously, he had discussed the possible relationship of brain size and intelligence during a conversation with one of his subordinates, W J McGee (who spelled his name without periods after the initials and who, eccentricities notwithstanding, was characterized by Gifford Pinchot as "the scientific brains of the Conservation Movement"). Powell had wagered that his brain was larger than McGee's, though McGee was a bigger man whose hat size was probably larger than Powell's. Arrangements were made for their brains to be removed upon death and placed in preserving fluid. Each man bequeathed his brain to the other. The survivor was to arrange for both brains to be examined by a noted brain specialist, Dr. Edward Spitzka, who had aroused the interest of anthropologists by examining the brains of unusual people. In due course, Powell's brain was delivered to McGee, who then asked Gifford Pinchot to convey both brains to Spitzka after McGee's death.

W J McGee died in 1912, and Pinchot carried out his trust. Dr. Spitzka carefully measured both brains. Major Powell's was the larger. The doctor then reported (with a certainty that would have amused later, more sophisticated brain specialists) that "Major Powell was endowed with a superior brain." It is now known that small differences in the size of normal human brains are not correlated to intelligence, but regarding Powell's brain, Dr. Spitzka made a final remark that cannot be argued: "He used it well."

Another assessment, by the historian Robert V. Hine, is perhaps more germane. In *The American West, An Interpretive History*, he calls Powell "more than a naturalist and institutionalizer," for Major Powell lived during a period of "massive attack by private interests on the resources of the West. The first serious challengers to the superabundance illusion were scientists with a high moral passion. John Wesley Powell, the best example . . . said that men and laws must be closely related to the environment from which they emerge."

Chapter 8
JOHN BURROUGHS
AND THE LITERARY
PUBLICISTS

"The most precious things of life are near at hand," John Burroughs said, "without money and without price." If so simple a declaration was hardly to be called philosophy, neither could it be dismissed as platitude, founded as it was on minutely detailed observation of nature's tapestry. It was the affirmation of an old man, expressed only a year before his death and included in his preface to an appreciative biography, *John Burroughs, Boy and Man*, written by his literary secretary, Dr. Clara Barrus. Reflecting on his own perpetual mood of wonder at nature's bounty, "Each of you," he continued, "has the whole wealth of the universe at your very door. All that I ever had, and still have, may be yours by stretching forth your hand and taking it."

By his own definition he was not a "scientific naturalist"—one who enlarges the body of known facts by indefatigable researches into minutiae; instead, and at times almost apologetically, he described himself as a "nature essayist" whose interest (and appeal to his readers) was primarily aesthetic, artistic. In 1919, a year before the Barrus biography appeared, he published a volume entitled *Field and Study* in which an essay on "The Pleasures of Science" explained his approach to field investigations:

200

My science is an unprofessional as my religion. I tarry under the trees, muse by the streams, and commune with my own soul through the living and non-living forms that surround me. Science only seasons my observations. If I do carry home a flower, it is for its beauty, or its association; if I gather a zoölogical specimen, it is because it has more than a zoölogical interest. Exact knowledge is good, but vital knowledge is better; details are indispensable to the specialist, but a knowledge of relations and of wholes satisfies me more.

All the facts of natural science that throw light upon the methods and the spirit of nature are doubly welcome. I can assimilate them. I can appreciate their ideal values. I can link them up with my intellectual and emotional experiences. . . . The ground underfoot becomes a history, the stars overhead a revelation, the play of the invisible and unsuspected forces about me and through me a new kind of gospel.

Yet I seem to approach nature through my understanding and desire for knowledge more than through any ethical or purely poetical craving. There is little of the moralist or preacher in me, but a good deal of the philosopher and investigator. I want to know the reason of things, and the relations of things, their intellectual rather than their moral values. I do not want the precise figures of the astronomer, nor the detailed proofs of the geologist, nor the formulae of the chemist, nor the data of the zoölogist; what I want is light upon the whole of Nature—her methods, her laws, her results, her non-human ways. What I get out of botany would hardly be available for the classroom; what I get out of biology would not go into a textbook. I love geology because it tells me much of the past of my own landscape . . . it is like the story of one's own family written large in the valleys and on the mountains.

Burroughs was instrumental in establishing a tradition of contemplative nature writing that has been illuminated by such chroniclers of American field studies as William Hornaday, George Bird Grinnell, Aldo Leopold, William Beebe, Adolph Murie, Rachel Carson, Paul Errington, Joseph Wood Krutch, John Kieran, Stephen Jay Gould, and many more. He added little to the store of scientific fact—no original geological researches as did Agassiz and Powell; no accumulation of data in ornithology (his earliest and deepest interest) or mammalogy as did Elliott Coues; no explorations of glacial phenomena as did Agassiz and John Muir. He was a successful fruit farmer—a horticulturist like Muir and Luther Burbank—but he devised no significant experiments, unraveled no botanical knots of mystery. He had more in common with Muir than with Coues or Burbank, for he was less a discoverer than a proselytizer in behalf of the study and love of natural history. (To Muir, however, whose scientific aspect was as unprofessionally, mystically religious as that of Burroughs, writing was a burden undertaken for the sake of a cause; he was more of a mountaineer than a geologist, more of a preservationist than a botanist, more of a political missionary than a writer of natural history, and he is more accurately classified as a pioneer of conservation than of nature study.)

By the time these contemporaries were at work, the foundations of natural science in America had been built. Burroughs lived during the twilight of true—often primitive—pioneering among naturalists. Yet he was the most influential of pioneers in another sense. As the foremost literary publicist among all of America's naturalists, he kindled public (and, indirectly, professional and governmental) interest in the study of nature. The writer and cultural impresario Elbert Hubbard declared at the turn of the century—fifteen years before Hubbard and a number of fellow passengers aboard the *Lusitania* died in the onslaught of submarine technology—that Burroughs did more than any man to inaugurate a "Nature Renaissance." The conservation historian John F. Reiger has averred that "Burroughs did more than any other individual to establish the American 'nature essay' as a literary *genre*."

The assertion will puzzle a generation that has rarely encountered Burroughs except in an underbrush of college-text footnotes but has waded the long miles through Thoreau's little pond at Walden. The fact is that Thoreau had an exceedingly limited audience, hence negligible effect, during his lifetime and for many years afterward, whereas Burroughs became one of the country's most widely read living authors, a "required subject" in many secondary schools and colleges. In an article appearing in *The Nation* on January 27, 1876, Henry James, Jr., called him "a sort of reduced, but also more humorous, more available, and more sociable Thoreau."

Thoreau was a philosopher who happened to be a nature-lover; Burroughs was a naturalist-philosopher, a significant distinction in the present context. Burroughs was influenced by Thoreau's philosophy but justifiably considered most of his accounts of nature to be superficial. Thoreau, like Emerson, was to be read for his abstract thought and his use of language, not for his insights into the ways and things of nature. A stronger influence on Burroughs was his friend and literary idol Walt Whitman, whose poetry and earthy grasp of the American scene more closely approached his own view of Nature—and Man as a part of Nature. Earthiness, or simplicity, gave Burroughs a kind of metaphysical strength in his descriptions of natural phenomena.

His background, if hardly auspicious for a man of letters, was sufficiently earthy for any naturalist. Born on a homestead near Roxbury in New York's Catskills on April 3, 1837, he was the son of Chauncey A. and Amy Kelly Burroughs, the seventh of their ten children and the only one with scholarly aspirations. His brothers and sisters could barely read and write. His ancestors had been drawing a living from the soil of the region for several generations; the farm was largely self-sustaining, and the world of the Burroughs men was limited by its horizons. Chauncey Burroughs read his Bible, an occasional newspaper, and little else. In later years, he did not trouble to read the writings of his famous son; he seemed to regard John as a source of pride and puzzlement in about equal measure. Amy Burroughs was puzzled, too, but she had a more pensive mind and she encouraged her son's early hunger for learning, even persuading her husband to buy books for him. When the boy was five, she wove a white-striped cotton suit for him and sent him off to the little stone schoolhouse about a mile from the farm.

After he reached the age of twelve, however, he was permitted to attend school only during winter months when he was not needed to help with the haying, the pasturing and milking of cattle, the building of stone fences, the dipping of candle wicks in melted beef fat, the churning of butter, and dozens of other chores. Butter, the family's principal source of income, gave him his initial glimpse of a larger world—a memorable first sight of the Hudson River, complete with a steamboat—when he was allowed to drive a wagonload of butter (a ton of it, more than three-hundred dollars' worth) fifty miles to the town of Catskill.

Burroughs told his biographer, Clara Barrus, that he thought his intense interest in nature had probably first been awakened on a Sunday in May when he was seven or eight years old. Hunting for wintergreen with his brothers, he sprawled on the ground to rest and gazed up into the branches of the trees. Flitting overhead was an unfamiliar bird, a small bluish songbird with a white spot on each wing. Though his brothers neither knew nor cared what it was, the sight aroused a strange tingle of emotion in him; it seemed to him he was watching a mysterious visitor from some distant land. He remembered the bird so clearly that almost twenty years later, when he gained access to the works of Audubon, he recognized the black-throated blue warbler (*Dendroica caerulescens*) as the species that had beckoned him to his life's work.

He recalled other incidents that had deepened his early interest. Once, armed with a musket, he waited on a hillside to intercept a fox being pursued by hounds. The fox came close, then paused to look back at the dogs. The boy was so fascinated by it that he forgot to shoot, and afterward he offered the embarrassed excuse that he had been encumbered by his mittens. On another occasion a flock of passenger pigeons lit in the beech woods adjoining his home. This time, too, he neglected to shoot as he became entranced by the actions of the birds foraging for beechnuts. "From childhood," he wrote, "I was familiar with the homely facts of the barn, and of cattle and horses; the sugar-making in the maple woods in early spring, the work of the corn-field, hay-field and potato-field; the delicious fall months, with their pigeon and squirrel shooting, threshing of buckwheat, gathering of apples and burning of fallows; in short, everything that smacked of, and led to, the open air and its exhilarations."

Like Alexander Wilson, John Wesley Powell, and a number of other naturalists, he began earning his livelihood as a country schoolteacher. It was at Tongore, New York, where he conducted his first classes in 1854, that he met his future wife, Ursula North. He married her in 1857. "Sulie" North Burroughs was not an ideal marital partner for a writer, or for a naturalist who delighted in cluttering his home with specimens. She had so little conception of his work's importance that she was to advise him years later, when he had achieved a measure of success, to find a different trade, one that would bring more money and less mess. She was to become suspicious and jealous when he became a celebrity, constantly surrounded by visitors who often included charming, sophisticated women and pretty young girls. Literally obsessed with the neatness and cleanliness of her home, she objected when papers were strewn about his desk and she denied him the use of a room in which he had planned to do his writing. Eventually he would build a separate cabin for himself, to be used as study, guest house, and retreat where he could escape the squabbles and dreariness of his home.

In fairness to Ursula Burroughs, it nust be said that her husband had his own obsession—his obsession with nature and writing—which often led to thoughtlessness and self-absorption. His ego, though tempered by gentleness, humor, and ironic self-awareness, was evidently of a size proportionate to his achievement.

While employed at Tongore, Burroughs attended the Hedding Literary Institute at Ashland and then spent three months at Cooperstown Seminary—the culmination of his formal schooling. After Tongore, he taught for a short time at High Falls, New York. Yearning to see more of the country and to earn a better livelihood, he also taught school briefly in New Jersey and Illinois. But it was in his native state, while teaching near West Point, that he began to form a vague idea of what his true career might be if he could escape the impoverished life of a rural schoolmaster. Here he first met Ralph Waldo Emerson, whose work he had begun to read at Cooperstown, and Emerson encouraged his study of literature. Here, too, in 1863 at the library of the Military Academy at West Point, he found Audubon's works—including the painting of the black-throated blue warbler that had thrilled him two decades before. Though still uncertain of the precise course his labors would take, he evidently saw that they would have to encompass both writing and the study of nature.

He also saw that he would have to find some interim employment by which to support himself and his wife. He had begun to write literary and intellectual essays; in 1860 several were published in the New York *Saturday Press* and one appeared in the *Atlantic Monthly*, and the following year his first nature essays, columns under the heading "From the Back Country," were printed in the New York *Leader*. They were well received but brought very little money.

For several months in 1862 he studied medicine with a physician at Tongore. Doctoring was not for him, but the experience gave him some knowledge of biology and made him a better observer and analyzer of animal and plant life; it affected his way of seeing things and was reflected in his occasional use of medical terms like *stomachic*.

It was also during this period that he began a forty-year friendship and correspondence with Myron Benton, a popular poet who was also a successful farmer, enjoying the kind of life Burroughs wanted for himself. Benton, a Transcendentalist and an admirer of Thoreau and Emerson, must have brightened the outlook of his young friend whose prospects appeared so dubious. Burroughs, though somewhat despondent over his poverty, felt a mystical optimism which he expressed in a poem written at this time. Entitled "Waiting," it became the most popular of his many verses. It was also one of his best, though by no means an example of great poetry. Burroughs, the master essayist and virtuoso of natural descriptions in prose, was a mediocre poet. The importance of "Waiting" lies in what it tells of John Burroughs at the beginning of his career:

> Serene, I fold my hands and wait,
>   Nor care for wind, nor tide, nor sea;
> I rave no more 'gainst time or fate,
>   For lo! my own shall come to me. . . .
>
> What matter if I stand alone?
>   I wait with joy the coming years;
> My heart shall reap where it hath sown,
>   And garner up its fruit of tears. . . .

Burroughs did not always realize that he was writing prose-poetry when he wove some of his finest images and rhythms into the fabric of thought in his better works, his essays: "Time, geologic time, looks out at us from the rocks as from no other objects in the landscape. Geologic time! How the striking of the great clock, whose hours are millions of years, reverberates out of the abyss of the past! Mountains fall and the foundations of the earth shift as it beats out the moments of terrestrial history. Rocks have literally come down to us from a foreworld. The youth of the earth is in the soil and in the trees and verdure that spring from it; its age is in the rocks; in the great stone book of the geologic strata its history is written."

Perhaps he was equally unaware that some of his finest work rested as mere jottings in his journals, observations to be incorporated into essays, notes for future poems rather than finished stanzas, as in the free-verse "Notes for an April Poem" that were to be scrawled on journal pages in 1894:

> The soft maples are crimson and the buds of the
> elm swarm like bees in its branches.
> The bee comes home with golden thighs from the
> willows, and honey in her bag from the arbutus.
> School-children pass with their hands full of hepaticas
> and arbutus.
> The newly-ploughed fields glow like the breasts
> of robins.
> I walk in the new furrow in the strong sunlight
> till it is photographed upon my spirit. . . .

Those lines were obviously and deeply influenced by the writing of Walt Whitman, a close friend and literary exemplar ever since their first meeting in Washington, D.C., in 1863. Burroughs came there—almost penniless after his family refused to lend him money for the trip—partly to learn at first hand about wartime activities and perhaps find government employment, and partly to meet Whitman, whose poems he had been reading since 1859 or 1860. A mutual friend, E. M. Allen, introduced the two writers and they quickly became comrades. Whitman accompanied Burroughs on tramps through the woods and took him along on some of his visits among wounded soldiers in the hospitals near the capital.

Allen found temporary work for Burroughs in the Quartermaster General's Department. Some months later Burroughs became a clerk in the Currency Bureau of the Treasury Department, with the primary duty of guarding a steel vault holding millions in bank notes. Each day he sat at a desk before the vault, with little to do but read and write. Having set up housekeeping in Washington with Ursula, he accelerated his study of natural history, raised a vegetable garden where the Senate Office Building now stands, and carried a little cane-gun with which to shoot an occasional bird for use as a specimen.

During the next couple of years, he and Whitman had many long discussions regarding natural science, philosophy, and literature. The *Atlantic Monthly* for May, 1865, carried an essay entitled "In the Hemlocks," in which Burroughs described "the finest sound in nature—the song of the hermit thrush . . . rising pure and serene, as if a spirit from some remote height were slowly chanting a divine accompaniment." A few months later he wrote to Myron Benton that Whitman was "deeply interested in what I tell him of the Hermit Thrush, and says he has used largely the information I have given him in one of his principal poems."

Perry Westbrook's perceptive critical biography *John Burroughs* points out that the hermit thrush and its song were thus introduced into the peom "When Lilacs Last in the Dooryard Bloom'd"—as a major symbol "and as the occasion for the finest lyric passage Whitman ever wrote." Whitman's thrush and the spiritual solace and serenity it symbolizes have a clear resemblance to the impressions described in the Burroughs essay.

Soon afterward, Burroughs wrote an article about Whitman—rejected by the *Atlantic* but published in *Galaxy*—and then he began work on a book devoted to the subject. Published in 1867, *Notes on Walt Whitman as Poet and Person* was his first book and a worthwhile contribution to literary criticism. An enlarged edition appeared four years later; it was followed by some fifty articles on Whitman and, in 1896, by another volume, *Whitman: A Study.*

The public never came to regard Burroughs primarily as a literary critic, despite such additional volumes as *Birds and Poets* in 1877, *Indoor Studies* in 1889, and *Literary Values* in 1902, but his views in this area were respected. There is no doubt that Burroughs had a vital role in gaining recognition for Whitman as a major American writer. In fact, as Westbrook remarks, "his influence was incalculable in establishing the controversial poet's reputation."

While so engaged (and amid such interruptions as a mission to England in 1871 for the transfer of bank notes—a trip during which he met another writer he admired, Thomas Carlyle) Burroughs continued to observe and write about flora and fauna. In 1871, he published *Wake-Robin*, his first volume of nature essays. The title, suggested by Whitman, is a popular name for *Trillium grandiflorum*, the white trillium that flowers in early spring as if to signal the return of the birds. In the introduction, Burroughs called the book "an invitation to the study of Ornithology." It has achieved the rank of a minor classic, often compared to Gilbert White's *The Natural History of Selborne*. This volume and his ensuing books and articles made Burroughs America's best-known ornithologist. He was not the country's most scientific ornithologist—nor was that his aim—but neither did he let his inherent optimism inject cheap sentiment or unwarranted anthropomorphism into his reportage of field investigations.

At a time when some writers were romanticizing nature to the point of imbuing wildlife with a penchant for practical jokes and moral judgments, he observed and recorded animal behavior as it actually occurred. "The Return of the Birds," the first essay in *Wake-Robin*, contained a chilling account of a blacksnake's assault on a catbird nest:

> Three or four yards from me was the nest, beneath which, in long festoons, rested a huge black snake; a bird two thirds grown was slowly disappearing between his expanded jaws. As he seemed unconscious of my presence, I quietly observed the proceedings. By slow degrees he compassed the bird about with his elastic mouth; his head flattened, his neck writhed and swelled, and two or three undulatory movements of his glistening body finished the work. . . . I could but admire his terrible beauty.

But nature's amorality was a concept unacceptable to nineteenth-century America. Even for an American like Burroughs, with his scientific and metaphysical acceptance of nature's ways, truly objective observation of animal behavior sometimes proved almost impossible. Moments after admiring the snake's "terrible beauty," he was so revolted by the scene that he could not let nature take its course; he picked up a stone and knocked the reptile from the nest to the ground. Still, in his insistence on detail and accuracy rather than preaching and romance, he was closer to the spirit of modern behavioral investigators—a Konrad Lorenz or a George Schaller—than to the nature writers of his own time. In the spring of 1903, he was to create a furor by writing for the *Atlantic* an article on "Real and Sham Natural History." Apparently having lost his usually mild temper, he scathingly attacked the type of nature writing, at that time very popular, in which the romantic humanizing of animals was presented as fact proven by scientific inquiry.

He himself could liken animal actions and even emotions to those of humans, but his comparisons were supportable by field observations. And he had no quarrel with fantasy presented as such. What enraged him was the kind of mawkish tale, offered to the public as factual reporting, in which a fox lured a pursuing hound onto a railroad trestle just in time for the dog to be hit by a train; or in which a beast committed suicide or poisoned its young to stave off captivity; or in which a bird fashioned a cast of mud over a cracked egg. Concerning the story of the fox and the hound—a perpetration of Ernest Thompson Seton—Burroughs suggested that the fox must have been equipped with a railroad timetable. His attack particularly singled out Seton and the Reverend William J. Long, noting that Seton's *Wild Animals I Have Known* could more appropriately have been called *Wild Animals I Alone Have Known,* and that the birds described in Long's *School in the Woods* merited diplomas.

President Theodore Roosevelt read the *Atlantic* article and sent Burroughs a letter of support and congratulation. Roosevelt was annoyed that the popularization of scientific studies should be adulterated, thus perpetuating misconceptions among most laymen, and he was especially angry over the fact that schoolchildren were reading fictitious accounts which could undermine the value of the Burroughs essays then being used as natural-history texts. It was Roosevelt who coined the term "nature fakers" for the purveyors of ersatz natural history. (Several commentators subsequently adopted another version of the term—"nature fakirs"—feeling perhaps that a *double entendre* would be doubly scathing.)

At first, Roosevelt refrained from entering the controversy publicly, and the charges and rebuttals among nature writers continued for several years. But in 1907, he permitted *Everybody's Magazine* to print an interview in which he sharply expressed his opinion, and shortly afterward the same magazine published the views of a panel of professional naturalists who supported the Burroughs-Roosevelt contention. With the opposition crushed, there ensued an almost Lutheran reformation (though a far from total or permanent one) in the popularization of scientific inquiry in the United States.

Roosevelt himself was a very competent field naturalist, and he and Burroughs genuinely liked and admired each other. Their association also had the mutual benefit of favorable publicity. Though the President's hunting exploits had made him a hero to many, there were many others who attacked him for killing animals. Some of the critics were respected and influential; indeed, a few were fellow-conservationists who were otherwise well-informed but could not accept man's participation in the natural environment as a predatory species. A revealing anecdote concerns John Muir's advice to the President regarding his sport—a succinct suggestion that he ought to "grow up." Burroughs, on the other hand, defended the President persuasively in reply to a woman's suggestion that Roosevelt, being a big-game hunter, could not share his love for the larger animals. Burroughs said that Roosevelt must love them more, because "his love is founded upon knowledge, and because they [big-game animals] had been a part of his life." So effective had Burroughs been in awakening a national interest in natural history that once, while he was traveling with Roosevelt, Burroughs received the more enthusiastic cheers from welcoming crowds at waystops.

Ornithologists, in particular, were influenced by his meticulous field observations, and they made pilgrimages to his home. One such eminent naturalist was Frank M. Chapman, who came to see Burroughs in 1896 and recorded the visit in his *Camps and Cruises of an Ornithologist*. In *Wake-Robin* and in subsequent writings, Burroughs had plumbed a new depth of field reporting by his simple emphasis on accurate detail regarding animal behavior. This is not to imply that previous naturalists had not made similar attempts. Many had—from the Bartrams to Audubon. But Burroughs did it better. His work was the popular counterpart (and to a certain degree the inspiration) of more scientific contemporary researchers like Spencer F. Baird and Elliott Coues.

On one occasion, he timed the repeated trips of a chipmunk as it transferred grain to a new den from an old one that had been disturbed, and carefully noted an average of ten minutes per trip. Curious about the amount of food stored by this species, he watched another chipmunk for three days, making estimates of the loads the little animal could hold in its cheek pouches, and finally arriving at a calculation of one whole bushel of chestnuts, hickory nuts, and corn kernels in the three-day period. On another occasion—June 3, 1905—he logged one of his experiments in the timing of bird songs: "My little field sparrow sings five times a minute. I timed him at 8 and 11 A.M. on different days; and he has sung since April! He does not sing much in afternoon. He probably sings 300 times an hour, for seven or eight hours, or 2,000 times each forenoon. As yet he shows no hoarseness in his song." Once, mustering greater detachment than usual, he conducted a surprisingly cold-blooded experiment for the sake of observing a predator-prey relationship; he released a "gigety"—a red squirrel—in a currant patch to see if it could elude his dog. Fortunately, it did.

His descriptions of flora were based on similarly careful and detailed observation. In *Signs and Seasons*, published in 1886, he reported that after the very severe winter of 1880–1881 the fragrance of hepaticas was sweeter than usual and there were more white ones; he had found that white hepaticas tend to smell sweeter than those of other colors, but elsewhere he cautioned that color is an unreliable key to fragrance. Counseling against dogmatic assumptions about nature, he remarked in the same book that for more than twenty years he had failed to find honeybees visiting the blossoms of trailing arbutus and had therefore concluded that they did not use the nectar of those flowers. Then one April day he found the conclusion to be premature, for he observed a swarm of honeybees crawling under leaves and moss to get at arbutus blossoms.

The praise of literary critics, acceptance by the scientific community, and a growing affection among the reading public did not quickly reward Burroughs with a comfortable income. He might have had to abandon nature study and writing had he not received a government appointment as a bank examiner in 1873. He was good at the work. He had no special love for it, but the occupation permitted him to settle in the Catskills, within a day's journey of his boyhood home, to travel occasionally, and to have sufficient leisure for continued scientific and literary pursuits. He retained the position until 1886, shortly after the publication of *Signs and Seasons*.

Upon becoming a bank examiner, he purchased a small fruit farm at West Park, near Esopus, overlooking the western banks of the Hudson almost opposite Hyde Park. There he raised grapes (his chief and most profitable crop), apples, pears, berries, and (in later years) celery. In 1874, he completed the building of a stone house, which he named Riverby, and moved in with his wife. Burroughs was not a practical designer and builder like the elder Bartram (or, for that matter, like Julian Burroughs, the son his wife bore in 1878 after she and John Burroughs had almost despaired of ever having a child). Riverby had a badly located cistern, too little light, rooms that were too small and others that were too cold, a fireplace that looked quaint but drew poorly, and a lack of fire-stops in the walls. The original building was gutted by fire in 1947, killing the mother-in-law of his granddaughter.

The house was spiritually as well as physically depressing, for Burroughs could not work well in the spotless, cold formality created and insistently maintained by his wife Ursula. His second nature book, *Winter Sunshine*, appeared in 1875; it had been nearly completed in Washington and Burroughs once commented that if there had been any winter sunshine in Riverby he might have been too contented ever to produce another book. Ursula Burroughs lived until 1917, four years before his own death, and he never seemed to lose his love for her, but the friction between them is well documented and there is little doubt that he sought escape for progressively longer, more frequent periods—fishing, hunting, camping alone or with friends and later with his son, traveling, honey-gathering, or merely tramping the local woods to contemplate the flora and fauna.

The years at Riverby brought fame and grief. His parents died; his brothers and sisters, one by one, all died during his lifetime; Walt Whitman's death in 1892 was a crushing blow, and Whitman was but one of a number of old friends who passed from the scene; even a succession of beloved dogs died unexpectedly—victims of accidents, attacks by other dogs, and once a malicious poisoning by neighborhood boys. Sometimes when sorrow came, Burroughs was unable to study or write, and sometimes he reacted by immersing himself in work.

Winter Sunshine contained nature studies and an account of his European visit of 1871. It also contained descriptions of freedmen around Washington. Burroughs had little in common with John Wesley Powell, and no claim can be made for him as an anthropologist or ethnologist, but his approach to the black man was an admirable blend of the scientific and humanitarian. Perry Westbrook points out that "Burroughs' main interest, whether he is discussing a southern Negro or an Englishman, is in a human being's relationship to the soil, to the climate, and to the resources of his environment. . . . Burroughs' attitude is certainly less condescending than that of most writers of his day who claimed to be well-disposed toward the Negro—Whitman, for example."

This second nature book was followed by *Birds and Poets,* then *Locusts and Wild Honey,* and, in 1881, *Prepacton.* Much of the material in that book was the fruit of a short exploratory voyage along the Prepacton—the upper reaches of the Delaware's East Branch—which probably had never before been explored by a white man in a boat. Characteristically, Burroughs made part of the trip in the company of two small boys who abandoned their makeshift raft to go with him. Six years later, in 1887, a Chicago schoolteacher named Mary E. Burt persuaded the Board of Education to purchase three dozen copies of *Prepacton* for her sixth-grade reading classes. Some of the words and concepts had to be explained to the children, but the book delighted them. So successful was this imaginative experiment that Houghton, Mifflin & Company, which had published most of the Burroughs works, engaged Miss Burt to edit texts by Burroughs for classroom use. She did so with a light, tactful, and successful hand. Nature study—often mingling science and English lessons—blossomed in schools all over the country. The most popular texts were slender editions of Burroughs, which were published for the purpose at intervals until 1923.

The year *Prepacton* was published, Burroughs built himself a small cabin—a study and retreat—on a wooded hill east of his home, and near it he then had a summerhouse erected. The venture was a precursor of Slabsides, a retreat and guesthouse he built in 1894 and 1895 in a nearby swamp clearing. The Slabsides chimney was rough stone, the outer walls a medley of textures and tones produced by slabs of hemlock, birch, and chestnut. Burroughs had learned much from the Riverby experience about designing a home to fit its natural environment. In 1908, he refurbished a house on the ancestral farmlands at Roxbury as a summer home and named it Woodchuck Lodge. He was even happier there—or perhaps more comfortable in the woods of his boyhood—than at Slabsides, but it was Slabsides that became an amateur naturalists' mecca and most popular literary shrine of its era.

The aging Burroughs—white-bearded, balding but haloed with snowy hair, bespectacled, gently twinkling—looked rather like a slimmed Saint Nicholas. Long before he died he was being called the Seer of Slabsides. Discomfited by the throngs who visited him, he had no wish for the oracle's pose but he had involuntarily become the philosopher of naturalists, the guru of nature lovers.

Burroughs Societies were formed in many parts of the country for the promotion of nature study and conservation. Shortly after his death, the John Burroughs Memorial Association was established and headquartered at the American Museum of Natural History in New York City. Its activities focus chiefly on conservation. The Association awards a John Burroughs Medal annually (but withholds it if there is no worthy recipient) to the author of a distinguished piece of nature writing. There is a kind of poetic and natural irony in the fact that Ernest Thompson Seton, having contributed some of his better work in the years after he was ridiculed by Burroughs, was among the earliest writers to receive the medal. Other recipients have included William Beebe, Rachel Carson, Joseph Wood Krutch, and John Kieran.

After *Prepacton* came *Fresh Fields, Signs and Seasons, Indoor Studies, Riverby, Whitman: A Study, The Light of Day* (a theological and philosophical work), *Literary Values, John James Audubon, Far and Near, Ways of Nature, Bird and Bough* (his only book of verse), *Camping and Tramping with Roosevelt, Leaf and Tendril, Time and Change, The Summit of the Years, The Breath of Life, Under the Apple-Trees, Field and Study*, and *Accepting the Universe*. Two final volumes, *Under the Maples* and *The Last Harvest*, were nearly completed before his death. They appeared posthumously, edited by his literary executor Clara Barrus.

Dr. Barrus had been a resident psychiatrist at Middletown State Hospital until she gave up her practice to devote her life to Burroughs as his typist, secretary, and companion. At first, of course, Ursula Burroughs was suspicious of her motives, but Dr. Barrus eventually won the confidence of all the Burroughs household through diplomacy, tact, and obvious devotion. On one occasion, in fact, Mrs. Burroughs refused to join her husband on a visit to the West Coast unless Dr. Barrus would agree to meet them there.

Clara Barrus had come to Slabsides in 1901 to see the man whose nature writings she most admired. Soon she was typing his book on Audubon, and eventually she became part of the Burroughs household. Her first books about him, *Our Friend John Burroughs* (1914) and *John Burroughs, Boy and Man* (1920) suffer somewhat from their author's uncritical adulation. But her two-volume work, *The Life and Letters of John Burroughs*, published in 1925, remains the most comprehensive account of the naturalist's life. Her final contribution, *Whitman and Burroughs, Comrades*, appeared in 1931 and provided more letters, previously unpublished bits of manuscript, and a detailed account of the friendship between Whitman and Burroughs.

Eventually the unassuming and somewhat reclusive Seer of Slabsides revisited Europe and traveled to Canada, Hawaii, the Caribbean, and with John Muir to Alaska on one occasion, to the Grand Canyon and the Yosemite on another. He camped and tramped not only with Roosevelt but with Henry Ford, Thomas A. Edison, and Harvey Firestone. He came to know Grover Cleveland, William Howard Taft, Woodrow Wilson, and Herbert Hoover.

Although he enjoyed his rank as an international celebrity, he probably would have preferred to read about it in the intellectual press instead of experiencing it, for he was a reserved, unpretentious man. He shared John Muir's concern for the preservation of wilderness and conservation of wildlife, but he could not bring himself, as Powell and Muir did, to lobby and politick for reform. Only once did he labor as an activist, in behalf of the Weeks-McLean Act of 1913 (which assigned responsibility for migratory game birds to the federal government, thereby providing a basis for regulatory legislation to protect waterfowl and shorebirds). In support of the bill, he lobbied in Washington and signed four hundred and fifty letters.

He never again involved himself in such direct propagandizing, but indirectly—as the foremost literary publicist for the study of natural history—his reverent attitude toward the unspoiled natural world made him a singularly influential champion of reform. He had been recognized as an able biologist for decades, and in his later years as a competent geologist, and he was an internationally acknowledged expert on birdsong and bird habits; with such credentials, he had only to express his views in order to influence public opinion regarding the need to study nature and protect it. Even on such controversial subjects as Darwinian evolution—a theory Burroughs was quick to accept—he helped to influence both scientific and public opinion.

In 1921, after wintering in California, he boarded a railroad train for a last long journey home. He was almost eighty-four years old and in failing health. He did not expect to live long but he hoped to see the Catskills once again. Perhaps he dreamed of his native woods as he fell asleep for the last time, in Ohio on March 29, 1921. His last words were a question; he wanted to know how far he was from home. He had long ago said all the important things. In 1908, speaking both as scientist and visionary conservationist, he had issued a prophetic warning:

> One cannot but reflect what a sucked orange the earth will be in the course of a few more centuries. Our civilization is terribly expensive to all its natural resources; one hundred years of modern life doubtless exhausts its stores more than a millennium of the life of antiquity. Its coal and oil will be about used up, all its mineral wealth greatly depleted, the fertility of its soil will have been washed into the sea . . . its wild game will be nearly extinct, its primitive forests gone. . . .

And four years later, with the mingling of reasoned alarm and optimism that so often characterizes a scientific reformer, he had amended the prophecy:

> We can use our scientific knowledge to improve and beautify the earth, or . . . poison the air, corrupt the waters, blacken the face of the country, and harass our souls with loud and discordant noises . . . we can use it to mitigate or abolish all these things.

Selected Bibliography

ADAMS, ALEXANDER B.
—*Eternal Quest: The Story of the Great Naturalists.* New York: G. P. Putnam's Sons, 1969.
—*John James Audubon, A Biography.* New York: G. P. Putnam's Sons, 1966.
AGASSIZ, ELIZABETH CABOT (Cary)
—*Louis Agassiz, his Life and Correspondence.* 2 vols. Boston: Houghton Mifflin, 1885. (Also listed as coauthor; see *Agassiz, Louis.*)
AGASSIZ, G. R. (ed.)
—*Letters and Recollections of Alexander Agassiz; with a sketch of his life and work.* Boston: Houghton Mifflin, 1913.
AGASSIZ, LOUIS
—*Contributions to the Natural History of the United States of America.* 4 vols. Boston: Little, Brown & Co., 1857–1862.
—*An Essay on Classification.* London: Longman, Brown, Green, Longmans & Roberts, 1859. (This book is also available in a modern edition: *Essay on Classification*, edited by Edward Lurie. Cambridge: Belknap Press of Harvard University Press, 1962.)
—*Geological Sketches.* [first series]. Boston: Ticknor & Fields, 1866.
—*Geological Sketches* [second series]. Boston: Houghton Mifflin, 1886.
—*Methods of Study in Natural History.* Boston: Ticknor & Fields, 1863.
—*Studies of Glaciers, preceded by the Discourse of Neuchâtel.* (Translated and edited by Albert V. Carozzi.) New York: Hafner Publishing Co., 1967.
AGASSIZ, LOUIS and AGASSIZ, ELIZABETH CABOT (Cary)
—*A Journey in Brazil.* Boston: Ticknor & Fields, 1868.
AUDUBON, JOHN JAMES
—*The Birds of America; from original drawings by John James Audubon.* 4 vols. London: Havell, 1827–1838.
—*Delineations of American Scenery and Character.* (Essays from the first three volumes of *Ornithological Biography*, with an introduction by Francis Hobart Herrick.) New York: G. A. Baker & Co., 1926.

—*Ornithological Biography; or, An Account of the Habits of the Birds of the United States of America; accompanied by descriptions of the objects represented in the work entitled, "The Birds of America," and interspersed with delineations of American scenery and manners.* 5 vols. Edinburgh: A. Black, 1831–1839. (Also issued in 5 vols. by J. Dobson, Philadelphia, 1831–1839.)

AUDUBON, JOHN JAMES and BACHMAN, REV. JOHN

—*The Quadrupeds of North America* [smaller edition of *The Viviparous Quadrupeds*; see listing below]. 3 vols. New York: V. G. Audubon, 1851–1854.

—*The Viviparous Quadrupeds of North America.* 3 vols. New York: J. J. Audubon, 1845–1848.

AUDUBON, MARIA R.

—*Audubon and his Journals* (with zoological and other notes by Elliott Coues). New York: C. Scribner's Sons, 1897.

BARRUS, CLARA

—*John Burroughs, Boy and Man.* Garden City, N.Y.: Doubleday, Page & Co., 1920.

—*The Life and Letters of John Burroughs.* 2 vols. Boston: Houghton Mifflin, 1925. (This book is also available in a modern reprint of the original edition; New York: Russell & Russell, 1968.)

—*Our Friend John Burroughs.* Boston: Houghton Mifflin, 1914. (This book is also available in a modern reprint of the original edition; New York: Haskell House, 1970.)

—*Whitman and Burroughs, Comrades.* Boston: Houghton Mifflin, 1931. (This book is also available in a modern reprint of the original edition; Port Washington, N.Y.: Kennikat Press, 1968.)

BARRUS, CLARA (ed.)

—*The Heart of Burroughs's Journals.* (Reprinted from journal excerpts published before 1931, when Dr. Barrus died.) Port Washington, N.Y.: Kennikat Press, 1967.

BARTRAM, JOHN

—*Observations on the inhabitants, climate, soil, rivers, productions, animals, and other matters worthy of notice. Made by Mr. John Bartram, in his travels from Pensilvania to Onondago, Oswego and the Lake Ontario, in Canada. To which is annex'd, a curious account of the cataracts at Niagara. By Mr. Peter Kalm.* London: J. Whiston & B. White, 1751. (Also listed as coauthor; see *Stork, William.*)

BARTRAM, WILLIAM

—*Botanical and Zoological Drawings, 1756–1788.* (Reproduced from the Fotergill Album in the British Museum; edited, with an introduction and commentary, by Joseph Ewan.) Philadelphia: American Philosophical Society, 1968.

—*Travels through North and South Carolina, Georgia, East and West Florida, the Cherokee country, the extensive territories of the Muscogulges, or Creek confederacy, and the country of the Chactaws; Containing an account of the soil and natural productions of those regions, together with observations on the manners of the Indians. Embellished with copper-plates.* Philadelphia: James & Johnson, 1791.

—*Travels.* (Modern edition, edited, with commentary and an annotated index, by Francis Harper.) New Haven: Yale University Press, 1958.

—*The Travels of William Bartram* (Modern edition, edited, with notes, by Mark Van Doren and containing all 13 original illustrations plus facsimiles of original copyright, title page, and dedication—a paperback republication of the 1928 Macy-Masius edition.) New York: Dover Publications, 1955.

BONAPARTE, CHARLES LUCIEN JULES LAURENT, *prince de Canino.*
—*Observations on the nomenclature of Wilson's ornithology.* Philadelphia: A. Finley, 1826.

BURROUGHS, JOHN
—*Bird Courtship and Other Papers.* Boston: Houghton Mifflin Co., 1923.
—*The Birds of John Burroughs: Keeping a Sharp Lookout.* (Eleven essays reprinted from the Riverby Edition of *The Writings of John Burroughs.* Edited, with an introduction, by Jack Kligerman; foreword by Dean Amadon; drawings by Louis Agassiz Fuertes.) New York: Hawthorn Books, 1976.
—*Notes on Walt Whitman as Poet and Person.* New York: American News Co., 1867.
—*Wake-Robin.* New York: Hurd & Houghton, 1871.
—*The Writings of John Burroughs.* (Contains most of his books, from *Wake-Robin,* his first nature volume, through *Field and Study.*) 20 vols. Boston: Riverby Edition; Houghton Mifflin, 1904–1919.
—*The Writings of John Burroughs.* 23 vols. New York: Russell & Russell, 1968.
—*John Burroughs' America; Selections from the Writings of the Hudson River Naturalist.* (Edited, with an introduction, by Farida A. Wiley; foreword by Julian Burroughs.) New York: Devin-Adair, 1951.

CAHALANE, VICTOR H. (ed.)
—*The Imperial Collection of Audubon Animals: the Quadrupeds of North America.* (Plates and excerpts of text by John James Audubon; edited, with an introduction, notes, and additional text concerning the fauna, by Victor H. Cahalane; foreword by Fairfield Osborn.) New York: Bonanza Books, 1967.

CANTWELL, ROBERT
—*Alexander Wilson: Naturalist and Pioneer, a Biography.* Philadelphia: Lippincott, 1961.

CATESBY, MARK
—*The Natural History of Carolina, Florida, and the Bahama Islands.* (Revised, with additional material, by George Edwards.) 2 vols. London: C. Marsh, 1754; also London: B. White, 1771.
—*The Natural History of Carolina, Florida, and the Bahama Islands.* (Portfolio of fifty color plates from Catesby's originals.) Savannah, Ga.: Beehive Press (distributed through Johnson Reprint Corp., New York), 1974.

CLEMENT, ROLAND C.
—*The Living World of Audubon.* (Selection, in color, of sixty-four plates from *The Birds of America,* presented together with photographic studies of those species featured in the plates; edited, with an introduction and explanatory text, by Roland C. Clement.) New York: Grosset & Dunlap, 1974.

CONNORS, DONALD FRANCIS
—*Thomas Morton.* (An analytical biography in the American Authors Series.) New York: Twayne Publishers, 1969.

CORNING, HOWARD (ed.)

—*Letters of John James Audubon, 1826–1840.* 2 vols. Boston: Club of Odd Volumes, 1930.

COUES, ELLIOTT

—*Key to North American Birds.* (Contains "Historical Preface" in which Coues combines biographical notes with erudite evaluations of early American naturalists.) Salem, Mass.: Naturalists' Agency, 1872.

CRUICKSHANK, HELEN GERE (ed.)

—*John and William Bartram's America; Selections from the Writings of the Philadelphia Naturalists.* (Foreword by B. Bartram Cadbury.) New York: Devin-Adair, 1957.

DARLINGTON, WILLIAM

—*Memorials of John Bartram and Humphry Marshall.* Philadelphia: Lindsay & Blakiston, 1849. (This book is also available in a modern reprint of the original edition; Hafner Press, New York, 1967.)

DARRAH, WILLIAM CULP

—*Powell of the Colorado.* Princeton: Princeton University Press, 1951.

DAVENPORT, GUY (ed.)

—*The Intelligence of Louis Agassiz; a Specimen Book of Scientific Writings.* (Selected, with an introduction and notes, by Guy Davenport; foreword by Alfred S. Romer.) Boston: Beacon Press, 1963.

DEANE, RUTHVEN (ed.)

—"Unpublished Letters of John James Audubon and Spencer F. Baird." Cambridge, Mass., *Auk,* n.s. vol. 21, no. 2 (pp. 255–259), 1904.

DELLENBAUGH, FREDERICK S.

—*A Canyon Voyage; the Narrative of the Second Powell Expedition Down the Green-Colorado River from Wyoming.* New York: G. P. Putnam's Sons, 1908.

DWIGHT, EDWARD H.

—"The Autobiographical Writings of John James Audubon." St. Louis: *Missouri Historical Society,* vol. 19, no. 1 (pp. 26–35), 1962.

EARNEST, ERNEST

—*John and William Bartram, Botanists and Explorers.* Philadelphia: University of Pennsylvania Press, 1940.

ELMAN, ROBERT

—*The Living World of Audubon Mammals.* (Selection, in color, of sixty-two plates from *The Viviparous Quadrupeds of North America,* presented together with photographic studies of those species featured in the plates; edited, with a biographical introduction and explanatory text, by Robert Elman.) New York: Grosset & Dunlap, 1976.

FAGIN, NATHAN BRYLLION

—*William Bartram, Interpreter of the American Landscape.* Baltimore: Johns Hopkins Press, 1933.

FORD, ALICE

—*John James Audubon.* Norman: University of Oklahoma Press, 1964.

FORD, ALICE (ed.)

—*Audubon's Butterflies, Moths, and Other Studies.* (Compiled and edited by Alice Ford.) New York: Studio Publications in association with T. Y. Crowell, 1952.

FRICK, GEORGE FREDERICK and STEARNS, RAYMOND PHINEAS
—*Mark Catesby: the Colonial Audubon.* Urbana: University of Illinois Press, 1961.
GEISER, SAMUEL W.
—*Naturalists of the Frontier.* Dallas, Tex.: Southern Methodist University Press, 1948.
GROSART, REV. ALEXANDER B. (ed.)
—*The Poems and Literary Prose of Alexander Wilson.* 2 vols. Paisley, Scotland: A. Gardner, 1876.
HERRICK, FRANCIS HOBART
—*Audubon the Naturalist; a History of his Life and Time.* 2 vols. New York: D. Appleton & Co., 1917. (This two-volume biography is also available in a modern reprint of a 1938 edition; New York: Dover Publications, 1968.)
HOLDER, CHARLES FREDERICK
—*Louis Agassiz; his Life and Work.* New York: G. P. Putnam's Sons, 1893.
JORDAN, DAVID STARR
—"Louis Agassiz, Teacher." Lancaster, Pa., *Scientific Monthly,* vol. 17 (pp. 401–411), 1923.
KELLEY, ELIZABETH BURROUGHS
—*John Burroughs: Naturalist.* New York: Exposition Press, 1959.
KIERAN, JOHN (ed.)
—*John Kieran's Treasury of Great Nature Writing.* (With comments and biographical notes by John Kieran.) New York: Doubleday & Co., 1957.
LAWSON, JOHN
—*The History of North Carolina.* London: Taylor and Baker, 1714. (Lawson's first version of this work, entitled *A New Voyage to Carolina* and published in 1709, is available in a modern edition; edited, with an introduction and notes, by Hugh Talmage Lefler; University of North Carolina Press, Chapel Hill, N.C., 1967.)
LURIE, EDWARD
—*Louis Agassiz; a Life in Science.* Chicago: University of Chicago Press, 1960.
MARCOU, JULES
—*Life, Letters, and Works of Louis Agassiz.* 2 vols. New York: Macmillan & Co., 1896.
MATTHIESSEN, PETER
—*Wildlife in America.* New York: Viking Press, 1959.
MEADOWS, PAUL
—*John Wesley Powell: Frontiersman of Science.* Lincoln: University of Nebraska Studies (New Series No. 10), 1952.
MIALL, LOUIS COMPTON
—*The Early Naturalists; their Lives and Work (1530–1789).* London: Macmillan & Co., 1912.
MIDDLETON, WILLIAM SHAINLINE
—"John Bartram, Botanist." Lancaster, Pa. *Scientific Monthly,* vol. 21 (pp. 191–216), 1925.
MILLER, WILLIAM HUBERT
—"Mark Catesby, an Eighteenth Century Naturalist." Richmond, Va. *Tyler's*

Quarterly Historical and Genealogical Magazine (pp. 167–180), Jan., 1948.
MORTON, THOMAS
—*New English Canaan.* Amsterdam: J.F. Stam, 1637. (This book is also available in a modern edition; edited, with introductory matter and notes, by Charles Francis Adams, Jr.; New York: Burt Franklin, 1967.)
PEATTIE, DONALD CULROSS
—*Audubon's America; the Narratives and Experiences of John James Audubon.* Boston: Houghton Mifflin, 1940.
—*Green Laurels; the Lives and Achievements of the Great Naturalists.* New York: Simon & Schuster, 1936.
PLATE, ROBERT
—*Alexander Wilson.* New York: David McKay Co., 1966.
POWELL, JOHN WESLEY
—*Canyons of the Colorado.* (Revision, with photographs replacing many original woodcut illustrations, of *Exploration of the Colorado River* as published by the Government Printing Office in 1875; see listing of 1875 edition.) Meadville, Pa.: Chautauqua Press/Flood & Vincent, 1895.
—*Down the Colorado.* (Excerpted diary of the first trip through the Grand Canyon, 1869, with photographs and epilogue by Eliot Porter; foreword and notes by Don D. Fowler.) New York: E. P. Dutton, 1969.
—*Exploration of the Colorado River of the West and Its Tributaries, Explored in 1869, 1870, 1871, and 1872.* (Bound volume, illustrated with woodcuts and diagrams, containing the report submitted to the Smithsonian Institution in 1874; also contains unrelated zoological papers by Elliott Coues and G. Brown Goode.) Washington, D.C.: 1875. (This report is also available in a modern reprint; Dover Publications, New York: Government Printing Office, 1961.)
—*The Exploration of the Colorado River.* (Abridgement of the 1875 edition of Powell's report to the Smithsonian; with an introduction by Wallace E. Stegner.) Chicago: University of Chicago Press, 1957.
—*Indian Linguistic Families of America, North of Mexico.* Washington, D.C.: Government Printing Office, 1891.
—*Introduction to the Study of Indian Languages, with Words, Phrases, and Sentences To Be Collected.* Washington, D.C.: Government Printing Office, 1877.
—*Report on the Lands of the Arid Region of the United States.* Washington, D.C.: Government Printing Office, 1878. (This report is also available in a modern edition, edited by Wallace E. Stegner; Cambridge, Mass.: Belknap Press of Harvard University Press, 1962.)
—*Truth and Error; or, The Science of Intellection.* Chicago: Open Court Publishing Co., 1898.
ROBBINS, PEGGY
—"John James Audubon." Harrisburg, Pa., *American History Illustrated* (National Historical Society), vol. 9, no. 6 (pp. 4–9 & 38–44), 1974.
SMALLWOOD, W. M.
—"The Agassiz-Rogers Debate on Evolution." Baltimore, *Quarterly Review of Biology*, vol. 16 (pp. 1–12), 1941.

Spitzka, Edward Anthony
—"A Study of the Brain of the Late Major J. W. Powell." Lancaster, Pa.,
American Anthropologist, n. s. vol. 5, no. 4 (pp. 585–643), 1903; also published as a reprint under the same title by New Era Printing Co., Lancaster, Pa., 1903.

Stegner, Wallace E.
—*Beyond the Hundredth Meridian: John Wesley Powell and the Second Opening of
the West.* (With an introduction by Bernard De Voto.) Boston: Houghton
Mifflin Co., 1954.

Stone, Witmer
—"A Bibliography and Nomenclator of the Ornithological Works of John
James Audubon." Cambridge, Mass., *Auk,* n. s. vol. 23 (pp. 298–312), 1906.
—"Bird Migration Records of William Bartram, 1802–1822." Cambridge,
Mass., *Auk,* n. s. vol. 30 (pp. 325–358), 1913.

Stork, William and Bartram, John
—*An Account of East Florida, with a Journal Kept by John Bartram.* London:
W. Nicoll & G. Woodfall, 1769.

Teale, Edwin Way (ed.)
—*Audubon's Wildlife.* (Illustrated selections from the writings of John James
Audubon, with commentary by Edwin Way Teale.) New York: Viking Press,
1964.

Terrell, John Upton
—*The Man Who Rediscovered America: the Life of John Wesley Powell.* New York:
Weybright & Talley, 1969.

Westbook, Perry D.
—*John Burroughs.* (An analytical literary biography.) New York: Twayne Publishers, 1974.

Wilson, Alexander
—*American Ornithology; or, The Natural History of the Birds of the United States,
with plates coloured from original drawings taken from nature.* 8 vols. (plus one
posthumous volume, completed by Charles Lucien Bonaparte and George
Ord, published in 1829); Philadelphia: Samuel Bradford, 1808–1814.
—*American Ornithology* . . . (Work listed above, with a sketch of Wilson's life
by George Ord.) 3 vols. New York: Collins & Co., 1828–1829.
—*American Ornithology* . . . (Wilson's original work, with the additions by
Charles Lucien Bonaparte, edited by Robert Jameson, and with illustrative
notes and a biography of Wilson by Sir William Jardine.) 3 vols. London:
Whittaker, Treacher, & Arnot, 1832.
—*The Foresters: a poem, descriptive of a pedestrian journey to the falls of Niagara, in
the autumn of 1804. By the author of American Ornithology.* Newtown, Pa.:
S. Siegfried & Joseph Wilson, 1818.
—*Watty & Meg; or, The Wife Reformed.* Paisley, Scotland: G. Caldwell & Co.,
1830[?].

Index